XTRAORDINARY

XTRAORDINARY

THE ART AND SCIENCE OF REMARKABLE LEADERSHIP

GERARD PENNA

Praise for book and author

'The magic in this book is not just in the great examples of leadership in a variety of settings or the explanation of the science behind certain behaviours, but through the challenge Gerard leaves us at the end of each section to deeply examine ourselves – our motivations, values and feelings and in the end appreciate what we have to offer as leaders. It is through this introspective challenge that we can truly learn and grow. I recommend this book as a great learning guide to help us navigate and grow in ALL of our relationships and lives.'

Nino Ficca, non-executive director Transurban Qld, Australian Energy Market Operator and Deakin University Councillor

'I loved it. The book *Xtraordinary* is an essential tool for all leaders navigating our complex and changing world to deliver outstanding outcomes. In his book, Gerard Penna has taken his 30-plus years of leadership observation and development and succinctly defined what makes extraordinary leaders. A must read for all leaders, experienced and emerging. Bravo!'

Katrina Blair, Chief Financial Officer, Tennis Australia

'There is no better time for a leader to read this deeply insightful book by Gerard Penna. Leaders now face more complexity and ambiguity than ever before. Despite living in a world of data abundance, we all strive (and struggle) to make smarter, faster and more informed decisions. This book emphasises the transformation value that leaders can bring by exhibiting a combination of strength, warmth and a vision for the extraordinary. These qualities when harnessed effectively help "catalyse the release of energy and commitment from a diverse range of people" to deliver Xtraordinary outcomes. This is one of those leadership manuals that I look forward to reading time and time again.'

Richard Bartlett, Senior Vice President, BP

'In *Xtraordinary*, Gerard Penna offers a compelling, practical and nuanced roadmap for enhancing your leadership. This book is both relentlessly optimistic and brutally realistic about what you can accomplish. Penna has developed a rich framework and set of useful tools that show how synthesizing strength and warmth is not only possible but essential to enable you to achieve more effective, lasting, and impactful results.'

Marty Linsky, long-time Harvard Kennedy School faculty, and co-author of *Leadership on the Line* and *The Practice of Adaptive Leadership*

'In a time where extraordinary leadership is needed more than ever before, Gerard Penna's book *Xtraordinary* could not be more timely. This practical and insightful book shows the reader what extraordinary leadership looks like and why it matters. Most importantly it explores the eight habits on how to become an extraordinary leader. Full of examples and stories, this book not only provides the know-how but the inspiration to become the best leader you can be.'

Gabrielle Dolan, best-selling author of *Magnetic Stories* and *Stories at Work*

'Many of us in leadership roles today use the words volatility, uncertainty, complexity and ambiguity to describe the times in which we lead. Navigating such times requires extraordinary leadership, and Gerard Penna offers the learnings from a long career developing extraordinary leaders.

'Penna offers us a choice – to remain ordinary in our leadership, or become something more remarkable, inspiring those we lead to make a difference. This is a book that prompts reflection on your own behaviours, and then through Penna's own X model, offers a path from the way you lead now towards extraordinary leadership.'

Andrew Maher PhD, Group Managing Principal, Eminence, Digital & Innovation, Aurecon

'I thought *Xtraordinary* to be fantastic book in a number of ways. The Xtraordinary leadership model was really helpful in focusing my own thoughts on where I sit as a leader in a simple, clear and concise way.

The reflections at the end of each section further enhanced self-assessment and accountability to be honest with myself and finally, I found the habits of Xtraordinary leaders an incredible framework to facilitate me becoming a more consistent and more effective leader. A great read, highly recommended.'

Peter Chapman, Chief Financial Officer, Great Western Bank (NYSE:GWB)

'In this book Gerard Penna asks the critical question, "How do we create more extraordinary leaders in a world that needs them?" In so many ways he answers this question through a brilliant distillation of his 30-plus years of leadership experience. It is clear from the depths of this book that this is Gerard's life's work, with engaging stories, thought provoking reflections, and "how to's" that give leaders great direction on their own extraordinary leadership development. A must-read for anyone wanting to lift their own leadership.'

Michelle Sales, author of *The Power of Real Confidence*

'Gerard has brought us an Xtraordinary book that blends both his knowledge of psychology and his years of in-depth work developing leaders. It's a great book with so many key teachings that will help all leaders get a clearer perspective on themselves, and how great leaders learn to adapt to engage others with both strength and warmth. Clearly these are powerful concepts and I'll be using them to coach myself and my clients in the days ahead.'

Colonel Lee Ellis (retired), President, Leadership Freedom LLC and author of *Leading with Honor*

'In his book *Xtraordinary: The art and practice of remarkable leadership* Gerard Penna shares with us his well-thought-out and deeply practiced approach for breaking with the dangerous confines of ordinariness, both in the way one considers leadership in the 21st Century and in the way one considers the true potential of those we are invited to inspire and influence. As a leader, you are given a gift. Don't take it for granted.'

Dawa Tarchin Phillips, CEO, Empowerment Holdings, President of the International Mindfulness Teachers Association, and author of *Mind Your Business*

'There's no better human than Gerard Penna to write a book about extraordinary leadership. Gerard's gift to us all is his unique ability to skilfully combine leading-edge leadership theory with his lived experience. If you are looking to truly embrace what it takes to fully step up into extraordinary leadership this is a must-read book.'

Mark Le Busque, author of *Being Human* **and** *The Little Book of Human*

'Gerard has had an amazing impact.'

John Rogerson, Chief Executive Officer, Alcohol and Drug Foundation

'What a difference Gerard has made ... Ground breaking!!'

Fred Harrison, Chief Executive Officer, Ritchies Supermarkets

'A wealth of knowledge, experience and strategy is what I feel I get with Gerard, and a feeling of learning and progress after every session is a consistent outcome ... Would highly recommend.'

Larry Kestelman – Founder of Dodo, Owner of the National Basketball League, Chairman LK Group

'I would recommend Gerard to any business leader who is ready to step out of their comfort zone and challenge themselves to improve their leadership.'

Chris Dean, Chief Executive Officer, Choice Energy

'Gerard has a unique combination of intelligence, compassion and insight that has led to significant progress on key relationships and strategies ... Without his ability to "align the stars", we would still be navel-gazing!'

Ned Coten, Chairman, Basketball Australia

'Gerard has played a key role on our journey to high performance.'

Shane Bonello, Managing Director, Hallmark Cards

'We really advanced the performance of our team as a result of Gerard's expert guidance.'

Andrew Clark, Managing Director, Boston Consulting Group

' … the most valuable coaching I have experienced.'
Anthony Schinck, Chief Executive Officer, City of Ballarat

'Initially, Gerard conducted a two-day leadership training workshop that was a major awakening for most of our leadership team. It was an amazing two days and an equally amazing outcome. At our subsequent monthly management meeting we "debriefed" and the effect was startling.'
James Egan, Owner and Director, Freedom Facilities Management

'Gerard's work with our senior leadership team and our broader leadership group has been tremendously valuable.'
Adrian Spadafora, Learning & Development Manager,
Little Real Estate

'Gerard has outstanding skills in facilitating strategic conversations that results in real direction and outcomes for the client.'
Mike Anderson, Chief Operations Officer, Minor Hotels

'[Gerard] brings a strong, confident polish coupled with an operating style that enables him to build credibility quickly … '
Jason Gindidis, Learning and Development, Medibank

'He was able to teach our entire team to listen and appreciate each other's style better. We've seen great change as a result. Gerard really broke through the barriers with each individual and built trust.'
Sharon Robinson, General Manager People and Safety,
South East Water

'What really stands out to me was his authenticity. He is confident without arrogance, and super smart with the ability to make things practical and real for people.'
Susan Beardsley, Head of HR Australia and New Zealand, Hallmark

About the author

Gerard Penna is the CEO and founder of Xtraordinary Leaders. For over 30 years, he has been researching, teaching and practising leadership. Today, he is a leadership advisor and coach to billionaires, CEOs, boards and senior executives.

Gerard's clients include highly regarded Fortune 500, FTSE 100, ASX 200 and other leading global companies.

He designs and delivers award-winning leadership programs as well as consulting on multibillion-dollar business transformations and turnarounds, while also providing pro bono services to charities and social enterprises.

Gerard has taught thousands of leaders around the world, from supervisors to senior executives, in many diverse scenarios, including jungle mining camps and high-tech start-ups, and from sprawling factories to corporate boardrooms perched atop skyscrapers.

Gerard is the former chairman of a fast-growing international firm of business psychologists and past director of the global consultancy DDI. He has also worked as a senior manager with the strategy firm Bain and Company, and held in-house senior roles within large national and global businesses.

Gerard lives with his wife and two children on the beautiful Mornington Peninsula in Australia, where he surfs and swims all year round.

First published in 2021 by Xtraordinary Leaders

© Gerard Penna 2021
The moral rights of the author have been asserted

All inquiries should be made to the author.

A catalogue entry for this book is available from the National Library of Australia.

ISBN: 978-1-922553-42-3

Printed in Australia by McPherson's Printing
Project management and text design by Publish Central
Cover design by Oliver & York

The paper this book is printed on is certified as environmentally friendly.

Contents

Preface

The world we live in, with all of its attendant challenges, has placed increased attention on the quality of leadership we are experiencing. Satisfaction with our political, corporate and community leaders is at an all-time low, and distrust in the organisations and institutions they command is at an all-time high. The gap continues to grow between what we need of our leaders, and what they are delivering.

Throughout 2020, the global COVID-19 pandemic caused the tide to go out on many of our leaders. Across our countries, businesses and communities, the pandemic and its flow-on effects continue to expose the failings of the typical, ho-hum, garden-variety version of leadership that we commonly find out there.

A quick trawl through media commentaries and 'state of the nation' reports into our attitudes towards the quality of leadership in our lives reveals that we are extremely dissatisfied. Many of us are yearning for something different – a version of leadership that is better able to engage us and galvanise the innovation and transformation that our communities and institutions so desperately need.

Of course, dissatisfying leadership is nothing new, and we tolerated (and resisted) it long before the events of 2020 exposed it more fully. However, the range of crises and problems we now face has thrown a collective spotlight on this kind of leadership. The challenges and opportunities we face emerging from the pandemic will only intensify our focus on the quality of leadership we have, compared to that which we need.

If we are disengaging with our leaders, and the data certainly supports that view, we need to cultivate a way of leading that is better at engaging each other, releases greater energy for what we all need to do, and leaves us more satisfied with our experience as we are leading and being led.

For, without doubt, if leadership at its core is about influencing and mobilising other people, we need more leaders who are remarkable in their ability to engage others and build their contribution and commitment to the goals, outcomes and aspirations that we share.

Perhaps you also desire to become more extraordinary in your leadership, because your own dreams, hopes and desires are inextricably linked to your ability to engage, influence and mobilise the people whose support you need.

I have spent much of my career seeking to understand this more extraordinary version of leadership. The acceleration of change, and the challenges this change has brought over the last several years, has only heightened my desire, and increased my sense of urgency to find answers to these compelling questions: What does a more extraordinary version of leadership look like? What can it do that ordinary leadership does not? How can we develop ourselves to become more extraordinary in our own leadership?

This book is the product of this long investigation, and many of the answers I've found to these questions.

Introduction

Let's begin in what might seem a strange place to start a book about extraordinary leadership – with a general knowledge question. See if you know the answer.

The word 'Anablep' describes:

A. a type of star found in the Milky Way galaxy
B. the name of a heavy metal band competing in the Eurovision song contest
C. a genus of unique freshwater fish found in Latin America.

The correct answer is C. The Anablep[1] are extraordinary fish native to Honduras and Mexico, unique in having eyes raised above the top of the head with each eye divided into two different parts, upper and lower, allowing them to see above and below the water surface at the same time. They are sometimes referred to as the 'four-eyed fish'.

This evolutionary adaptation helps the Anablep with two basic drives that all animals share: access to food and avoidance of predators. Being able to see above and below the water simultaneously means the Anablep can snatch terrestrial insects from on or above the water surface, while also snacking on invertebrates and small fish below the water line, maximising their food opportunities. Their bifocal vision also helps them identify and avoid dangerous predators that may approach from the sky above, or rise stealthily from the water column below.

The Anablep is indeed a remarkable species that's evolved to better meet the demands of its environment. So too have we humans, and some of those adaptations now play a disproportionate role in how leadership works.

YOUR BRAIN EVOLVED TO BE SOCIAL

Homo sapiens and our ancestors evolved over millions of years. Our bodies, brains and behaviours are the product of a multitude of adaptations that allow us to survive and thrive more effectively in the world in which we live.

These adaptations included many outward changes, such as the development of a more upright stance. This enabled us to reach higher to collect fruit and nuts and (along with the ability to sweat) facilitated easier travel over longer distances, a distinct benefit for nomadic hunter-gatherers moving across vast grasslands and arid deserts in search of food and resources.

However, changes to the human genome didn't just affect our bodies. As outlined by historian Yuval Noah Harari in *Sapiens: A Brief History of Humankind*, our brain anatomy and functioning also adapted to the major features of our environment – of which one of the most significant was *other people*. Indeed, our ability to access food, stay safe and reproduce was entirely dependent on our interactions with other people, and remains so today.

When meeting new people is life or death

As social beings, every new social interaction we have with a stranger can represent an opportunity – however, it can just as easily represent a threat. For our ancestors, meeting someone new or unfamiliar could lead to benefits such as improved access to resources, increased safety, or even the chance to mate with someone who had good genes. At the same time, new social connections presented potential risks – such as diseased individuals who should be avoided, danger from those intent on physically harming us, or even from those who might cheat, lie or steal.[2] It was, therefore, beneficial to our species to evolve effective responses to those opportunities and threats.

Thinking fast, and slow

Speed of thinking was essential, though. In order to take advantage of opportunities or avoid the dangers that arose when interacting with other people, our decision-making needed to evolve to be lightning fast. If we were too slow in our decisions and actions we could miss out on opportunities, or be harmed or even killed.

The fast survival thinking our ancestors developed, which we all now possess, is probably familiar to you. Anyone who has experienced the rapid fight, flight and freeze urges generated by our primitive reptilian rear brain knows what it feels like when it's activated. I know I have.

As a keen fly fisherman, I sometimes frequent the cooler Australian high country streams and rivers when the lowland waters become too warm during the summer months. These areas are also home to highly venomous snakes such as tiger, copperhead, brown and black snakes.

One trip in mid-summer, on a hot afternoon, I was walking along the banks of the Cobungra River. Rounding a corner, I spotted a striped, curved shape lying across the sun-dappled path. *Oh sh …!* Within milliseconds my muscles contracted and I froze, stopping mid-stride and halting the trajectory of my foot through the air. I immediately retracted my leg and took a step backwards. A second or two later, with my heart still pounding, I realised the shape was not a snake but a broken branch, with the dappled sunlight creating a striped effect like that of a tiger snake. The more recently evolved pre-frontal region of my brain had finally caught up with the action and was informing the ancient and primitive rear brain that there was no danger. Stand down!

Nonetheless, I was thankful that my survival reaction had been so fast, even if inaccurate. If a real tiger snake had been lying across the path, my slow-thinking modern brain would have allowed me to stand right on it. Being an extremely aggressive snake, it may have attacked me repeatedly, and I would possibly have had to deal with being envenomated by one of the world's deadliest snakes many miles from help.

In this way, and as psychologist and economist Daniel Kahneman outlines in detail in *Thinking, Fast and Slow*, lightning fast, instinctual responses deeply coded into our primitive rear brain can be more helpful to our survival than the powerful but slow and laborious thinking we do with our modern frontal brain.

AVOIDING DANGERS AND ACCESSING OPPORTUNITIES

Of course, dangers come not only from other species such as snakes, spiders and sharks – of which we have plenty in Australia! Human beings sometimes represent just as real a danger – and, indeed, we often use phrases such as, 'Look out, he's a shark' or 'She's a snake in the grass' to describe these threats.

On the flip side, others can also represent valuable opportunities to us. Perhaps that's why we use phrases such as, 'She's a gem' and 'He's got a heart of gold' to communicate the value of others. But, as with real precious stones and metals, competition may exist in finding and taking advantage of the social opportunities that come from new networks, collaborations and relationships – such as access to resources, belonging, and maybe even love. Others may beat us to these social opportunities, so we need to be just as quick in capitalising on their benefits.

Therefore, being able to identify and act on these social dangers and opportunities quickly is an advantage. As a result, our social cognition – how we think and feel around other people – has evolved to be instinctive and lightning-fast.

Those of our ancestors whose brain structures and functions incorporated these beneficial fast-thinking adaptations were more likely to survive and thrive, and so more likely to pass on their genes to future generations. You are the product of these evolutionary adaptations.

Not surprisingly, those same instinctive social cognition responses now exert a major influence in our daily lives at work, at home and in our communities, especially through the impressions we form of others.

Speedy first impressions

The most important form of fast social cognition occurs when you encounter someone for the first time and your brain instantaneously forms an impression of them. Without prompting, and outside of your control or awareness, your brain will size that person up and make a critical judgement about them, with the results shaping what you think of them, how they make you feel, and whether you are willing to engage with them or otherwise avoid them.

Surviving and thriving from first contact

As already discussed, the almost instantaneous speed at which first impressions are formed – less than three-tenths of a second – was especially important to helping our hunter-gatherer ancestors survive.[3]

Moving across the landscape in relatively small groups, your ancestors were highly likely to have regularly encountered members of other tribes – who might be hostile or friendly.

Imagine being an early human living a hunter-gatherer existence. One day while out looking for food, you emerge from a forest into a clearing and see a stranger crouched over a freshly killed animal just a few metres away. As he turns his head towards you, your brain has to make an extremely rapid assessment of this person and the situation. Are you now in danger? Or might there be some benefit in hanging out with this person for a bit?

Two attributes assessed at first contact

In the past, people had to make this assessment rapidly if they were to survive, by considering two critical characteristics of the stranger:

1. What can I discern about their intentions towards me?
2. Do they appear to have the ability to carry out those intentions?[4]

Our brains still make the same speedy assessments, and the answers our instinctive thinking generates to these questions, within split seconds, largely dictates our subsequent responses, thoughts and feelings about the person, and the type of relationship we form with them.

For example, continuing the early human hunter-gatherer scenario, if the stranger's intentions appear cold or hostile towards me and he looks strong enough to harm me, I would probably experience a feeling of fear and run. If, however, his intentions seem hostile but he looks weaker and slower than me, I might think, *I can take this dude, and the fresh meat, no worries.*

If, on the other hand, the stranger smiles warmly and I assume his intentions are good, I might consider moving closer and engaging with him, perhaps with the hope of trading something for the food and improving my situation. If especially strong and competent as well as well-intentioned, I may even decide some benefit exists for me or my tribe in attempting to establish a deeper social connection with this individual.

CONSIDERING WARMTH AND STRENGTH: TWO CRITICAL ASSESSMENTS

Because we are the offspring of generations that evolved this rapid assessment capability (and our brains have not really changed since the emergence of *Homo sapiens* around 300,000 years ago), perhaps unsurprisingly our brains still make the same powerful split-second judgements of another person in two critical areas – their warmth and strength. And we still use these judgements to decide whether we should engage and co-operate, or disengage and resist.

The answers to these questions have enormous implications for our attitudes towards others and the relationships we are likely to have with them – especially our leaders.

Choosing to follow

Leaving behind the prehistoric world of our hunter-gatherer ancestors, here's a modern-day scenario for you to contemplate.

Imagine it's day one in your role as a department manager in a new organisation. It's a great role and real step up. You've even moved cities to take up this opportunity and, after a lot of packing, logistics and a long drive across the country, here you are on your first day, understandably excited and slightly nervous about what's in store.

So far, the only people you have met are your boss, Jenny, and the HR manager, but that's all about to change. Before you started, Jenny told you a team meeting was scheduled for 10 am on your first day for all her direct reports. These people will be your teammates and will play a role in your success or otherwise.

Having little yet scheduled in your calendar, you have plenty of time to make your way through the labyrinth of corridors to the assigned meeting room. Arriving a few minutes early, you scan the room as you enter, noticing one person seated at the meeting table focused quietly on her laptop and another standing at the back of the room having a loud and animated conversation on his phone.

You decide to take up a seat opposite the quiet woman seated at the table, offering a warm hello and introducing yourself as you sit down. After a moment of silence, she lifts her head shyly, makes fleeting eye contact and says, 'Hi, I'm Helen' in a small and quiet voice before going back to intently typing on her laptop.

It's not much of an invitation to strike up a conversation so after a moment you decide to make your way to the side table to grab a coffee. Standing near the coffee station is the fellow on his phone, a tall dark-haired man who seems agitated and tense. The diary he is carrying has the name 'Rex Black' embossed on it. As you are making your coffee you hear Rex finish the call with a raised voice, shouting, 'I don't care, just do it!'

After a moment he notices you, looks you directly in the eye and asks brusquely, 'Who are you?' You share your name, explain that you're new here and extend your arm for a handshake, but he's been distracted by your boss Jenny entering the room and brushes past you with a perfunctory hello as he zeroes in on her. 'Nice fellow' you remark quietly to yourself as you sip your coffee by the window while other people come in and seat themselves at the table, finishing phone calls and typing messages.

Just as the clock strikes 10 am, one final person rushes into the room, fumbling his laptop and some documents as he looks at his watch, apologising to everyone for being late (even though he isn't). Noticing you at the back of the room, he makes a beeline for you with big strides and a huge smile on his face. 'Hi there! I'm Kurt. You must be our new teammate. It's a real pleasure to meet you,' he says in a fast, almost breathless, way as he drops some papers to the floor. Reaching for them he continues without skipping a beat. 'When Jenny told me you were joining us I was so excited. You have terrific experience and great qualifications, and I'm sure you will be such a great fit in our company.' Almost rambling now, he continues on as he fumbles and drops some more papers. 'I'm such a klutz and I'm not very good at time management either; I can't believe I was almost late for your first team meeting. Everyone always gives me that feedback, and I've been working on it but...'

Kurt is interrupted by Jenny asserting herself over the chatter in the room. 'Shall we get started? Our time together is valuable, and we have a lot of important issues to address.' As everyone else moves to be seated, Jenny makes her way around the table to where you are standing, smiling as she approaches to give a firm and warm handshake. 'I'm so pleased to finally have you here. We can really use your help with some of the big goals we have for this year. Come sit next to me,' she says before asking, 'Would you like me to introduce you to the team, or would you like to introduce yourself?'

This scene may have elements or characters that are familiar to you, so you may not have to think too hard about your response to this question: Of the four people you spoke to that morning, who would you rather be led by?

Two critical characteristics of leaders

Odds are that, like most people, you've picked Jenny as the person you'd prefer to be led by. Many people report they need little time to debate the pros and cons of each person, with the selection of Jenny almost instinctual.

That's because our brains are hardwired to look for the two critical bits of information that are central in identifying who is likely to be a good ally – and, in our modern setting, who is most likely to be the better leader, and the kind of leader most of us would rather work for. This is someone who possesses both warmth (has good intentions towards us) and strength (appears capable and competent).

In the example scenario, Jenny is the only person who behaves in a way that suggests she is both warm towards us and strong enough to lead. Kurt is likeable but appears weak and lacking the competence or confidence to lead. Rex appears strong and dominant but also lacks warmth – to the extent that his behaviour even seems hostile. Helen is withdrawn and passive and so lacks both warmth and strength.

The fact is, and research certainly bears this out, that we have a preference for being led by someone who is both warm and strong above any other combination.

By understanding the role that strength and warmth play in us preferring one person over another to lead us, we actually move one step closer toward distinguishing ordinary from extraordinary leadership. Indeed, through the research and evidence I present in this book, strength and warmth are shown to play a starring role in the formation of extraordinary leadership, the sort that is better able to engage, influence and mobilise people.

I highlight throughout this book that your ability to harness the gifts of strength and warmth has far-reaching consequences for your leadership success, determining whether you are able to initially gain others' attention and trust, and then over time whether you can engage with them in a way that encourages their best efforts, and releases their full potential and contribution to what you believe to be important.

While the story I tell may begin with first impressions, it continues on well past the first few seconds or minutes into the weeks, months and years that you exercise leadership with others. In other words, these critical aspects of strength and warmth ultimately determine whether your leadership throughout your life is simply ordinary, or something more extraordinary.

STRENGTH, WARMTH AND THE STORY OF EXTRAORDINARY

I sometimes feel surprised finding myself referred to as an expert in leadership, partly due to how I started as a leader. I was thrust into my first leadership role, entirely unprepared at the age of 21, and I am still eternally grateful to this day that no-one died or was badly injured under my leadership!

It was my last year of university ... well, to be truthful it was my fourth year of a three-year course. I had failed a subject the previous year owing to social commitments that conflicted with a scheduled class (I was at the pub or at band practice, I can't remember which) and needed to complete this one last subject to graduate.

Given one subject wasn't a terribly demanding workload, I had started working as a labourer for a builder named Len on a small apartment block construction site. The work was hard manual labour, but I felt it fitted well with my Italian working-on-the-land roots, and I felt comfortable digging trenches, breaking through brick walls and moving many barrows of wet concrete across muddy work sites.

As the project progressed, Len needed more labourers, so I started recruiting mates from college and the odd relative. Naturally, once our labouring gang got to a reasonable size a fair amount of supervision was needed, which Len was happy to provide – until we broke ground on a second construction site.

Promoted beyond my competence

Len was becoming really stretched as he tried to supervise two sites, and we started experiencing delays at the first site because he wasn't around to provide direction or fetch supplies that we needed to do the work. Len's solution was to promote me to the role of supervisor. I was chuffed that Len thought enough of me to ask me to do that, so my ego said yes. The truth is I had no idea what I was doing. I didn't know the best way to get things done, and I didn't know how to properly care for people.

My leadership style was a mix of issuing orders and commands in areas I thought I had the authority – sometimes followed by a weak sugar-coating and pandering – and sycophantic back-pedalling when anyone with more experience than me pushed back. I must have looked similar to a 'Jekyll and Hyde' character to anyone watching. It hardly bears saying that our productivity was less than optimal as I struggled to learn leadership on the job and on the fly.

Looking back, I can also see how under my supervision we continued some really unsafe practices. The site was non-unionised, and Len's normal approach to safety was slack. Our safety training boiled down to one piece of advice: 'Just make sure your hands, feet or any other part of your body are not in the path of whatever you're cutting or bashing and you'll be right.' I still get a knot in my stomach whenever I think back to how far we stepped over the boundaries of safe working – including grinding concrete without face masks, leaning out over rooflines with no harnesses and even cutting through walls and eaves without any breathing protection whatsoever. Possibly the most perilous activity was using Len's old rusted Valiant Charger to collect trailer-loads of bricks, overloading it so badly that the dragging tow ball produced sparks on bumpy roads, the suspension bottomed out with large bangs and groans, and the car swerved violently and unpredictably to either the left or right under anything other than the lightest application of the brakes. We'd created a death trap.

But not just physical safety was at risk – psychological safety was too. Although never condoning it, I allowed the bullying of one crew member, who while being incredibly annoying to everyone on site, never deserved the tricks played on him or the denigrating nicknames.

We were on track for something bad to happen but fortunately the gods smiled on us – I finished my final year of university with all of my body parts undamaged and so did my crew. In truth, simple dumb luck or good fortune gave me the gift of my next 30 years, spent trying to analyse and address the harm that may have been caused by my poor leadership and other examples like it. I still look back with regret on what I didn't know as a leader, and curiosity about what would have made a difference.

Working to understand leadership using three big questions

So, for the last three decades I have studied, practised and taught leadership. My work has centred on three big questions related to leadership, each question (and its subsequent questions) taking at least a decade to find an answer that was even close to being satisfying. The big questions emerging during each of those decades were:

- **My twenties:** What is this thing called leadership? What does it *do*, what is its purpose, what does it typically look like, and how do you *do* it?

- **My thirties:** Is there a difference between ordinary and extraordinary leadership? What situations need something more than average or ordinary leadership, what *impact* does this extraordinary version of leadership have, and what distinguishes this more remarkable version from average, typical, ho-hum leadership?

- **My forties:** How do we create more extraordinary leadership in a world that needs it? How do we cultivate it, how can more leaders *become* extraordinary, how do we accelerate the transition, and how can we teach it?

The gifts from my study and experience of leadership

The truth is I only started to realise the importance of extraordinary leadership halfway through my career, along with the disproportionate role that the attributes strength and warmth play in the exercise of it. While I can't go back in time and present the gifts I've uncovered since then to the 21-year-old me on the construction site, I can share them with others who might need them today.

Here's what I've learned strength and warmth provide in extraordinary leadership:

- **Simplicity:** Strength and warmth provide a simple way to understand leadership. I have found that most leaders understand the basics pretty quickly, and then it's up to them to work out how far they want to take it – which can be towards quite amazing things.

- **Systematic thinking:** Strength and warmth form the foundation of a systematic way of thinking and practising your leadership. This is the opposite of a disparate or eclectic mix of ideas and concepts that have been thrown together in some disjointed version of leadership theory. This systematic approach that comes from focusing on strength and warmth allows you to build your competence and confidence much faster.

- **Scientific approach:** The benefits of combining strength and warmth and the related research I present throughout this book come from peer-reviewed scientific evidence and actual measurable business results, not from outdated beliefs or unfounded claims from the kinds of self-proclaimed experts that abound on the internet. Drawn from contemporary findings in neuroscience, social psychology, anthropology, strategy and management, the data collated here is solid and compelling.

- **Artistic performance:** Leadership is also a creative art form that evolves through our practice of it. It's the experience of experimenting, innovating and creating new ways of engaging and influencing people through warmth and strength that allows our leadership to organically grow and develop – and become a performance art.

- **Practical techniques:** Ultimately, strength and warmth produce techniques, tools, strategies and structures that are intended to be used practically to do the work of leadership. As I heard one senior leader recently quip in true Aussie fashion, 'It's okay to talk about getting shit done; it's another thing altogether to actually get shit done.' Presented in this book are the results of decades of practical experience from myself, my clients and colleagues in how to get more shit done.

My 10,000 hours (and then some)

Journalist Malcolm Gladwell wrote in *Outliers* that 10,000 hours of deliberate practice in any area of endeavour are required to achieve mastery. By my simple calculations, I've been deliberately working on my knowledge and practice of leadership for a little over 50,000 hours. I share this not to self-proclaim mastery, but to communicate how many opportunities I've had to observe leaders in all walks of life, some of whom were masterful and truly extraordinary.

During that time, I've also seen countless people become better leaders, and generate better results. Whether the ultimate goal is sales, profit, customer satisfaction, teamwork, engagement, efficiency, quality, innovation, productivity, change agility, or any other outcome, I have found that if you can improve your leadership, you can achieve better results.

I've also seen leaders transform relationships with others, turning them from fractured and dysfunctional to productive and collaborative, not only helping to produce better results, but also significantly improving the quality of their everyday experiences with team members, peers and bosses. After all, no-one wants or needs problematic and dysfunctional relationships in their life.

If you will indulge me ... (drum roll please)

Who has trusted me to coach, teach, guide and generally improve their leadership? Yes, this is the 'establishing my bona fides' bit and, as you'll see a bit further on in this book, establishing your competence is a useful, indeed essential part of leadership – provided you don't overdo it. People do need to believe that you know what you are doing if they are to trust your leadership, just so long as you don't appear egotistical and arrogant. With this in mind, I'd like to offer up a little about my experience in developing leaders, hopefully providing enough to satisfy your need to understand my competence. (If, however, you are pretty relaxed about my competence and think I seem to know what I'm talking about, you can skip the next couple of paragraphs.)

For over 30 years, I have guided, coached and taught tens of thousands of leaders – from billionaires to CEOs, from blue-collar shift supervisors and white-collar professionals, to no-collar start-up entrepreneurs, and across all industries, sectors, occupations and many countries. I've plied my trade in boardrooms perched at the top of skyscrapers, in remote mining camps in steaming jungles and bone-dry deserts, and in noisy lunchrooms surrounded by grinding, screeching industrial processes. I've worked with leaders in huge profit-minded Fortune Top 100 global companies, right through to leaders in smaller social-oriented not-for-profits as well as government departments and agencies.

This all means that, whatever your situation, I have likely worked with leaders in similar contexts and with similar challenges – and I have brought some of that diverse experience into the teachings, stories and examples in this book.

My wish for you

What then is my wish for you, and by extension your world, in writing this? I hope that, wherever you are on your leadership journey – emerging or established, struggling or feeling like you might be making some advances – you find a way for your leadership to continue to evolve from ordinary to extraordinary, from good to great. It seems that now, among the turmoil of divided politics, climate change, social upheaval, pandemics and the other challenges of change in our work and personal lives, is probably no better time for extraordinary leadership. If this book helps you evolve your leadership to something more extraordinary, in some way it is helping others, and the world in which we live. These extraordinary times call for extraordinary leadership.

SPOTTING EXTRAORDINARY LEADERS

Unfortunately, extraordinary leaders are not as common as we would like, and looking around you for examples may not yield great results. Tomas Chamorro-Premuzic, a psychology professor at University College London and Columbia University, suggests that this lack may be because up to half of our leaders (most of them male) are not sufficiently competent to do their jobs properly.[5] This is supported by other studies that show ineffective leaders make up half of today's organisational management pool.[6]

So how do we spot the more remarkable leaders? What should we be looking for? I have found they are easily recognisable by their ability to perform two important tasks that average or common leaders cannot. Extraordinary leaders:

1. get and hold people's attention – they are engaging and influential
2. catalyse the release of energy and commitment from a diverse range of people – they help others contribute their best.

The test of extraordinary leadership

The commonsense logic of these two markers of extraordinary leadership is easily tested by asking these related questions:

1. If people are unwilling to listen to you, or engage with you, how can you *lead*?
2. If you are unable to release the full potential of every person that you need to lead, formally or informally, how can you *lead well*?

The answer that emerges is that you can't lead well unless you are able to engage others, build trust *and* release their energy and contribution. In the absence of being able to do so, your leadership is unlikely to be seen as remarkable or beyond average.

The ordinary world of extraordinary

Part of the challenge of observing extraordinary leadership is that it often shows up without fanfare, quietly going about its business in our organisations and communities. While our attention is grabbed by the daily news feed of global and national leadership crises, the opportunity for extraordinary leadership is showing up much more frequently in commonplace and everyday situations. These include:

- influencing groups of people via team meetings, presentations, town halls and speeches
- establishing productive relationships with new partners, colleagues or team members
- mobilising people to engage with difficult and challenging changes in work conditions and their lives
- motivating team members, peers and even bosses who have different styles and needs
- influencing people with whom you have no formal authority
- leading unfamiliar people in virtual and project team settings
- coaching and managing the performance of team members to a higher level
- resolving entrenched destructive conflict between team members or groups
- responding to a crisis where you don't have all the answers.

This is not an exhaustive list, but it does describe many of the more common situations in which both new and experienced leaders find their everyday leadership challenges. They are also the moments in which you, as a leader, can show up as ordinary, or indeed something more extraordinary.

YOUR LEADERSHIP POTENTIAL IS UNKNOWABLE

The good news that you have a choice – you can remain ordinary in your leadership, or become something more remarkable. The experiences I've had leading, coaching and teaching prove that if you are prepared to do the work, how extraordinary your leadership can become is unlimited. Your leadership potential is unknowable.

Yet fewer of us share this belief than is healthy or helpful. I believe this is because most people have not had the opportunity to observe up close the *becoming* of an extraordinary leader. If you have not seen the transformation firsthand, how can you know it is possible?

Instead, we are more likely to have found ourselves surrounded by lots of leaders stuck in the unchanging habits and patterns of the ordinary. The same ho-hum, less-than-satisfying status quo, served up on a daily basis.

Sure, a few extraordinary leaders may have shown up in your regular life along the way, although you likely only noticed their remarkable ways because they had already travelled much of the path towards becoming extraordinary. Chances are, you did not get to see the start of their 'becoming'.

Witnessing the 'becoming' of extraordinary things

Similarly, we do not get to see the becoming of the butterfly as it transforms from its caterpillar state. In springtime and summer, caterpillars are usually easy to find on the leaves of trees and plants, munching away before moving into the pupal stage. And no doubt you notice the glorious, patterned butterflies they become after hatching. If you are especially observant, you may even see the camouflaged cocoon hanging from a tree branch, hiding the chrysalis as the pupa metamorphoses into the butterfly. But you don't get to see the actual change and transformation. The *becoming* of the butterfly is hidden from us, happening quietly and privately.

Hidden moments of transformation

In much the same way, the path to becoming an extraordinary leader is a mostly unheralded affair, conducted in moments of solitary reflection, unannounced experimentation and repeated practice. In a way, this is similar to the path to becoming a sporting star. Fans of the remarkable sportsperson Michael Jordan, for example, didn't see the countless hours of learning, experimentation and practice he undertook over many years to master even the fundamentals.

Even those parts of the extraordinary leader's journey shared with others are often intimate and private – whether it be conversations with confidantes, coaches and mentors, or participation in intensive leadership programs with like-minded colleagues.

As a result, it's quite possible that you will have insufficient observational evidence that becoming extraordinary is a journey, and not something that just happens. You may, therefore, struggle to truly believe in your own potential, and so be less willing to do the work necessary to evolve into a remarkable leader.

Allowing this state of affairs to remain unchallenged, and for you not to realise your limitless potential, would be a disservice. I've had the privilege of observing and guiding many leaders through their transformative stages and through the chapters in this book have shared much of what I have seen with you – to help you understand your potential to become extraordinary.

MAKING THE JOURNEY

This book contains many examples of leaders who realised their potential to become more extraordinary. If you are like them and also wish to display more remarkable leadership, this book is written in three parts to help you make progress:

- Part I, 'Hidden in plain sight', addresses *what* extraordinary leadership looks like. It does so by revealing how the two critical aspects of strength and warmth create hidden dynamics present in all human interactions, which have especially profound effects on how a leader acts and how they are experienced. I then introduce my Xtraordinary Leadership Model, a simple yet powerful model that reflects these dynamics along with the four patterns of leadership associated with them – one of which is extraordinary. This 'X' model is especially valuable to you in making better sense of your own leadership dance and identifying what may help or hinder your own growth towards 'Xtraordinary' leadership.

- In the chapters in the second part of the book, 'The leadership dance', I answer the question *why* Xtraordinary leadership matters, by bringing you up onto the 'balcony' to reveal new insight into your leadership dance and how it affects your ability to engage, influence and mobilise team members and others. Using the X model further, I explore the practical and oh-so-critical implications for engagement, culture and business results of Xtraordinary leadership. In doing so, I build a clear and compelling case to help you see how your own success can be improved, and also that of your team and organisation.

- The chapters in the third and most substantive part of the book, 'The habits of Xtraordinary leaders', reveal the *how* of remarkable leadership – through the exploration of eight habits. In these chapters, I provide practical and powerful skills and techniques that real-life leaders use to engage, influence and mobilise others. Packed with familiar situations, practical examples and real-life stories, these chapters guide you along the path from concept to application. The end-goal here is your enhanced ability to apply these ideas in your own life and, in doing so, accelerate your leadership from ordinary towards Xtraordinary.

At the end of each chapter, I also provide Reflection points, to allow you to process the information provided through the chapter, and see how you can apply it to yourself and your own leadership situation.

Getting started

Speaking of you, an important question right now is: Why are you reading this book?

What leadership challenges or growth opportunities are you currently experiencing that you would like to make progress with? What problems or goals would you like to solve by shifting your leadership and influence toward something more remarkable? Make some notes (either here or on your preferred device) and keep these in mind as you progress through the book.

My leadership challenges/opportunities/problems/goals:

_____

_____

_____

_____

_____

_____

_____

_____

_____

_____

_____

_____

_____

_____

_____

_____

_____

_____

_____

_____

_____

_____

_____

_____

_____

_____

_____

PART I

Hidden in plain sight

In the introduction to this book, I cover the critical aspects of strength and warmth in my initial exploration of extraordinary leadership and influence. That's because they play a disproportionately large role in the difference between ordinary and more remarkable versions of leadership. In this part of the book, I explore exactly how these two critical characteristics can produce either ordinary or more extraordinary leadership.

Chapter 1 helps you understand what I really mean by strength and warmth, and how they show up in leadership and more broadly in life. Chapter 2 reveals a critical difference in how ordinary and extraordinary leaders relate to strength and warmth. Chapter 3 then describes the three main patterns of ordinary leadership that are produced by unhelpful ways of thinking about and showing strength and warmth. Extraordinary leadership involves a different pattern, produced by more remarkable mindsets and behaviours, which I describe in chapter 4. I then share the powerful Xtrarodinary Leadership Model with you in chapter 5 to help you make sense of all this in a simple, practical and useful way.

1

Strength and warmth: The big two in extraordinary leadership

Despite the title of this chapter, strength and warmth are not only critical for extraordinary leadership. Psychologists actually call strength and warmth the 'big two' because they play a major role more broadly in our lives. Indeed, as outlined by psychologist David Bakan in *The Duality of Human Existence*, they are the primary dimensions that humans use to navigate social interactions and relationships with others, and they represent the two most fundamental modalities of human existence.

Strength and warmth can be described as shown in the following table.

Strength	Warmth
Focus is on the self and separation	Focus is on others and connection
Concerned with expressing the self in the world	Concerned with relating to others
Reflects your existence as an individual and your separateness from others	Reflects your participation in something larger, such as your family, team or organisation
Facilitated by your drive and ability to exert your will on the world	Facilitated by your desire and ability to make sense of the world and respond to it with and through others

TO BE IS TO BE … HOW STRENGTH AND WARMTH HELP US MAKE SENSE OF OUR WORLD

These two psychological forces are so prevalent and influential in human behaviour that they have been the subject of a huge swathe of psychological research for the last 70 years. An enormous amount of scientific research has investigated strength and warmth to explain the human experience and how we interact with each other.

Even though different words have been used at times for these two characteristics, research[1] has linked them to many aspects of existence, including:

- how you see yourself
- how you think, reason and problem-solve
- how you recall and describe past events and experiences
- how you perceive and respond to other people
- your personality
- your perception of gender and sex roles in society
- your coping strategies and defence mechanisms
- what is likely to stress you
- physical and mental health problems you may be prone to
- changes in how you think and feel as you get older
- your ethnic cultural identity
- how you see yourself in the world.

In other words, strength and warmth explain a huge amount about how we make sense of our place in the world, and how we respond to the opportunities and challenges it presents – including how we lead.

In this chapter, I explore these two forces in much more detail, starting with strength.

The impressive competence of Dr Wang

My mother was recently admitted to hospital with severe back pain. We discovered she had a degenerative spinal condition requiring an operation, and were referred to a neurosurgeon. My mother is 79, so my family (especially my father) were concerned about the risks of surgery. Indeed, my father became increasingly anxious over the few days until the appointment.

However, from the moment the neurosurgeon Yi Yuen Wang entered my mother's hospital room, minds were put at ease. He had a quiet confidence about him that suggested he knew what he was doing, conveyed through his movements, tone and words. He answered my family's questions succinctly, factually, and in a to-the-point way. He shared the results of his surgeries, was open about the risks, and provided some insight into his experience with older patients. When he left the room my mother, father and siblings (as well as myself) all felt very confident in Dr Wang's skills and expertise.

When I asked my father how he had felt about Dr Wang, his response was, 'He appeared very confident and competent. I'm very comfortable with him being Mum's surgeon.' In a short time, Dr Wang had made a large impact, leaving no uncertainty in our minds that my mother was in safe hands.

A CLOSER LOOK AT STRENGTH

Strength describes your capacity to exert your will over the world. In the exercise of strength, you use mastery, competence and personal will to exert control and influence over your environment and others, and to enable you to solve problems, seize opportunities and create an experience of the world that reflects your needs and desires.

Strength is not just the exercise of physical effort, although it may sometimes entail it. It relates more broadly to what we do and say to make things happen, through actions and behaviours, as well as words and language that have control or influence over things and people.

Individuals with a moderate to pronounced strength orientation experience fulfilment and satisfaction through their individual contributions and accomplishments, as well as their sense of independence, autonomy and separateness.

Words often used in psychology to substitute for or complement the term 'strength' include agency, dominance, influence, power, mastery and competence.

When strength is absent

The opposite of strength or complete absence of it is referred to as weakness or submission, portrayed as a giving up or giving in to whatever forces are acting on you in your environment, situation or social group. Powerlessness, surrendering, acquiescence, passiveness and inaction are other words that describe an absence of strength.

Strength and leadership

Strength was a basic building block in the spectacular ascendance of humans as the dominant species on earth. Our drive to shape and control our environment and others around us has been at the core of the development of our civilisations, technology, advancements and cultures. We have a deep abiding drive to create a better tomorrow, which compels many human beings to make things happen today – for which strength is the primary ingredient.

Strength is, therefore, traditionally a highly valued characteristic in leadership and management because it makes things happen. If a principal reason for leadership is to mobilise action (and so get others to get things done), strength is a fundamental requirement in this.

Will and skill in the demonstration of strength

To demonstrate high levels of strength, a person needs the will – or the drive and motivation – to act and influence the world around them. They also need the requisite skills, knowledge and experience.

An absence of skill or will often results in lower levels of perceived strength; however, under certain conditions, a high level of drive or motivation attached to a high level of confidence can combine to mask a deficit of skill and competence.

Confidence and strength

Confidence is perceived by most humans as a reliable indicator of strength or competence. Confidence creates the impression that we are masterful, capable and willing to act. Even when we lack confidence, we are encouraged to 'fake it until you make it', if only for the reason that it will encourage others to believe we are competent. If their reactions towards us then signal that we are perceived as competent, it stokes our confidence and creates a positive cycle of affirmation and self-belief.

Unfortunately, the far-reaching and pernicious side effect of this 'fake it until you make it' approach is that many less-than-competent leaders bluff their way into roles well beyond their skill level because of overblown confidence. The reality is that confidence is not necessarily a reliable indicator of competence. As I mention in the Introduction, research by Professor Thomas Chamorro-Premuzic shows that close to half of all leaders, most of them male, are not sufficiently competent to do their role properly. Nonetheless, many are able to attain and retain these roles because they bluff their way through by portraying high levels of confidence.

Dominance and status

So why is confidence such a prized characteristic in many parts of our societies, and especially in leadership? Part of the reason is that when an individual shows up confidently in group social situations, they are often assumed to have higher status and more authority within the group. This is advantageous, because higher status individuals in any social hierarchy typically have more influence and power within the group – especially over individuals who have lower status, often identifiable by their more submissive and uncertain behaviours.

In this way, the exercise of strength goes beyond being merely based on the competence a person possesses (such as experience, knowledge, skills and qualifications) to also encompass their ability and willingness to act in an authoritative or dominant fashion.

Strength, task and results

As well as being valued in leadership, strength is also valued on an individual level, especially in our organisations and businesses – again because it's the key ingredient in human behaviour for getting things done.

This makes it especially valuable to organisations that are held accountable for producing results, such as the military, profit-producing companies, and government agencies where results and performance are constantly scrutinised. In my experience of these settings, and in much of the management literature, strength is therefore highly correlated to aspects such as task, action, results, outcomes, production and performance.

Strong competencies looked for in leaders

Not surprisingly, then, the competencies that we most frequently look for when selecting leaders for our organisations are traditional, strength-based competencies such as:

- accountability
- initiative
- opportunity recognition
- planning
- problem-solving
- results focus
- strategic direction
- tenacity
- visioning.

Strong body language

Strength can be easily identified through to our body language too; for example, through:

- looking confidently in any direction chosen
- moving deliberately and purposefully
- standing with a straight back, shoulders back and chin held high.

Strong verbals

Even the words we use and the way we deliver them can convey strength, such as through:

- avoiding filler words such as 'umm' and 'like'
- raising your voice
- speaking with a lower pitch
- using confident, active words such as 'can' and 'will', instead of 'maybe' or 'might'.

Strong behaviours

More complex behaviours can also reflect strength. These include:

- actively monitoring the execution of a plan
- arguing a point in a debate
- asking for what you want
- delegating a task
- forthrightly sharing your opinion or view
- identifying a problem, opportunity or solution
- letting someone know the outcome if they act or don't act
- making repeated attempts to get someone to listen to you
- presenting a case for a new idea or proposal
- putting together a plan
- speaking more loudly or deliberately to make sure you get your point across
- standing up to get people's attention
- trying to influence how others think or feel about a topic.

Western cultures especially value strength

Think about how many hero movies are built around one individual tenaciously overcoming adversity to succeed and triumph. Individual effort and self-agency are such valued traits in the western world that we have been trained since childhood to develop and demonstrate our competence, initially through our schooling system and then throughout our work careers. Exams, grades, job interviews and performance appraisals are nothing more than mechanisms to demonstrate our competence and strength.

We emphasise strength in ourselves but warmth in others

Interest in warmth-based competencies such as vulnerability, empathy and compassion has increased in recent times. However, we are still more likely to emphasise competence and self-determination as qualities we most admire in ourselves – even while we value and highlight warmth when we describe the qualities we most admire in others.

For example, when asked to recall stories about themselves that illustrate admirable qualities, people are more likely to share strength examples such as courage, persistence and resilience. When people are asked to share stories about others that illustrate admirable qualities, they are more likely to share warmth examples such as compassion, trust and selflessness.

We prefer others to develop warmth, but choose strength training for ourselves

European social psychologists Andrea Abele and Bogdan Wojciske showed that while we prefer that others learn how to become warmer, we choose training for ourselves that will make ourselves stronger and more competent.[2] Their research found that we are more likely to choose this kind of competence-based training for ourselves, such as strategic thinking and time management, over soft skills training.

However, the reverse is true when we choose training for others – we are far more likely to desire their participation in relational and humanistic skills training that develops warmth capabilities such as empathy and collaboration.

The personal benefits of strength

Personal benefits also come when we possess strength. A range of studies have shown significant psychological advantages associated with possessing a moderately pronounced strength orientation[3], including:

- higher wellbeing[4]
- better health

- greater self-esteem
- less anxiety
- lower incidence of depression.

Martine – a study in warmth

Martine is an accomplished accountant and leader. She is also a loving mother and partner. Somehow, she has found her way to balancing her home and work life so well that she has been awarded a prestigious women in leadership award, to be presented at a swanky dinner in front of hundreds of people. This, however, is where Martine feels at the edge of her competence. She is a petrified public speaker.

When the MC announces that after a short 15-minute break they will be presenting the main award for the evening, she whispers loudly to the person beside her, 'I feel terrified.' Of course, many others at the table hear her admission and spend the next 15 minutes letting her know exactly why she belongs up on stage and reassuring her that she will be fine.

When Martine is finally called up to accept her award and share some words, she steps on to the stage, approaches the microphone, smiles and says, 'I'm glad this is not an award for public speaking because I hate doing it. I almost want you to clap now rather than at the end when you will have discovered that I don't know what I'm doing up here.'

The room erupts into applause because, through Martine's authenticity, she has connected with the same fear that so many people in the room also have about public speaking. When their applause eventually dies down, she says, 'Thank you. It is an honour to accept this award on behalf of every woman whose struggle has allowed me to stand here. I am here to encourage more women to struggle and succeed and not give up.'

As she continues, there is an almost palpable sense that she is surrounded and held up by those many women she spoke of, and the many people in the room in which she stands.

A CLOSER LOOK AT WARMTH

Warmth refers to your capacity to relate to others and cooperate with them. It is present when you desire connection with others and move towards them physically, emotionally or intellectually. When a person demonstrates warmth, they are perceived to connect with and relate to others.

When you experience warmth from others, you are likely to feel a sense of belonging and being cared for, with warmth-oriented individuals experiencing fulfilment and satisfaction through their relationships and their sense of belonging.

Other words for warmth can include communion, connection, love and likeability.

The opposite of warmth

So what are we signalling to the world when we show the opposite of warmth? The logical answer is coolness (as in warm is the opposite of cold). However, cool, reserved, emotionally passive behaviours are not the only way to show an absence of warmth. Highly active and red-hot emotionally charged physical or verbally aggressive behaviours are also the opposite of warmth, declaring with hostility, anger and contempt that 'I don't care about you!'

Elie Wiesel was a writer, professor, political activist and Holocaust survivor. He was also awarded a Nobel Peace Prize in 1986 for his humanitarian work. One of his more powerful statements was that 'the opposite of love is not hate; it's indifference'.

I see this in myself. I know at times I can display indifference and an absence of warmth to others. This is not intentional, but it can show up nonetheless when I am being presented with a point of view that is different from my own. As I try to make sense of that other point of view and think about what I want to say in response, I withdraw into my own thoughts. In these moments, I lose eye contact, and my face becomes passive, cold, even distant – I have even been told by my daughter that when I think deeply, I sometimes have a 'resting bastard face'. If you were with me in that moment, you likely would not describe my behaviour as hostile but, nonetheless, I would no longer be showing up as warm.

The term 'disconnected' captures all these aspects, because it encompasses both the cool, passive and disconnected behaviours as well as the hot, aggressive and active behaviours that signal a lack of warmth.

Warmth in leadership

Warmth has traditionally not been as valued in leadership nearly as much as strength has been, particularly in western cultures; however, that seems to be changing as social standards and generational expectations change. This is reflected by the inclusion of more warmth-related competencies found in some leadership profiles today such as:

- acting authentically
- building collaborative relationships
- coaching
- cultivating trust
- developing others
- engaging with others
- giving and receiving feedback.

What warmth looks like

The following examples of warm behaviours provide some more concrete and specific ideas about what warmth looks like:

- adjusting your own views and positions to integrate what others have shared with you
- asking others to share what they know, think or feel
- involving others in conversations, meetings and decisions
- leaning forward
- making eye contact
- open and inviting body language – such as arms open, hands in view
- pausing and reflecting on what others have said
- paying attention to others in the moment rather than the task

- paying attention to the needs and motivations of others – what drives them and what they care about
- responding with empathy to others' emotional states
- saying what you authentically feel and think without needing to protect yourself
- sharing deeper thoughts, feelings and vulnerabilities
- showing emotions
- showing others that you have heard what they have shared with you
- smiling
- softening your voice – reducing volume and pace
- using pluralistic words such as 'we' and 'us' rather than singular words such as 'me' and 'I'.

Trust and warmth

Trust is a key element of warmth and comes in two forms: trusting others' intentions and trusting others' competence.

When you trust someone's intent, you're assuming that their actions towards you will reflect your best interests, not just their own. When you trust their competence, you're assuming they have the capabilities to make a meaningful contribution to improving your situation.

Your assessment of them in these two areas can determine whether you show warmth towards them, and whether you adopt an approach or an avoid strategy with them.

Likewise, their starting position on these two assumptions about you will affect whether they show up with warmth or not. People who generally assume that others' intent cannot be trusted, or that they are incapable or incompetent, will often signal low warmth in their behaviour, discouraging approach behaviours from others.

So trust signalling behaviours project warmth and promote openness and receptivity. An absence of trust signalling can result in closed and protective behaviours, typically resulting in lower levels of cooperation between people.

Emotional connectivity, warmth and trust

Emotional connectivity describes the relationship we have to other people's feelings and emotional experiences. It is an important element of emotional intelligence and is concerned with our ability to recognise and respond appropriately to other emotions.

When our behaviour signals that we are interested in and responsive to the feelings and emotions of others, we are displaying warmth. We are likely to be perceived as having good intentions towards the other person – that we have interest in their wellbeing, not just our own. This in turn promotes trust.

When our behaviour signals that we are uninterested in or dismissive of others' emotional experiences, we are not displaying warmth. We likely will be perceived as self-interested and lacking concern for their wellbeing. This promotes mistrust.

Warmth is universal

Interpersonal warmth is so intrinsically connected to the human experience that it is a word or concept that is used universally across all human cultures and societies. Each language may have a different word for warmth, but its meaning is exactly the same.

Warmth is valued by others

As revealed earlier in this chapter when discussing strength, social psychologists find that we value warmth more in others than we value strength – we are more likely to choose warmth-based training for those that we live and work with even though we are likely to choose strength-based training for ourselves. Likewise, when we hold positive images of others, we are more likely to emphasise their warmth characteristics when describing them.

Warmth is psycho-physiological

The feeling of relational warmth is actually correlated to biological sensations of temperature in the human body. In some quirky research experiments conducted at the University of Colorado, participants who briefly held a cup of hot (versus iced) coffee judged a target person as having a 'warmer' more generous and caring personality.

Conversely, another set of experiments by social psychologists found that when a person is excluded from a group and experiences disconnection, they will actually feel physically cold.

(As a sidenote, scientists hypothesise that the strong connection between physical warmth and interpersonal warmth is partially explained by the physical warmth we experience as foetuses in the womb, or when we are held closely as babies to the warm bodies of our carers.)

The benefits of warmth

A range of studies have shown significant psychological benefits are associated with possessing a moderately pronounced warmth orientation. These include:

- generally feeling more supported by others[5]
- actually having greater access to support from others, both tangible (for example, money and information) and intangible (for example, emotional support and advice)[6]
- a buffering effect that reduces the feeling of stress[7]
- lower incidences of depression and anxiety[8].

The benefits of warmth in leadership

Leaders and entrepreneurs who are perceived as being warm gain further benefits; for example:

- Warmth is essential to be considered a great leader, according to research by Jack Zenger and Joseph Folkman. In their research, involving over 50,000 leaders, each leader was rated in terms of their leadership performance and their likeability (aka warmth). They discovered that only 27 leaders were rated in the bottom quartile in terms of likeability at the same time as being rated in the top quartile in terms of overall leadership performance. In other words, the chances that a person who lacks warmth will be considered a great leader are only about one in 2000.
- When we are perceived to be warm, others are more likely to support our plans – as discovered by researchers who examined

the decisions investors made into start-up ventures in Silicon Valley.[9] When Mascha Wout and Alan Sanfey examined the investment decisions made by hard-nosed venture capitalists, they found that they favoured start-up entrepreneurs who showed stronger warmth behaviours such as smiling and use of pluralistic language.

RECAPPING STRENGTH AND WARMTH

To summarise the 'big two':

- Strength is all about dominance, influence, competence and agency. In other words, strength is about *making things happen*.
- Warmth is all about connection, communion, love and likeability. The essence of warmth is best expressed by the phrase *with and through others*.

Now that we established what strength and warmth are, in the next chapter I delve deeper into their relationship to each other.

Reflection

What do you describe as the attributes you look for in others?
Are these more warmth or strength related?

Think back to the leaders you've experienced through your life.
What did you value in them – warmth or strength?

What about the attributes you are most proud of in yourself?
Do you tend to focus on (and try to develop) your warmth- or strength-related behaviours?

2

How strength and warmth relate

How you think about the relationship between strength and warmth is important. Indeed, it has far-reaching consequences for the kind of leadership you produce.

You can see the relationship between strength and warmth broadly in two ways. I discuss both options in this chapter, and how we can move from an 'either/or' approach to one that is 'both/and'.

OPTION 1: WARMTH *OR* STRENGTH

The operative word here is *or*. From this view, strength and warmth are mutually exclusive, seen as opposites, with each occupying opposite ends of a spectrum (as shown in the following figure). You can choose *either* strength *or* warmth.

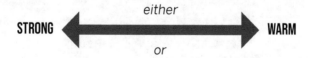

This mental model assumes that to show more strength in actions, we have to show less warmth, and vice versa. It also assumes that strength and warmth do not exist in high concentrations in the same space and time. Like a seesaw, for one to go up, the other must come down. To have a lot of one, you must have less of the other. In other words, they must be traded off against each other.

Here are some typical thought patterns that show how this 'trading off' mindset works:

- *I need to make this happen. Engaging with others will take time. I don't want to lose time. So, I won't engage with others.* (In this case, giving up warmth to preserve strength.)

- *I know how to make this happen. Others' ideas are not as good as mine. If I ask them, I might lose control. So, I will just tell them what will happen.* (Choosing not to act with warmth so that I can maintain strength.)

- *I value being connected to others. If I speak up, I might rock the boat. I might be disapproved of. I won't say what I really think.* (Giving up strength to show warmth.)

- *I like to get along with others. This argument is getting heated and might go nuclear. If I stand my ground any further our relationship will be damaged. I will back down, withhold my honest opinion, and agree with the other person.* (Giving up strength to preserve warmth.)

Have you noticed yourself experiencing any of these thought patterns? Do you notice yourself sometimes giving up strength to have more warmth or vice versa? I know that I do. When I 'debate' (a polite word for 'argue') with my wife, Tamsin, I sometimes notice myself becoming worried that she'll become cool and distant from me if I press my point too insistently. So, I don't. I dial down my strength ('Oh, I suppose it doesn't matter that much.') and turn up the warmth ('You're probably right, darling. Let's do it your way.') I also notice the opposite sometimes happens with my children when they are not doing what I've asked. My voice gets louder – dialling up the strength – my face becomes sterner, and my language becomes less inclusive and warm.

The tyranny of *or*

These kinds of 'either/or' thought patterns and behaviours are subject to what social philosopher Professor Charles Handy terms 'the tyranny of or' in his book *The Empty Raincoat*. This applies to thought processes where our mind is presenting to us a binary option – A or B; this or that. You can only choose one; you can't have both.

It's not just modern minds that have grappled with this dilemma. Niccolò Machiavelli was an advisor to the rich and powerful in the highly political and influential middle states of Italy around the time of the Renaissance in the 15th and 16th centuries. His book *The Prince* instructs how to exercise influence within the high stakes power plays of that time. His ideas were unique, and even today we use the term 'Machiavellian' to describe anyone who has been cold, dispassionate and calculating in their exercise of leadership to achieve their own aims. A basic question asked by Machiavelli was, 'Is it better to be loved or feared?' He acknowledged it was very difficult to possess strength and warmth simultaneously so suggested that if you are forced to choose, then choose strength – perhaps not his exact words but precisely his sentiment.

These sentiments continue to be expressed in the 21st century. John Neffinger and Matthew Kohut advise American politicians and company leaders on how to influence people from their headquarters in Washington DC, a modern-day hotbed of politics and influence. In *Compelling People: The Hidden Qualities that Make Us Influential*, they highlight the critical role that strength and warmth play. Their observation is that 'it is very hard to project both at once' because they are in direct tension with each other and are subject to a 'hydraulic effect'. Like a pipe filled with fluid and with a rubber bulb reservoir at each end, if you squeeze at one end, the other end will expand and vice versa.

Importantly, however, Machiavelli as well as Neffenger and Kohut acknowledge the possibility that strength and warmth can exist in the same space and time, although it can be difficult to do so and, therefore, much rarer to find in leaders. This is exactly why the expression of strength and warmth showing up together is the 'x factor' of leadership – rare, elusive, and extraordinary when it does appear.

Why the tyranny of *or*?

Over the years, I have observed many leaders caught in the dichotomous mind trap of seeing strength and warmth as mutually exclusive. Why are so many held by the tyranny of *or*? Two main hypotheses explain it: one based on society and one on biology.

Hypothesis A: Societal conditioning

Societal expectations surround us from birth and have an enormous impact on our thinking and our behaviour. In the context of strength versus warmth, the different expectations of what being male and female looks and sounds like are a significant influence.

Strength and warmth have long been gendered in our societies, especially in the west. Females have traditionally been socialised to manifest principally as warm, caring, nurturing, loving and connected. Males are encouraged to take up the traditionally 'masculine' characteristics of strength, action, dominance and independence. In many people's eyes, to at least some extent, to be male is to be strong and masculine. To be female is to be warm and feminine.

Categories

Human beings also have a built-in and irresistible drive to categorise things that they observe as a way of making sense of the world and surviving. For example, if I see something that is large, has sharp teeth and is running towards me, I know it is probably in the category of things that are dangerous, and I should take evasive action.

Many of our categories are binary: big or small; heavy or light; fast or slow; soft or hard; good or bad; safe or dangerous.

Binary is good for speedy decision-making, such as in the lightning-fast reactions our brain needs to activate in survival situations. If our automatic and non-conscious survival brain only has to decide between two options, faster decisions result.

Gender as an either/or category

One of the earliest binary categorisations most of us are exposed to as very young children is whether we are classified as male or female. I am a boy, you are a girl. In our simple young minds, we learn and entrench in our understanding of the world a universal truth that you are a boy, or a girl, and that only two options are possible. You can't be both. This, of course, is not biologically true but very few of us have experiences in life that enable us to learn early that biological sex is not always black and white.

At the root of gender bias

Thus, we have the necessary ingredients for the tyranny of *or* to be embedded as gender bias. It goes something like this: our non-conscious brain is taught by the world around it that women are supposed to be warm and men are supposed to be strong. It also learns that being male or female is a binary, either/or classification. You can't be both male and female, so therefore you cannot be both strong and warm.

When strength and warmth are embodied in binary gender classifications, and gender has such a large range of powerful associations with how we should be in the world, it seems inevitable that the non-conscious brain of the average person estimates the possibility of being strong and warm is the same as being simultaneously male and female – very low to zero.

The consequence is a world view that sees men as strong but not warm and women as warm but not strong.[1]

Challenging bias

So much is at stake with these non-conscious associations. They create unhelpful gender bias as well as limit our capacity to appreciate gender ambiguity and diversity.

They are implicated in the ongoing challenge we have of increasing female participation in leadership roles. Given that leadership and strength are highly correlated, the bias against women being seen as strong is a distinct disadvantage for them in accessing leadership roles as easily as their male counterparts.

What's more, the gendering of men as exclusively tough and strong and not warm leads to tremendous psychological damage to boys and men who are consequently not taught or encouraged to express their fears and emotions in constructive ways, and can instead learn to direct their displaced frustration, anger and rage towards violence against others, and violence towards themselves (through self-harm or suicide).

Making progress

If sociological conditioning is a major mechanism behind the 'tyranny of *or*' thinking when it comes to strength and warmth, I hope this book can make even a small contribution to the elimination of gender bias by encouraging the *and*: women can be strong *and* warm, men can be warm *and* strong – indeed all of us can be *both* warm and strong. Perhaps by doing so, more women can take up the leadership roles they deserve and more men can be encouraged to show greater compassion and emotional connectedness.

Hypothesis B: Neurological mechanisms

While still in the early stages of understanding the full complexity of how our brains work, experts have outlined two ways in which its functioning can facilitate the tyranny of *or*.

First, our brains have a number of neural networks, each facilitating different types of thinking and behaviours. Neuroscientist Anthony Jack from Case Western Reserve University showed through fMRI imaging that activating the neural network in your brain responsible for analytical and task-focused thinking actually supresses the neural network responsible for social and emotional reasoning, and vice versa. As explained by Jack's colleague Professor Richard Boyatzis, this means that the brain of a leader primarily focused on solving problems and getting things done in in the workplace may not even notice the people around them.

Boyatzis acknowledges, however, that the brain of a more effective leader is capable of cycling back and forth between the task and social neural networks extremely quickly, measuring the rapid switching in fractions of a second. This is usually the result of having been trained to notice task and people issues equally well, and to strengthen the operation of the less dominant neural network.

In addition to neural structures, our brain chemistry exerts powerful effects and provides a second pathway for the binary approach of warmth *or* strength thinking and behaviour. Testosterone and oxytocin specifically are two hormones that appear to be heavily implicated in strength and warmth behaviours respectively; however, the effect of one may reduce the effect of the other. Here's how neuroscience explains it.

Testosterone and oxytocin

Testosterone is associated with activating dominant, aggressive and competitive tendencies.[2] In other words, testosterone activates behavioural tendencies related to strength.

Oxytocin plays an important role in social cognition, mentalisation and empathy.[3] In other words, it is crucially implicated in our ability to read social situations and other people accurately and respond in a warm and connected manner. In fact, in one experiment researchers found that after giving a group of male subjects a single dose of oxytocin, they were better able to interpret subtle facial cues and the emotions and feelings that other people were likely to be experiencing. Oxytocin is also sometimes referred to as the 'love drug' because it is associated with feelings of empathy, closeness and connection to others.

In summary, testosterone promotes strength and oxytocin facilitates warmth.

Testosterone blocks oxytocin

Both of these hormones are essential in the proper functioning of the human brain and body; however, elevated levels of testosterone appear to have an inhibitory effect on oxytocin. This is because the brain receptors that oxytocin binds with become blocked by elevated testosterone levels.[4] When this happens, oxytocin is unable to play its usual role in stimulating or maintaining warm feelings towards others.

For example, imagine that you and I are having a conversation face to face. We like each other but, nonetheless, find ourselves in an argument. In an attempt to win, you dial up your strength and try to dominate me through your words, tone and body language. In response, testosterone is released in my body and activates any tendencies I may have towards dominance, competition and aggression. At the same time, my elevated testosterone levels block the path of oxytocin in my brain, and – voila! I am unable to maintain a warm and connected feeling towards you as a result.

Testosterone also inhibits impulse control

A secondary effect of testosterone also plays out. Another target of oxytocin is our pre-frontal cortex[5], the more recently evolved part of our brain that controls our impulses and regulates our thinking and emotions. High levels of testosterone impair thinking in this part of the brain, making it difficult for us to maintain calm and deliberate control of our impulses, actions and behaviour, and not be triggered into highly emotional or overly reactive states such as frustration or anger.

Testosterone and oxytocin just don't get along

The overall effect of these hormonal mechanisms is to make it quite hard to maintain warmth and manage strength to an appropriate level. I know from personal experience when in arguments with my wife, Tamsin, just how hard it can be sometimes to find the presence of mind and exert enough willpower to pull myself back from the brink of high strength–low warmth feelings of frustration and rising anger.

It is, therefore, possible to argue that to some extent strength and warmth are biologically incompatible given the opposite behavioural effects[6] created by the interaction of testosterone and oxytocin[7] with each other.

This means the view of strength and warmth as binary opposites may have its roots in our lived experience of our own biology.

Mastering our behaviour

I do not believe, however, that any of us should use neurobiology as an excuse for poor behaviour or ineffective leadership. We are not a species that is powerless to reshape our neural networks or resist the impulses of our primitive survival brain mechanisms. We have no reason to believe we cannot train our brains to adopt more balanced thinking patterns or master our impulses towards aggression or overly competitive behaviour.

We can show up with strength and warmth if we choose to. We simply need awareness, the right intentions, training, and repeated experimentation and practice until we learn how to master the genius of strength *and* warmth.

OPTION 2: WARMTH *AND* STRENGTH

A 'both/and' approach is a different way of thinking about the relationship between strength and warmth, and a shift in mindset is required that is revolutionary for many. Copernicus changed the way we see our place in the universe when he proposed that the earth revolved around the sun, not the other way around (as people had believed for thousands of years). For many leaders, changing the way that they see strength and warmth relating to each other is similarly eye-opening.

The operative word here is *and*, where it is understood that strength and warmth are separate constructs that exist independently of each other. This belief assumes that strength and warmth can, therefore, theoretically coexist in the same space and time and are not mutually exclusive, as shown in the following figure.

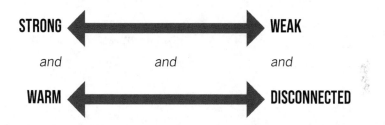

This perspective acknowledges that, even if difficult, you can have high levels of strength behaviours alongside high levels of warmth behaviours – or any other combination for that matter.

This thinking has significant implications. It means you don't have to give up strength to have warmth, or vice versa – although you can choose to if the situation requires it. Strength and warmth can exist in the same space and time and might even be mixed together to respond to a specific situation or need.

In other words, strength and warmth don't exist as polar opposites on the far ends of a single continuum. They are like yin and yang in traditional Chinese philosophy. They both exist and are both needed. In balance, they are helpful and desirable. Out of balance, they can cause unintended problems and consequences.

The proposition that strength and warmth are not opposites, and in fact stand at right angles, is also made by social leadership expert Adam Kahane in *Power and Love*, where he examines the leadership required to guide people through very complex and devastating problems such as ensuring global food security or finding the path to peacefully transition to a genuine democracy in post-apartheid South Africa.

Here are some thought patterns that illustrate how strength and warmth can co-exist:

- *We need to make this happen.* (Strength) *Engaging with others will take time but is essential to generating their commitment and buy-in.* (Warmth) *I don't want to lose time, but we'll lose a lot more if people don't get on board. How can we still move fast enough and engage others?* (Strength and warmth)

- *I know how to make this work.* (Strength) *However, other people's ideas might be better than mine.* (Warmth) *If I ask them their ideas, I might have to rethink my approach, although the outcome would be more successful. I'll ask for their ideas and remain open to considering them if they will improve the result.* (Strength and warmth)

- *I respect others and value being connected to them.* (Warmth) *If I speak up* (strength) *I might rock the boat, but am I being truly respectful of others if I hold back my view? It's best that I speak up.* (Strength and warmth)

The genius of *and*

This belief system that strength and warmth can co-exist reflects a phenomenon that is the antidote to the 'tyranny of *or*' thinking. Instead, this is the 'genius of *and*' thinking, in which we challenge the paradigms and assumptions that lead us to binary 'either/or' thinking.

Adjusting our thinking in this way is not always easy – firstly because some of our binary assumptions are so automatic and habitual that we are not even aware they might be in operation, and secondly because finding the *and* answer where it has not existed before requires real effort and struggle.

Today, binary thinking is behind the struggle that we encounter with some of our more pressing problems. Consider the climate debate – often a pitched battle between valuing the economy *or* the environment. Left-leaning socialists endlessly debate with right-wing capitalists as to whether people or profit is more important.

Professor Charles Handy, introduced earlier in this chapter, proposed that it is intellectually lazy and defeatist to assume something is an either/or proposition – although it is convenient because when you choose a side you don't have to do the hard work to think through the numerous tensions and complexities that might be required to find the genius of *and*.

Indeed, as you read on further, you will discover just how important this *and* thinking is in producing the more extraordinary and energising version of leadership that you crave from others, and aspire to yourself.

Reflection

How do you think about strength and warmth – as an *either/or* proposition? Or as an *and/both* relationship?

What about your behaviour? Do you sometimes trade off warmth and strength, giving up one when showing more of the other?

Think of the very best leaders that you have experienced. To what extent did they appear to balance or integrate both strength and warmth into their leadership?

3

Ordinary leadership patterns

In this chapter, I draw together what has already been covered about strength and warmth to reveal three ordinary patterns of leadership behaviour.

These three ways of leading – control, relate and protect – and how they relate to strength and warmth are shown in the following figure. They are commonly seen in most organisations, with each bringing helpful as well as unhelpful behaviours to the workplace.

Control, Relate and Protect: Ordinary leadership patterns

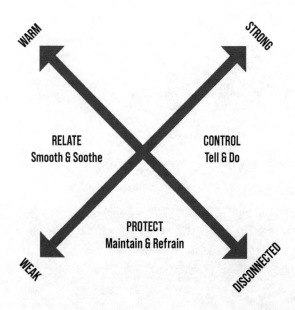

WARM

STRONG

RELATE
Smooth & Soothe

CONTROL
Tell & Do

PROTECT
Maintain & Refrain

WEAK

DISCONNECTED

I provide a full description of each pattern, along with the pros and cons of each, in the following sections.

CONTROL: TELL AND DO

When you encounter strength without warmth, you'll see the exercise of dominance, action and agency. This kind of behaviour is all about control, and about telling and doing. It is interested in getting things done, but not that interested in people, their thoughts, feelings, or ideas. Where this Control pattern of leadership sits in relation to strength and warmth is shown in the following figure.

Control leadership: Strong and disconnected

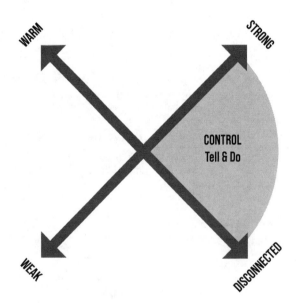

Getting things done

This pattern of behaviour is characterised by its focus on task and outcome. A physical action often conveys this intent to get things done – making plans, scheduling meetings, coordinating action, arranging materials, preparing a business case, making an argument, or wielding a tool or instrument. No matter what the action is, it instantly conveys the message that something is happening.

Body posture and facial gestures can also signal action – for example, a hard-set, businesslike face showing focus and determination; a strong, hands-on-hips stance signalling commitment and an unyielding position. Words can also indicate, convey and compel action and movement, such as 'I will' rather than the more tentative 'I could'. Tone will be certain, strong and convicted.

'I' not 'we'

At the same time, the low warmth behaviours in this Control pattern signal a focus on self rather than others. This behaviour prioritises the needs of the self over the needs of others. It signals a disconnection from other people's thoughts, feelings or involvement, and says, 'I don't really care about you; I'm more interested in me right now – my needs, my wants, my thoughts, my ideas.'

This focus on the self can be signalled in subtle ways, such as through lack of eye contact, arms crossed over the chest, little or no enquiry into others' thoughts or ideas, or a lack of evidence that they are even listening to what others are saying when they do speak. Words such as 'I', 'me', 'my' and 'mine' (instead of 'us', 'we', and 'our') are repeated frequently and signal an independence from others.

This focus can also be signalled in more obvious ways, such as micromanaging and over-controlling – which are both versions of 'do it my way' behaviour.

The pattern can even display an overt and hostile disconnection by actively rejecting the thoughts and contributions of others – as if to say, 'My ideas are the best ones. Yours are stupid and unhelpful.'

Situational judgement of when control might be needed

Without doubt, in some scenarios a leader may judge that a high level of supervisory guidance and instruction would be helpful, such as when employees are new to a task or are struggling and need plenty of instruction and coaching. High levels of control might also be needed when deviant behaviour would create negative outcomes, such as in a high-risk setting (working in a prison, for example) or when performing a potentially dangerous task (such as flying an aeroplane).

As a general rule, however, and as I explore further in chapter 11 (which looks at energising and motivation), a low-trust, high-control approach runs counter to modern theories of motivation and getting the best out of people. It is certainly counter to the expectations that many modern-day team members have of their managers, and is one of the reasons for low levels of engagement combined with high levels of staff turnover.

Task over relationship

Early in my career, I was taught that any human interaction in a workplace involves both practical needs and personal needs. The practical needs are the reason for the interaction – such as to solve a problem, agree on a plan or resolve a conflict. The personal needs also present are the needs of the people involved in the interaction – such as a need to be heard, respected and involved. The high-strength, low-warmth behaviour of the Control pattern is very focused on the practical needs of the interaction but not so much on the personal needs.

From this kind of leader, any social chitchat or small talk at the beginning of the conversation will be short, cursory and fleeting – if it occurs at all. Instead, it may be more likely to make an appearance at the end of the conversation once business has been attended to, as if connecting with others is a second-tier goal or lower priority than getting things done.

If this pattern of behaviour had its own motto it might be something like 'performance over people' or 'results over relationships'.

Apathy and antipathy

The general message you receive from a leader in the Control behaviour pattern is that they don't really care about what you feel. If you were to express emotion, they are likely to ignore it – although not always maliciously. The leader may just be so focused on trying to solve a problem or get a result that they skip straight past any acknowledgement of your feelings and instead focus on the facts – showing up, though, as apathetic, cold or uncaring.

At their worst, these kinds of leaders will not only ignore others' feelings and emotions but also criticise them, telling others that they are wrong to feel a particular way.

Either way, the lack of emotional responsiveness and connection has an erosive effect on trust and engagement of others.

Busy-ness people – expectations, stereotypes and extreme behaviour

Prioritising of results over people is not uncommon in companies and businesses that are principally interested in making profits. That is why they often (but not always) recruit, promote and reward businesspeople whose predominant pattern of behaviour is higher strength and lower warmth – but this doesn't always create the best results, as shown in the following example.

Results versus people?

Colin led a consulting team within a Fortune 50 global company. His team of highly skilled business consultants had led some massive innovations and improvements but were losing steam. While working incredibly hard and producing outstanding results, the latest employee engagement results were troubling. Disconnected leadership, zero tolerance for mistakes, little coaching and unyielding expectations were all showing up as issues in the engagement data, and they were taking a toll. Colin and his boss were especially concerned that if nothing changed, they might lose valued team members, as well as the energy, innovation and commitment of those who stayed.

Colin and the consulting leadership team were guided through a discovery and development process that allowed them to see that the way they were leading was prioritising results over people, causing burnout and unsustainable ways of working. Over several months, they turned their attention to collectively cultivating leadership that also showed concern for people, without giving up expectations for high quality work and results.

The results of their efforts to improve their leadership were extraordinary. When a follow-up engagement survey was conducted, scores across the function improved by nearly 50 per cent, with the items related to the quality of leadership driving the remarkable improvement. At the same time, the team continued to deliver outcomes to such a high standard that they were judged across the business as an aspirational role model for other consulting teams.

Take a brief moment to examine the word 'business'. It is the conflation of the elements of 'busy' and 'ness'. By its very nature, 'business' is about doing things and getting things done. It values action and productivity.

This was reinforced by renowned businessman and company turnaround expert Sir Archie Norman, who acknowledged that if you are forced to make a choice between high-strength and low-strength behaviours in the business world, you should choose the former. (Norman did, however, also value warmth – see chapter 8 for more on this.)

It's not surprising, therefore, that the archetypical businessperson portrayed in Hollywood stereotypes is a hard-nosed, profit-driven, cold and ruthless tyrant – a successful mogul, no doubt, but also not a very nice person.

These behaviours are not just Hollywood legends and myths. I remember that my very first boss displayed this acute version of strength without warmth. I was 15 and had just started as a casual employee at a local supermarket. My new boss, a large and gruff fellow, was taking me on a walking tour of the store when he became incredibly agitated and upset as we arrived at the fresh produce department. I clearly remember watching him berate a junior department manager, standing over him with spittle flying from the corners of his mouth, as he abused and criticised his helpless team member in a loud, shouting voice. I particularly remember the moment when my new boss threw a ripe eggplant on to the floor. I watched it explode, with pulp and seeds spattering over the department manager's shoes and trouser leg. The look of shame and embarrassment on the department manager's face remains seared in my memory.

This example might seem extreme; however, you might be surprised by how often I hear of this type of behaviour showing up in workplaces today.

Control patterns in everyday life

Of course, Control leadership behaviour doesn't have to be as acute as the preceding example, with shouting and abuse as the principal dominance strategies. A milder version shows up in many day-to-day life situations – for example, when you stop listening to what your partner is saying, and you are only interested in arguing your point of view; or the instance when you are focused intently on a task and your child asks you a question and you don't really hear them, instead giving them some automatic unthinking response.

Here are some of the typical and more moderate behaviours that accompany this Control pattern of high strength and low warmth:

- advocates a position with focus and intensity
- appears confident and acts with conviction
- assumes agreement without testing
- becomes easily irritated or frustrated
- counter-argues
- defends against feedback
- demonstrates little enquiry or genuine curiosity
- does not appear to hear or accommodate others' views
- refuses to accept 'no' for an answer
- gets straight to business – no small talk
- gives critical feedback
- ignores or shows apathy towards other emotional expressions
- impatiently listens
- interrupts and speaks over others
- listens to respond rather than to understand
- over-controls projects, processes and events
- rarely adjusts view or position
- seeks to win at any cost

- sets the agenda and topic of the conversation without consultation
- shows signs of impatience or appears fidgety when encountering resistance
- speaks first and speaks often
- speaks louder or faster to compel agreement
- tells others what to do and how to do it.

Under the hood

Most people have core guiding beliefs – slogans and catchcries that we use to orient our actions and justify our behaviours. 'Do unto others as you would have them do unto you' or 'Don't do in secret what you would be ashamed to do in public' are examples of these guiding principles.

So what might the catchcries and slogans of the Control pattern of behaviour be? Probably something like:

- 'It's my way or the highway.'
- 'Win at all costs.'
- 'Whatever it takes.'
- 'Produce or perish.'
- 'Just do it (or else).'
- 'Let me tell you how it is.'
- 'You can't make an omelette without breaking a few eggs.'
- 'When the tanks roll into town, kiddies get crushed.' (Yes, one banking CEO said this to his team.)

When it comes to high-strength and low-warmth leadership behaviours, the more persistent and acute examples are usually underpinned by typical beliefs and mindsets that perfectly explain the behaviour, as shown in the following table.

Control leadership beliefs	Typical behaviours produced
'I have all the answers.'	Argues so that own views and ideas prevail
	Gets louder or more insistent if resistance is encountered
	Listens to respond rather than listens to understand
	Remains closed to better or alternative ways
'I can't really trust others.' 'People need to be told.'	Doesn't empower when delegating or collaborating
	Issues detailed directives and instructions
	Looks for flaws in others' ideas or approaches
	Micromanages
'Do it my way ...or else.'	Rarely asks, mostly tells
	Demands compliance
	Punishes others who don't comply
	Minimises others who resist through sarcasm, belittling, scapegoating etc.

You can easily see why the Control pattern has earned the label of 'tell and do' leadership. When this kind of leader is not actually doing the work of the team, they're telling them exactly what to do, and precisely how to do it – my way ... or else!

The dark side of strength without warmth

Dr Martin Luther King, the well-known civil rights leader and political activist, had something to say about this pattern of behaviour when he exclaimed, 'Power without love is reckless and abusive.' I believe that he was commenting on the potential for this high-strength and low-warmth behaviour to be so focused on outcomes and results that it may be at the expense of people and is, therefore, experienced as self-serving and uncaring.

When it comes to the tough, uncaring, businesslike characteristics of an amped-up caricature of this high-strength plus low-warmth behaviour, I nominate the following real and fictional characters as the poster boys and girls of my generation:

- Donald Trump
- Margaret Thatcher, former British Prime Minister
- Gordon Gecko, fictional businessman in the movie *Wall Street*
- Lord Voldemort
- Darth Vader.

Reflection

Most of us have encountered this pattern of Control behaviour at school, work or in life in general. Where have you seen it?

Who among your bosses, coaches, teachers or parents have you seen demonstrate this kind of strong doing, controlling, 'win at all costs' and dominating behaviour?

Maybe even ask yourself a more challenging question – when has your behaviour showed up this way?

RELATE: SMOOTH AND SOOTHE

If the Control: Tell and Do pattern of behaviour is remarkable for its focus on task rather than people, this next pattern of behaviour is noticeable for being the opposite – focused on people, connection and relationships, with less attention to results, outcomes and getting things done. This focus, and its position in relation to warmth and strength, is shown in the following figure.

Relate leadership: Warm and weak

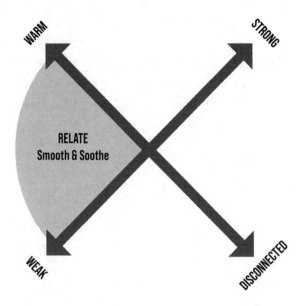

WARM

STRONG

RELATE
Smooth & Soothe

WEAK

DISCONNECTED

With and through others

When encountering the pattern of Relate: Smooth and Soothe behaviour, you may notice immediately the warmth being conveyed through body language – including eye contact, physical movement towards you, open body posture, and perhaps even a smile and a welcoming gesture. These are the hallmarks of warmth, and are clear signals that you are welcome and important.

These signals may be followed up with friendly words, an invitation to connect, or even an enquiry into how you are doing, again signalling that you matter, and that what you are experiencing and feeling is important.

Relate behaviour is interested in you – your thoughts, your ideas and your feelings. This interest may be conveyed through lots of questions and followed up with clear signals that what you are saying is being paid attention to, perhaps with vigorous head nodding and verbal encouragement such as, 'Ah ha' and 'Yes, yes'.

Of course, this pattern of behaviour goes beyond these actions. Warmth-oriented individuals make sense of the world with and through others. While high-strength individuals will respond to problems by analysing them independently and developing a solution that they will then try to influence others to adopt, leaders in the high-warmth Relate pattern need to engage and consult with others to even sense the problem and be able to see or pursue a way forward.

Of course, all of these behaviours signal something important: 'I trust you' and 'I am to be trusted'. Likewise, they signal 'I value you' and 'I would like you to value me'.

Unfocused but fitting in

At the same time, the low-strength behaviours of the Relate pattern produce something more passive and inactive when it comes to tasks, results or outcomes. The energy the behaviour has for building and maintaining relationships is not to be confused with the type of energy required for dominance, influence and agency. Leaders showing this kind of high-warmth but low-strength behaviour could conceivably spend a lot of time connecting without really getting anything done. As a result, conversations or meetings can seem unfocused, meandering and unbusinesslike.

What's more, the absence of strength, and of its accompanying independent thought and action, means that leaders showing this behaviour are highly susceptible to going along with the crowd, being highly agreeable and compliant, and saying yes to whatever is asked of them – even when they have no plan or capacity to follow through with real action. Sometimes these leaders can even agree with others when they actually hold the opposite view. By agreeing, however, they are able to avoid conflicts and tension in their relationships, and instead preserve the harmony they desire. Protecting relationships is a key facet of this pattern of behaviour.

#Keepingthepeace

Smoothing things over

This high-warmth Relate: Smooth and Soothe pattern values interpersonal harmony and belonging. As a result, leaders in this pattern struggle to engage with conflict or hang out with interpersonal tension. Instead of addressing conflictual issues candidly and openly, they will instead skirt around the issue, dancing on its edges but not really addressing the core problem. In a bid to avoid being disliked, they can also sugar-coat tough feedback and smooth over tensions that appear in relationships with others.

The warm but weak leader in this pattern may also flip-flop and back-pedal on contentious issues, adopting whatever is the prevailing mood or view rather than going against it – even when they think or believe something contrary. In this way, leaders in this pattern of behaviour will often say yes, even when they are thinking no.

Fused with others

One of the characteristics of leaders in this pattern of behaviour is that they connect intensely to others' emotional experiences. Their identification with the feelings others are experiencing is so intense it is as if the experience is being shared. Instead of empathy, it is sympathy. ('Sympathy' is when you share the feelings of another, whereas 'empathy' is when you understand the feelings of another but do not necessarily share them.)

This fusing of experience can leave the warm but weak leader in a position where they are now also held by the emotional state being experienced by someone else – for example, frustration, anxiety or fear. As a consequence, they cannot play their required role in helping the other person take clear-headed action to improve their situation. What's more, the overly sympathetic leader can be left unable to make tough or unpopular decisions because they will be seen to be betraying their team members. This can result in a lack of action on tough but important decisions.

If this pattern of behaviour had its own motto it might be 'relationships matter more than results' or, in a business context, 'people over profit'.

The usual habitat of Relate behaviours

Plenty of leaders showing Relate behaviours are, therefore, found in organisations and workplaces that place a premium on people and their human needs. Clubs and community groups in particular can be like this, where the principal reason for their existence is not to produce things or make widgets but to allow people to come together and connect. Many significant institutions also seem to have an abundance of leaders with these high-warmth behaviours, such as healthcare providers, churches, not-for-profits and charities. They are wonderful places to belong to, where people feel part of a community that is connected and cares.

However, a common complaint about the culture of these organisations (which I hear when I work with them) is that they are sometimes too 'soft', not performance-oriented enough, and that they prioritise harmony and collectivism too highly and, as a consequence, fail to have the hard conversations and build the robust performance culture that would deliver the full value to their customer and community stakeholders.

Certain occupational groups that value high levels of warmth also seem to attract high-warmth individuals who display the Relate pattern. Nursing, childcare and kindergarten teaching are stereotypical examples, as are the organisational functions of human resources ('I'm a people person, that's why I'm in HR') and marketing, which is sometimes unfairly caricatured as being more concerned with balloons, banners and fun than hard numbers, results and return on investment.

Can we do some work please?

Rob, a marketing director, would get incredibly frustrated with leaders displaying the Relate: Smooth and Soothe pattern – which was problematic because many in his leadership team often showed up this way.

Monday morning team meetings were particularly hard for him to bear as his team spent what seemed to him to be ages on sharing stories about their weekends and other non-business-related topics. As a self-described 'action man' and 'doer', his high-strength and low-warmth style really struggled when face with the opposite low-strength and high-warmth pattern.

What else you'll see

Some of the other typical behaviours that accompany this pattern of high warmth and low strength can include:

- agrees easily and quickly with the other person's suggestion, request or point of view
- avoids tough or conflictual conversations
- becomes uncomfortable when exposed to tension or heat in conversations
- compromises or gives in readily when views are in conflict with others
- engages in plenty of small talk and social chitchat
- enquires frequently into the other person's feelings or thoughts
- frequently smiles, nods or indicates agreement in other ways
- goes off on tangents
- is attentive to others' facial gestures and body language
- is highly responsive to what the other person says and does
- is overly compliant or agreeable
- is unfocused and easily distracted
- meanders without a sense of urgency
- rarely sets a clear purpose or agenda for conversations or meetings
- regularly overcommits
- shows sympathy for others' emotional states or expressions
- smooths over conflict
- struggles to say no to requests or demands from others
- uses humour too often to distract from helpful tension
- uses many words to say very little.

Fictional examples

Fictional characters – or even caricatures – who show likeable but weak behaviours include:

- Phoebe in the TV sitcom *Friends*

- Del Griffith (John Candy's character) in the movie *Planes, Trains and Automobiles*
- Simon the Likeable in the *Get Smart* TV series
- Gil Gunderson in *The Simpsons*.

Under the hood

The often-used phrases and catchcries of leaders in the Relate behaviour pattern can include:

- 'Let's just have a chat.'
- 'How was your weekend/how are the family, your dog, etc.'
- 'Don't worry, there's plenty of time.'
- 'If you have nothing good to say about someone, don't say anything.'
- 'Yes, yes, yes!'
- 'No worries.'
- 'Sure, I can do that.' (Even though the internal voice is saying, 'But I'm not sure how.')
- 'I agree with you.' (Although the internal voice says, 'Even though I disagree with you.')
- 'Are we okay? We're still friends, aren't we?'

Some of the beliefs and mindsets that can underpin the Relate pattern, and the typical behaviours produced, include those shown in the following table.

Relate leadership beliefs	Typical behaviours produced
'As long as others like you, they will do the right thing.'	Socialises extensively/lots of small talk
	Collegiate, warm and inviting
	Avoids being seen as critical
'Conflict or disagreement is always bad and should be avoided.'	Appeases easily
	Agrees and commits quickly
	Avoids conflict
	Feedback is unbalanced – only positive

Relate leadership beliefs	Typical behaviours produced
'It will all work out okay. We will be okay.'	Little planning
	Fails to address potential problems
	Overcommits

Can you be too nice?

Dr Martin Luther King had something to say about this pattern of behaviour when he stated. 'Love without power is sentimental and anaemic', cautioning us against the assumption that good intentions alone are sufficient to create meaningful change. In this simple statement, he points to the reality that care and warmth towards our fellow men and women are not enough to make progress with difficult problems and opportunities. At times, tough decisions and strong actions are also required. For example, while both Mahatma Gandhi and Nelson Mandela preferred non-violent protest, they also recognised that forceful action or even violence might be warranted if the only alternative was cowardly flight.

The other problem with too much warmth and not enough (or no) strength is a psychological phenomenon called 'over-communion'. As I mention in chapter 1, 'communion' is another term used in psychology for warmth. Over-communion occurs when an individual is so focused on satisfying the needs of others that they fail to pay attention to their own needs and wants – including their physical, emotional and financial needs. By constantly subordinating their own needs to the needs of others – whether their children, partner, team members or boss – they fail to look after themselves and, as a result, can become physically unwell, emotionally drained and economically disadvantaged. A 'martyr complex' can arise, as well as resentment towards dependent others that is repeatedly buried and not addressed – until at some point inevitably boiling toward the surface and, like a volcano, spewing out in a red-hot emotional eruption.

You can see an example of this in the Unikitty character from *The Lego Movie*, who aims to be always affable and nice, and suppresses any critical or negative thoughts or emotions about others, but finally blows her top and becomes a hyper-aggressive angry beast. For such individuals in the real world, self-care is sacrificed when caring for others, at significant mental cost.

Reflection

This is the Relate: Smooth and Soothe pattern of behaviour because it pays attention to relationships and people, as well as nurturing belonging within groups. To do so, leaders in this behaviour pattern learn to conform to the social norms of the group and their organisation and fit in. When overplayed, however, this pattern means that the leader's behaviour is too agreeable and avoidant of conflict in its attempt to not jeopardise acceptance and belonging.

You can probably supply examples of people from your own life. Who among your colleagues, friends and family regularly demonstrates some aspects of this pattern of behaviour?

What about yourself? When have you decided to play it nice or sugar-coat something to avoid conflict or an uncomfortable conversation?

PROTECT: MAINTAIN AND REFRAIN

When you observe an individual whose behaviour is low in both strength and warmth, you may be observing very little in the way of overt and immediately noticeable behaviour. Unlike the two previous patterns of 'or' behaviour we examined – the task-focused Control pattern and the relationship-oriented Relate pattern – this behaviour pattern doesn't declare itself with flashing lights and loud klaxons. It may be instead more identifiable by an absence of behaviour. This weak and disconnected behaviour forms the Protect pattern, as shown in the following figure.

Protect leadership: Weak and disconnected

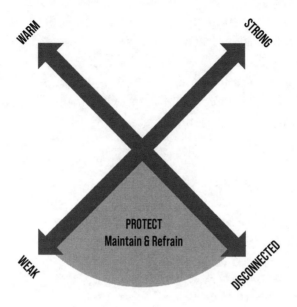

Hard to see, hard to read

The low-strength aspect of the Protect: Maintain and Refrain behaviour pattern shows up as passive, inactive and submissive. Leaders in this pattern are relatively inert in their environment, exercising little or no influence over the situations they find themselves in. Likewise, they appear reluctant to exercise influence over people to make something happen. If they see something that concerns them, their response may not be noticeable, or may be very subtle.

Stable and safe

The low-strength orientation of the Protect: Maintain and Refrain pattern means that leaders in this pattern are relatively unlikely to take significant action quickly or dramatically as issues arise. These leaders show up as 'even keeled' emotionally and are, therefore, very consistent and reliable, providing a predictable and non-impulsive response to situations and problems.

The behaviour of those in this pattern is to turn up on time and leave on time, but often no more and no less. They do what they're told, maybe even begrudgingly, but no more than that, without obvious additional initiative or proactivity.

This is the behaviour you will see when someone has decided that it's not a sensible course of action to do anything – and that speaking up or taking action probably won't change things anyway. It's the behaviour that follows the thought it's too hard or too risky to act, and so the person has made a decision to not try. Leaders in this pattern just accept, and even maintain, the status quo, avoiding change – which they see as unnecessary or risky.

If these leaders experience a situation they find uncomfortable, instead of actively seeking to change the situation, they just accept the situation, withdrawing further into themselves, becoming smaller, like a turtle withdrawing into its shell.

Unresponsive to others

The low-warmth aspect of the Protect pattern shows up as unresponsive – to others. When someone gives away little in facial gestures or body language to suggest what they are thinking or feeling, you are dealing with this low-warmth behaviour. When you ask a question and you get a vague or non-committal response, you are dealing with this low-warmth behaviour. When your enquiries are met with a one- or two-word answer, revealing very little, you are probably experiencing this behaviour.

It is possible, however, that this person is experiencing plenty of internal dialogue; it's just that you will have no idea what that dialogue is. They may care about what you are saying, or the topic being discussed, but it's not showing up in their behaviour. Instead, you are met with something that appears aloof, uncaring, unresponsive and disconnected from you.

Avoid and abdicate

At their most unhelpful, leaders in the Protect pattern of behaviour avoid taking accountability and abdicate responsibility for anything that is negative or even unpleasant, such as a poor result, a staffing change or a contentious decision. Instead, these leaders blame others or remain silent. Their most common catchcries include:

- 'It's not my fault. It's theirs.'
- 'It wasn't my decision. I'm just following orders.'
- 'You can blame finance/HR/operations/marketing (anyone else but me).'
- '…' (Saying nothing.)

Protect against risk

This pattern of behaviour can provide protection from the dangers that come from doing what feels risky. Speaking up, sharing your thoughts when you're not 100 per cent certain, and disclosing how you really feel: these can all feel like dangerous things to do for some people, or in some situation. Whereas remaining silent, keeping your head down and not engaging – these can all be behaviours that protect us from potential risk.

Maintain and refrain

Maintaining the status quo and keeping things just as they are is also a way of avoiding risk. Change often brings uncertainty and unpredictability, and stepping into the unknown in this way can feel uncomfortable. The current way things are, the status quo, is known – and even if we don't like some aspects of them, they may be preferable to an uncertain future.

This means keeping things just the way they are by criticising new ideas, resisting innovations and refraining from engaging in 'risky' change are hallmarks of this pattern of behaviour.

Passive-aggressive resistance

Leaders in the Protect pattern do not openly declare their resistance and hostility to risky ideas, plans or others. Instead, their behaviour helps illuminate what is meant by the term 'passive-aggressive', a term that many people use but struggle to define.

'Passive-aggressive' denotes a pattern of behaviour characterised by indirect resistance or hostility towards others, and an avoidance of direct confrontation. Indeed, this submerged hostility towards others makes passive-aggressive behaviour difficult to deal with. Unlike overt hostility, where you know exactly where you stand and which you can see and deal directly with, passive aggression doesn't announce resistance openly.

This can lead to the phenomenon of public compliance followed by private defiance. Most leaders have experienced this from their team or other leaders. No overt resistance is voiced to your idea or plan and you believe you have the support of others – only to find out later that somehow that agreement seems to have been undone. The reason for this is that the silence that greeted your suggestion or plan did not equal acceptance, even though you assumed it did.

Therefore, the Protect pattern of behaviour may choose to say nothing rather than publicly push back.

What Protect behaviour looks like

The typical behaviours that accompany this Protect pattern can include:

- abdicates responsibility
- argues for the status quo
- blames others
- complies publicly but resists privately
- corrects faults in others' work
- critically evaluates arguments and propositions
- holds back
- insists on extensive analysis before action
- is closed to others' ideas
- is cynical of innovation or change
- is emotionally detached
- is silent and disengaged
- looks for problems rather than opportunities in situations
- maintains distance
- provides no or little eye contact

- provides only blank or neutral facial gestures
- provides short and efficient responses
- rarely shares real feelings or deeper thoughts
- responds passively to problems
- speaks only when asked a question
- uses quieter vocal delivery, lacking dynamics of pitch or volume
- uses unresponsive body language
- withdraws from conflict.

Fictional examples

A list of characters (or caricatures, to be more precise) that display a noticeable aspect of the Protect behavioural pattern include:

- Stuart, the comic-book store owner in *The Big Bang Theory* TV series
- Eeyore the donkey from the *Winnie-the-Pooh* books
- C-3PO from the *Star Wars* franchise
- Marvin the Paranoid Android in *The Hitchhikers Guide to the Galaxy*.

Under the hood

The catchcries and slogans of Protect: Maintain and Refrain behaviour might be:

- 'No change is good.'
- 'We've tried that before, and it won't work.'
- 'It's not my responsibility.'
- 'It has nothing to do with me.'
- 'It's their fault.'
- 'We should wait a while before we respond.'
- 'Once bitten, twice shy.'
- 'Just keep your head down.'

The beliefs and mindsets that can underpin the Protect pattern, and the behaviour produced, are shown in the following table.

Protect leadership beliefs	Typical behaviours produced
'Don't rock the boat.'	Sticks to routine
	Avoids taking a strong stance
	Discourages disruption
	Cautious and non-committal
'Just do what is asked – nothing more.'	Reacts to requests; rarely shows initiative
	Blames others for tough messages or decisions
	Does not openly air disagreements
	Closed
'Keep your head down and don't take risks.'	Procrastinates for fear of making a bad decision
	Magnifies the risks and minimises the benefits
	Chooses the safe option even if sub-optimal outcomes result
	Guards against change

A unique ecological niche

So where do you find this Protect behaviour in greater concentrations than normal? In my experience, you find it anywhere it is safer to just comply, keep your head down, follow the rules, minimise risks and avoid bringing attention to yourself.

Many workplaces and organisations have cultivated this set of conditions. You have probably experienced it yourself as an employee or a client at least once in your life – and commiserations if you have to deal with it more often than that.

The stereotypical government department, lazy bank or telecommunications company that you may have had to deal with is a prima facie example. How much buck-passing, non-responsive, disconnected and bureaucratic behaviour have you had to endure from these types of organisations, where no-one seems to notice your existence, care for your problem, or take accountability for solving it?

> ## Reflection
>
> Keep in mind that I am talking about *behaviours* in this chapter (and throughout this book), not personalities or character. These are behaviours that even you are capable of adopting at any time.
>
> Think about it – when have you recently become unresponsive, disconnected and passive?
>
> Even momentarily, where have you just given up, stopped trying, and slipped into this pattern of Protect behaviour, playing it safe?

4

Catalyse: An extraordinary leadership pattern

In this chapter, I focus on the remarkable behaviours produced when a leader incorporates both strength and warmth into their repertoire. I call this the Catalyse: Challenge and Empower pattern, as shown in the following figure.

Catalyse leadership: Warm and strong

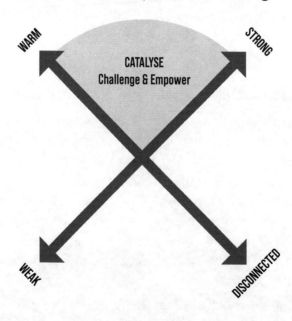

MAKING THINGS HAPPEN, WITH AND THROUGH OTHERS

The Catalyse pattern of behaviour does not signal that task matters more than people. Nor does it prioritise these aspects the other way around. This pattern of leadership seeks to make them both important. It is not results *or* people. It is results *through* people. Catalyse: Challenge and Empower behaviour recognises that by tapping into the desires and motivations of others, more can be unleashed collectively than can be by the leader working alone. By connecting people to a reason to act, greater energy and effort can be brought to bear on key opportunities and challenges.

Energetic and connected

For leaders in this pattern, energetic action also conveys intent towards getting things done. Body language, facial expressions and verbal communication all signal something is to be achieved. The behaviour shows up as confident and assertive without being egotistical or aggressive. Leaders in this pattern know what they stand for, and their interactions with others have purpose and meaning. Connection with others is also signalled through their action, body language and words – including eye contact, an invitation to engage, a request for ideas and a challenge to reach higher. These are all behaviours that acknowledge the presence of others and the role that they have to play.

Catalyst leadership – action with sustained energy

In science, a *catalyst* is a substance that is introduced to spark a reaction and cause a release of energy, but is not itself consumed in the process. In a similar way, Catalysing leaders spark a reaction without being consumed, seeing their role as unleashing the efforts of others rather than doing the work themselves. This means behaviours are oriented to challenging others to do the work, and supporting them to get it done, without taking away their responsibility. As the leader's energy is not consumed in the process, they are free to apply it to many more people and situations.

In contrast, leaders in the high-strength, low-warmth Control: Tell and Do pattern I outlined in the previous chapter take over the work, and by micromanaging and over-controlling must expend a significant amount of energy on each task and outcome. The inevitable outcome is that Control: Tell and Do leaders quickly tire and reach the limits of their abilities to get results through others. In this way, they actually become the bottleneck on team performance because everything must go through them. The opposite is true of the Catalyst leader, where the aggregate capacity of the team (rather than the individual leader) is the determining factor in how much gets done.

CHALLENGE: THE MISSING PARTNER TO EMPOWERMENT

The push for staff empowerment was a huge management fad in the 1990s. However, this push received a bad rap (and pushback) in some circles because ideas of 'empowerment' were often attached to ideas of providing latitude and freedom to team members to make decisions on what they did and how they went about completing work, but without this being accompanied by the necessary tension to perform to a required standard. Without clear setting of performance expectations, or the absence of a clear goal, leaders aiming for empowerment will fail to create the requisite conditions for accountability. Their intentions may be good, but without communicating their expectations for results and performance, their leadership may ultimately be weak and ineffectual.

This is where the idea of 'challenge' comes in. A Catalysing leader not only empowers but also challenges, inviting and demanding that people bring their best efforts and their best thinking to the problems and opportunities they are working on. They set clear goals and expectations, and monitor others' progress towards them. They also give feedback and support where it helps others make progress towards what was agreed. By doing so, they marry the warmth of empowerment to the strength of challenge.

Challenge and empower

As a result, two words perfectly summarise and signpost the combination of strength and warmth in this pattern of Catalyst leadership. They are 'challenge' and 'empower'. Catalyst leaders *challenge* themselves and others to do their best, question the status quo where it doesn't serve us well, and take accountability for the results created. They also *empower*, through acknowledging that the real work of leadership is to catalyse effort and application from others, to mobilise, guide and support team members, while also holding them accountable for tackling the tough challenges. By doing so, Catalysing leaders help others learn how to thrive, especially when the going gets tough.

Head and heart intelligence

The limitation for those who exhibit the more ordinary leadership patterns may be that they do not yet possess the sufficient mental complexity to unify strength and warmth. As the great American author F. Scott Fitzgerald wrote, 'The test of a first-rate intelligence is the ability to hold two opposed ideas in the mind at the same time, and still retain the ability to function.'

In his essay, Fitzgerald didn't elaborate on whether he was referring to the traditional intelligence of intellect (IQ), or emotional intelligence (EQ); however, the evidence indicates that great leadership requires both – extraordinary leaders use their IQ to optimise their strength, competence and mastery, and their EQ to cultivate their warmth, trustworthiness and connection.

A GROWTH MINDSET

The Catalyse: Challenge and Empower pattern of warm and strong leadership is one of growth and development. It is evident when you speak your mind and say what needs to be said, but at the same time are able to listen and change your perspective based on what you hear and learn. It shows up when you advocate your opinions convincingly but hold them lightly.

This pattern of behaviour produces an open system of growth – one that is receptive to new information, ideas and perspectives. Catalyst leaders seek, receive and consider feedback willingly because new information often leads to growth and improvement. For the same reason, they are willing to give feedback to others, even when tough love is being called for.

These leaders also take accountability and own their role in a mess rather than seeking to blame others and avoid responsibility. In the language of the management guru Jim Collins, Catalyst leaders look out the window during success and acknowledge others as the source of it, but look in the mirror during failure, accepting their part in the outcome and learning from their mistakes.

Expanded intelligence and co-creation

Leaders in the Catalyse behaviour pattern assume that others have more potential to express and that their intentions are good, so they willingly co-create solutions and outcomes with others to achieve better quality results, and gain higher levels of commitment. These leaders enquire into others' thoughts and feelings, and can show empathy and compassion so that others can progress in work and in life. Never believing that they have all the answers, leaders in this pattern do, however, think deeply about the key questions that will deliver new insights, galvanise people and challenge the status quo.

Novel and complex problems, for which one person cannot possibly have all the answers, are also approached more effectively by seeking and integrating the observations and interpretations of others before taking action.

The path less taken

The Catalyse leadership pattern is not as common as the three ordinary patterns of leadership I examine in the previous chapter (that is, Control, Relate and Protect). Two larger studies concerning the development of adults suggests that at any given time only 30 to 40 per cent of adults will possess the capacity to operate beyond the limitations of strength *or* warmth binary thinking.[1]

You may even struggle to think of many leaders you have worked with who were Catalyst leaders – although no doubt you remember any who were with gratitude and admiration. These leaders seem to be in the minority, although if you look carefully, you will find Catalyst leaders in many walks of life.

Catalyst leadership in the Twilight Zone

I have an enduring memory of another of my early bosses – but in this case one who demonstrated the Catalyst pattern of behaviour. He was young and relatively inexperienced, having recently graduated from the management training program of the company I was working for – a large department store. I was a casual employee, 16 years of age and working in what was possibly the most boring area in the whole building – the lighting department. This small, brightly lit alcove was located in the furthermost reaches of the top floor where customers rarely ventured. We called it the 'Twilight Zone'.

My colleagues and I were bored and unchallenged, while the department underperformed on a perennial basis. Into this challenging context came John, our new fresh manager. He quickly sized up the situation and made it clear that the status quo wasn't acceptable for him, us, or the business. He then challenged us by working with us to hatch a plan to promote the department and attract customers. We were all engaged with specific tasks that harnessed our unique abilities, and over several weeks we deployed the plan.

The following month, John greeted me at the beginning of my shift and showed me the management reports that displayed the trading results. Asking me to read out the month-by-month sales comparisons for the products we had promoted, he stood alongside me and listened quietly as I noted significant uplifts in many product lines. We had even beaten our total department sales budgets for the first time in living memory! When I finished speaking, he turned to face me, looked me in the eye and said, 'Thank you. It was your efforts and those of your teammates that made this happen. You should be proud.' Wow. I was so chuffed I could feel my chest swell with pride and gratitude.

At that moment I realised I could make a difference, that I had potential and that I was valued, even in a small, insignificant operation on the outer boundary of a business. This leader lifted me up, energised me and empowered me to do it again.

I realise now that this was the extraordinary impact of a leader who showed both strength and warmth.

The struggle for integration

Integrating and entwining warmth and strength in your leadership can be difficult. I've observed many leaders struggle at first to integrate both attributes, suffering from what I call the 'pendulum swing'. In a desire to be strong they give up warmth, with their behaviour swinging towards the Control pattern. When they realise they have lost their warmth, they give up their strength and swing back the other way towards the Relate pattern. At its extreme, this process looks like a Dr Jekyll and Mr Hyde version of leadership, as the leader swings between tyrant and sycophant. (You might recall from the introduction to this book that this is how I showed up in my first leadership role on the construction site.)

Catalyst leaders learn that you don't have to give up strength to add warmth, and vice versa. The goal instead is to maintain the warmth or strength you have, and just add more of the element you are missing. Add, don't subtract. Eventually, with experimentation, guidance and a good dose of persistence, you can work out how to integrate the two into your day-to-day behaviour.

WHAT CATALYST LEADERSHIP LOOKS LIKE

Here are some of the behaviours you might observe or experience when encountering this pattern of behaviour:

- challenges others to reach higher and achieve more
- challenges the status quo and asks, 'How can we make it better?'
- clarifies objectives and expected outcomes of interactions and meetings so they are productive
- holds self and others accountable for commitments
- accepts responsibility for errors, mistakes and unhelpful contributions
- asks for opinions, perspectives and ideas
- defines what needs to be achieved but allows choice in how it gets done
- gives both positive, reinforcing feedback and constructive feedback

- holds the necessary tension in conversations so real progress is made
- incorporates others' ideas into solutions and approaches
- inquires deeper into conflictual and competing views
- is open with own feelings and vulnerabilities
- is upfront with intentions to build trust and open dialogue
- listens attentively to others
- organises self and others to focus on desired goals and results
- pays attention to both facts and feelings
- pays disciplined attention to agreed plans and outcomes so they are executed
- reinforces and acknowledges others' contributions
- role-models courageous authenticity
- seeks feedback from others
- shares the rationale and the 'why' behind requests
- uses empathy and compassion to help others make progress.

Real-world examples

A small list of successful and impactful real-life leaders that regularly demonstrate (or demonstrated) this pattern of behaviour includes:

- Bob Hawke, former Prime Minister of Australia
- Jacinda Ardern, Prime Minister of New Zealand
- Nelson Mandela, anti-apartheid revolutionary and former Prime Minister of South Africa
- Sheryl Sandberg, author and COO of Facebook
- John F Kennedy, former President of the United States
- Meg Whitman, business executive and Republican candidate.

Under the hood

The catchcries and slogans of this Catalyst pattern of behaviour include:

- 'Results through people.'

- 'Together we are stronger.'
- 'Connect to others where they are.'
- 'Listen to understand not to respond.'
- 'Is a win–win possible here?'
- 'Accept your role in the mess.'
- 'Be the change you want to see.'
- 'Be strong enough to be vulnerable.'
- 'We learn more from our failures.'

Some of the underlying thoughts that underpin this pattern, and the typical behaviours they produce, are shown in the following table.

Catalyse leadership beliefs	Typical behaviours produced
'My job is helping others focus on the important work that we have to do.'	Focuses on important goals and results
	Shares why something matters, not just what needs to be done
	Challenges and invites others to contribute
	Demands that others express their full potential
'Trust is an important ingredient in collective success.'	Collaborates to achieve better outcomes
	Communicates openly and candidly
	Gives and receives feedback and support
'I don't know everything.'	Asks important questions and listens carefully for divergent views
	Demonstrates curiosity about others' views and perceptions
	Empathises with others' experiences in life

Reflection

Hopefully at some point in your career you have experienced leaders in this Catalyst pattern of behaviour, including those able to challenge and empower.

Where did you see this kind of leadership and what was its impact?

Now turn the lens on yourself. When do you believe you have shown up in this way?

5

The Xtraordinary Leadership Model: X marks the spot

To summarise the four patterns of Control, Relate, Protect and Catalyse leadership behaviour I created the Xtraordinary Leadership Model. This model shows all four leadership patterns and their relationship to strength and warmth. It also describes the typical behaviours associated with each pattern.

It's also designed to be a 'ready-reckoner' of sorts, a handy resource that you can use at any time and in any situation to make sense of your own and other people's behaviour.

The model is shown in the following figure.

The Xtrarodinary Leadership Model

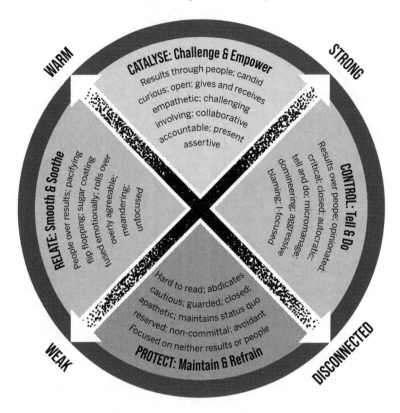

WARM

STRONG

CATALYSE: Challenge & Empower
Results through people; candid
curious; open; gives and receives
empathetic; challenging
involving; collaborative
accountable; present
assertive

RELATE: Smooth & Soothe
people over results; pacifying
flip flopping; sugar coating
fused emotionally; rolls over
overly agreeable;
meandering;
unfocused

CONTROL: Tell & Do
Results over people; opinionated;
critical; closed; autocratic;
tell and do; micromanage;
domineering; aggressive
blaming; I-focused

Hard to read; abdicates
cautious; guarded; closed;
apathetic; maintains status quo
reserved; non-committal; avoidant
Focused on neither results or people
PROTECT: Maintain & Refrain

WEAK

DISCONNECTED

I describe ways to use and build upon this model extensively through-out the rest of this book, so take a moment to familiarise yourself with it.

USING THE XTRAORDINARY LEADERSHIP MODEL

As you read through the descriptions of the four leadership patterns in the previous two chapters, and summarised in the Xtraordinary Leadership Model – or 'X model' for short – no doubt you were able to recognise many of the behaviours you've experienced from differ-ent people and leaders you know. You might also have seen some of your own behaviour in there.

To make the most of the X model and the leadership patterns it describes, the following sections outline a few things to remember.

Behaviour, not personality

This is a *behavioural* model. It describes a leader's actions – what we observe them to say, act and do, or what we observe them not saying or doing.

While personality traits and predispositions influence an individual to more consistently behave in particular ways over the long run, their behaviour can still be quite variable across situations and circumstances. Therefore, the words that are used to describe each leadership pattern in the X model – Control, Protect, Relate and Catalyse – are intended to describe behavioural patterns, not others' character or personality.

Behaviour shifts in different situations

Very few of us are so narrow and predictable that we only ever demonstrate one way of leading all the time. While a leader may behave in a dominant 'go to' or primary way, you will usually find their behaviour can shift into different patterns under certain conditions.

Behaviour changes according to context

Context is a major determinant of how we behave, and different situations can generate different behaviour. For example, when I'm in control and things are going well, I can easily stay within the Catalyse zone. If I'm feeling rushed, in crisis or under significant pressure, my behaviour can lose its warmth as I focus more on getting things done. This may result in my behaviour shooting towards the Control: Tell and Do pattern – including micromanaging, demanding and not listening.

Our behaviour can also shift according to the people we are interacting with. For example, I have noticed many leaders who are compliant and highly agreeable when interacting with their boss but show up as aggressive and overly critical with their direct reports. You may have a less pronounced variance when dealing with different people or groups, but like most people may show some variability nonetheless.

Likewise, I have noticed that some people and their behaviours seem to trigger my defensive tendencies, whereas others encourage a more open and collaborative style.

Most of us change our behaviour to some degree according to context – the situations we are in, and the people we are interacting with.

Sometimes actions are deliberate, sometimes not

Of course, our shifts in behaviour are not always conscious or deliberate.

Conscious shifts occur when I deliberately and intentionally adopt a different behaviour according to the context. For example, if I am meeting with my boss who has strong Control tendencies, entering his office with an agreeable and compliant high-warmth, low-strength stance may feel safer. Similarly, I might choose to dial up my strength and lower my warmth to take a forceful and tough position with a team member who is not listening.

Non-conscious shifts differ in that they are not consciously and deliberately activated. They occur automatically and spontaneously, without conscious thought. For example, have you ever noticed yourself losing self-control when in a conflict, and found yourself arguing without listening, becoming closed and unreceptive to the other person, maybe even shouting? You probably didn't choose to move into the high-strength, low-warmth zone. It just happened. Likewise, have you ever noticed that you have become quiet, withdrawn and unresponsive in reaction to someone else being overbearing and aggressive? This is likely an automatic and triggered response, not a deliberate and intentional choice.

MASKS AND MASQUERADES

Your decision to adopt a pattern of behaviour different from your usual way of operating is like wearing a mask. You may feel one way, but choose to show up a different way. For example, I may feel anxious or nervous before a big keynote speech in front of hundreds of people and might prefer to protect myself and not step onto that stage, but nevertheless I put on a warm and strong mask, and stride purposefully into the spotlight with a big smile on my face.

The truth is that all day long we are playing roles – perhaps that of parent, leader, partner or child – and sometimes need to wear a mask to show up in a more helpful way for other people.

Unfortunately, though, not all masquerades are helpful to others, or motivated by altruism. Some are self-serving, as well as being downright confusing and bewildering to others.

Many clients tell me a difficult combination to work with is when Control: Tell and Do intentions wear a Relate: Smooth and Soothe mask – that is, where you are dealing with someone who seems agreeable, warm and friendly, but you also find evidence later on that they have backtracked on everything you thought had been agreed, and they may even be sabotaging you and your efforts.

My daughter tells me this is called a 'frenemy' – a person who appears to be a friend to your face but backstabs and white-ants you behind your back. These behaviours are the result of a person who has self-serving 'I' intentions but puts on a collaborative 'we' mask for impression management purposes only.

Reflection

Take a moment now to think about your own leadership. Which of the four patterns most often show up in your leadership and how often?

Use the following blank model to assign percentages that describe how often your own leadership reflects each of the four patterns.

For any pattern that you allocate more than 0 per cent to, note the behaviours you typically demonstrate that explain that percentage.

As you do this work, remember that we all can demonstrate behaviours from each pattern depending on the situation we are in, and the people we are interacting with.

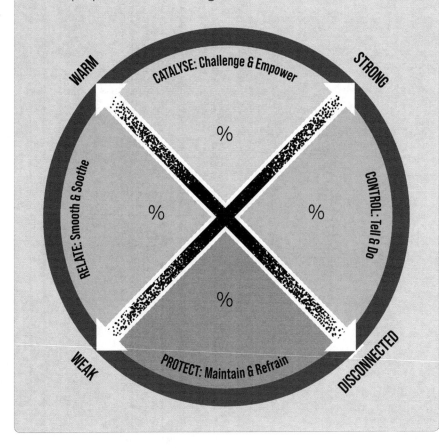

PART II

The leadership dance

One fine morning, two young coral reef fish are swimming side by side in a warm tropical sea. They encounter an old leathery groper fish swimming past them in the other direction. They share some brief smiles and nods as the elderly groper fish comments, 'The water sure is lovely this morning.' The young coral fish mumble, 'Sure, sure' as they watch the old groper swim away. Following a brief pause, one of the young coral fish turns to the other with a confused look on its face and asks, 'What's water?'

This story highlights the idea that we can be immersed in something and still be unaware of what surrounds us. A fish can't tell you about the properties of water, or about hydrodynamic principles or the complex biomechanics that allow it to swim. Nor can a bird flying gracefully across the sky describe to you the chemical composition of air, or how the physics of differentials in air pressure allow it to remain aloft as a glider would. These creatures are simply born into these environments and act instinctually to survive and thrive in them.

Immersed in a sea of behaviour

Human beings are much the same when it comes to the complex interplay of behaviours that occur between people, as well as the cognitive processes that produce our thoughts, feeling and actions related to those human interactions. The typical person doesn't think about these behaviours and interactions too deeply, instead relying on instinctive actions and responses.

This lack of analysis is rather problematic for the exercise of leadership, though – and especially if some of our habitual and instinctual responses to others limit our ability to engage and influence them. If these actions and responses remain unexamined, they can leave us powerless to improve our leadership. If you are unaware of the dance that you do, how can you change it? How can you become a leader others want to follow? And how can you create a culture of extraordinary results? The chapters in this part explore these ideas further, discussing why each is so important.

6

The hidden dance: Beyond awareness

In this chapter, I reveal some powerful but often hidden processes in human cognition and behaviour that have an enormous impact on our ability to take up leadership in a way that is beyond typical or usual and move us towards extraordinary.

Here's a summary of these key ideas that I'll be focusing on in this chapter:

- **First impressions rule:** In particular, I look at the effect of non-conscious snap judgements (based on limited strength and warmth data) on others' initial willingness to engage and be influenced by us.

- **Stubbornly resistant impressions:** I reveal some of the other brain rules that can make some first impressions much more resistant to being changed.

- **Self-fulfilling prophecies:** Here I consider a process similar to the well-known butterfly effect, looking at the way in which small variances in initial impressions can create widely divergent outcomes in leader–follower relationships over longer time frames.

- **Spiral dynamics:** I focus on the challenge of pulling out of unhelpful relationship dynamics once they have been established between a leader and someone else.

FIRST IMPRESSIONS: FORMED IN MILLISECONDS

Psychological research shows that strength and warmth are so influential in human dynamics that within one-tenth of a second of meeting a new person, our brains have already made assessments of them. For example, studies from Princeton University's Social Perception Laboratory showed people took less than 10 milliseconds to decide whether others looked trustworthy (warm) or aggressive (not warm).[1] That's as long as it takes to blink.

If we make a positive judgement, we will be predisposed to trust and engage with that person. A negative assessment will instead trigger feelings of caution and wariness or even a full-blown flight or fight response.

Given that these judgements are made within fractions of seconds, for all practical purposes, we are making these judgments almost instantaneously.

A fist fight at 30,000 feet

The evening following our wedding, Tamsin and I caught an overnight flight to Thailand to start our honeymoon holiday. A few hours into the flight, as we travelled through the vast and empty darkness of a night-time sky, like most other passengers I was attempting to sleep in the dimly lit cabin.

Only lightly snoozing in my cramped aisle seat, I became aware of someone walking past me with heavy footsteps, heading towards the front of the cabin. Opening my eyes, I caught a quick glimpse of the person's face as he pivoted quickly to turn back towards the rear of the plane. Without conscious thought my body reacted instantly to this fellow's face, knowing with certainty that he was bad news.

I became instantly awake and alert as my conscious mind caught up with my initial non-conscious assessment. The look of anger, the veins bulging in his neck and muscled arms, the staggering gait of a drunk all instantly combined to form one impression. *Uh oh, this can't be good*, I thought to myself. Careful not to make direct eye contact, I kept my eyes slitted as if I were still asleep, but kept my limited vision locked on his face and his arms as he came back past me, only then hearing the angry muttering under his breath. After passing my seat, I twisted around to watch him, thankfully, disappear into the gloom of the rear cabin. *Good. Sleep it off*, I thought to myself after waiting a while to see if he would reappear. I then tried without much success to settle back into proper sleep, instead dozing uneasily.

Crash! Bang! Grunts of pain, the sound of fists hitting flesh, cries of alarm and panic. I awoke to mayhem, the fog of sleep instantly lifting, knowing instinctually that the angry man was somehow involved in what I was hearing. A few seats back, in the middle of the centre row, two men were violently grappling as passengers around then scattered into the aisles. One of the men was the angry one I'd seen earlier. 'Help me,' the other man cried out as he tried desperately to stop the angry man's drunken punches from landing. 'Stop it, stop it!' a woman passenger screamed at the angry man. 'HELP ME!!' the other man pleaded again. Simultaneously a few of us moved quickly across the space and grabbed hold of the angry man from behind, pinning his bloody arms to his sides and pulling him away towards the back of the plane, past the surprised and bewildered faces of our fellow passengers.

This event is seared in my memory, and what I perhaps remember most is the instantaneous feeling of knowing that the angry man posed a risk to my safety and that of others on the plane, well before I had access to the facts that supported that assessment.

Warmth is assessed first

One of the classic findings in the study of first impressions is that the most immediate and influential assessment is that of interpersonal warmth.[2] Ample evidence suggests that the assessment of others' intentions is completed before the assessment of their strength. This has an adaptive survival advantage[3] in that it is more important to determine if a stranger is nasty or nice before we answer the question as to whether they are competent or not.

Assessments are based on limited data

Research also suggests our brains make rapid 'nasty or nice?' warmth assessments using very limited data. This also enables a better survival response. If our brains were instead like a grand jury, having to consider mountains of evidence tabled over months, we would possibly be dead, harmed or taken advantage of before our brain rendered its verdict.

Facial expressions, body movement and anything verbalised that signals something about our warmth or strength in those first few moments are all key sources of data that are used in the rapid formation of first impressions.

Assessments can be predictive ...

While made quickly, these initial assessments are surprisingly predictive.[4] Several studies have shown that initial impressions of strength and warmth formed within moments are highly predictive of assessments made over much longer periods of time. In one experiment at Princeton University, researchers asked two groups of students attending lectures to evaluate the same professors and lecturers in the same sessions. One group was asked to rate the staff after only a few seconds of exposure. The other group rated the staff at the end of the semester. The assessments of both groups were remarkably similar. This demonstrates how our initial impressions can be quite accurate predictors of others' strength and warmth.

In another experiment, the same researchers studied voters' perceptions of politicians who were standing for election. Research subjects who had no exposure to or interest in a particular election were asked to look quickly at each candidate's face and decide which one looked more competent. The test subjects were not told they were looking at candidates for political office or asked to predict the winner. Those they selected as more competent were also the actual winners of their elections about 70 per cent of the time, demonstrating that initial impressions can also greatly influence voting outcomes.

... But also prone to error

My wife, Tamsin, is an attractive and confident woman. She exudes strength, dresses well and appears stylish even when shopping for our groceries. She is also incredibly warm and welcoming – although at a distance strangers sometimes don't realise this, only seeing an attractive and confident woman, and someone who is the epitome of strength. And, as I discovered, this can create interesting first impressions.

Midway through a social function we were attending, while Tamsin was off talking to some friends of ours, I was waiting to order some drinks when I felt a tap on my shoulder. 'Excuse me,' said this stranger, a middle-aged woman. 'I just wanted to come over and tell you how delightful your wife is. I've been speaking with her tonight and she has such a lovely personality. I've only ever seen her from a distance in the village and I'd stereotyped her as stuck up and self-absorbed. But I was so wrong. She is gorgeous on the inside as well!'

Of course, I agreed completely with the stranger, thanked her for the compliment and told her that I would pass it on. That moment has stuck with me since as a very good illustration of how inaccurate first impressions can be.

The 'smoke detector' principle

It's perhaps not surprising that rapid-fire, automatic inferential judgements such as first impressions can result in errors. What may be news to you, though, is these errors are skewed towards making *negative* judgements of a stranger's warmth when the data available is ambiguous or incomplete. That is, our brain has evolved to be more likely to make the error of assuming someone else's intent is hostile, rather than assuming that their intent is warm. This is because errors that produce inaccurate negative assessments enhance survival outcomes, whereas errors that produce positive assessments detract from survival outcomes – that is, they lead us to believe it's safe to approach this person when it's actually not.

Our instinctual judgements, therefore, follow the 'smoke detector principle', as described by psychiatrist and founder of evolutionary medicine Professor Randolph Nesse.[5] Smoke detectors, such as the ones that you and I have in our homes and offices, are purposely designed to produce false-positive errors rather than false-negative errors. A false-positive error occurs when the smoke detector reacts to particles in the air that are not produced by fire, such as dust or chemicals. This results in the smoke detector activating even when no real danger is present, which at the time is extremely annoying and frustrating for anyone who is nearby. It also explains the number of times fire brigades are called out for 'false alarms'.

A false-negative error is one in which the smoke alarm fails to recognise or discounts airborne particles that may in fact be associated with a fire or combustion event. The outcome of this kind of error can be catastrophic – which is why engineers purposely design the smoke detectors to err on the side of caution.

Playing it safe

The human brain also appears to play it safe in making social perception judgements, having evolved to err on the side of making 'safer' errors when inferring the potentially dangerous traits or intentions of others. This means your brain is more likely to mistakenly assess a good person's intentions as untrustworthy, rather than the other way around.

Here is a practical example. Imagine you have just joined a large company in a mid-level role. On your first morning you see the CEO, whom you have not yet met, walking across your floor of the office building. He is headed for a meeting that you are going to be part of. He is close enough for you to notice he is walking at a quick pace, holding his phone to his ear, with a furrowed brow, narrowed eyes like Clint Eastwood in a *Dirty Harry* movie and tight lips. As he walks across the floor, he does not make eye contact with anyone.

So, what does your brain make of this data? Based on the available data, it can make at least two reasonable interpretations. A furrowed brow, slitted focused eyes, and tightly set jaw and lips can indicate anger and hostility. They are, however, the exact same facial signals of many people when they are concentrating and thinking intensely about a problem. No additional data is available at this stage to indicate which of these two interpretations is the more accurate one, but nonetheless your brain will very likely err on the side of caution and infer hostility and, therefore, danger. Perceived angry faces also grab and hold our attention more so than any other facial expression,[6] contributing to higher levels of alertness. Seeing your new CEO in the way described will then predispose your thoughts, feelings and actions towards caution, trepidation or anxiety when entering that meeting room for the first time.

STUBBORNLY RESISTANT

Initial impressions can also be quite resistant to change. Once your brain has initially made up its mind about the strength and warmth of another person, persuading it otherwise can be difficult. One classic study by Stanford University psychologists Lee Ross, Mark Leper and Michael Hubbard in the 1970s illustrated just how stubborn the human mind can be once it is made up.[7] In this study, observers were given feedback on how well a group of test subjects (people) had performed on a certain task, from which the observers formed positive or negative impressions of them. The researchers then revealed to the observers that the results had been manipulated and the feedback they had been given on each test subject was, therefore, inaccurate. Despite the observers then being provided with new data that should have reversed their original impressions of the test subject, the researchers found that the observers generally persisted in believing the original assessments.

Inferring trait from state

One of the reasons first impressions are resistant to change is because of an extraordinary leap of reasoning made by our non-conscious brain.

When first impressions are formed, the human brain doesn't just make behavioural observations and instead goes much further, performing large inferential leaps to deduce a stranger's personality. This is a product of our 'personality judgement instinct',[8] which first appears in early childhood and is such an essential life skill that by adulthood nearly everyone can do it well enough to get by.

This instinct is behind such statements as, 'I am good at reading people' – which actually means, 'I am good at taking a small amount of information about someone's behaviour and using it to predict what they are really like – including their personality, character traits and predispositions.'

Psychologists call this 'inferring trait from state', where we take a relatively fleeting observation of a person's momentary state, such as a smile, and assume that it is indicative of a trait that is stable over time – that is, this person is smiling (state), so they are a friendly person (trait).

This means that if I offered an effusive 'Hello!' in the morning, you'd likely generate a first impression of me as an extroverted, optimistic and enthusiastic person. A tired and lacklustre, 'Hi', delivered later after a very tough and challenging day could result in a first impression of me as an introverted, pessimistic or unenthusiastic person.

What if, however, I lie somewhere in the middle of extroversion and introversion, with no significant predisposition either way – as a reasonable number of people in the world do. This means that the first impression gained in the morning of an extroverted person was not accurate, nor was the evening's first impression of an introverted person.

To demonstrate these deductive acrobatics, in another study at Princeton University's Social Perception Lab, researchers measured test subjects' reactions to a series of photos of the same person making different faces. They found that the slightest change in expression could elicit an entirely different reaction in the viewer. Depending on which photos were shown, the same person could be classified as both extroverted and introverted. Yet participants used a stable personality trait (such as extroverted) rather than a fleeting emotion (such as happy) to describe the faces they saw. In other words, when you think you can judge people's dispositions from their faces, all you're really getting is a moment-in-time observational snapshot of their current mood and associated behaviours.[9]

Because personality is more fixed and stable over time, this can lead to us making more permanent and resistant-to-change judgements about others based on personality, rather than allowing for a more temporary placeholder judgement based on behaviour and emotion.

Biases that keep us safe

Another reason our first impressions are resistant to change is a function of biases that affect the thinking our brain does.

A bias is simply a non-conscious weighting in our brain towards a certain way of thinking or feeling when encountering certain conditions.

Clearly, a negativity bias exists when it comes to forming our initial impressions of others' intentions. We have already established that the human brain is biased towards making negative first impressions (because it's safer) and will do so using limited data (because it's faster).

A bias also exists against new information that may conflict with the original assessment of intentions. Researchers have found that a negative first impression of warmth will persist even in the face of contradictory information.[10] This means that if I initially assess you as lacking warmth or having negative intentions towards me, I'll need a lot of convincing, with loads of contrary evidence over a potentially long period of time, before I shift my initial assessment.

A second, relatively well-known form of bias may play a role in this. *Confirmation bias* is a tendency for our brains to take notice of new data that supports an existing belief but ignore data that may disprove or conflict with that belief.

But how do first impressions become so entrenched as reliable truths in our minds so quickly? The answer lies in understanding the psychological underpinnings of the phenomenon commonly called a 'self-fulfilling prophecy' – the topic of the next section.

SELF-FULFILLING PROPHECIES

The problem with first impressions is not that we form them. The problem, as we have now established, is that they are often inaccurate and can be long-lasting, which then leads to undesirable interactional effects. In other words, they can produce difficult-to-change relationship dynamics that are unhelpful to our ability as leaders to get the best from others, or for others to get the best from us.

The phenomenon that produces these effects is commonly referred to as a 'self-fulfilling prophecy', first defined by the distinguished sociologist Robert Merton. Merton described the process behind this phenomenon as one where an initially false definition of the situation evokes certain behaviours, and these in turn make the original false perception come true. In other words, through our behaviour we make real our originally held belief – even if it were inaccurate.

Interpersonal expectancy effects

The technical term used in psychology for a self-fulfilling prophecy is an 'interpersonal expectancy effect' or IEE.[11] This effect was first recorded in some of the earliest research into first impressions created in job interviews during the 1950s and 1960s. Given that job interviewing is a classic high-stakes example of the importance of first impressions, many early studies naturally focused in this area.

Numerous studies showed that in situations where interviewers had formed a positive first impression of a job candidate, the way that interviewer conducted themselves in the interview also changed.[12] When a resume or application created a more positive first impression, the interviewers were observed to smile more, display more open body language and ask fewer deliberately challenging questions. They also attempted to sell the job and the company more to the candidate.

In turn, the greater the positive signalling by the interviewer, the more positive the applicant's behaviour became, which led to a more positive impression of the candidate, generating a self-reinforcing cycle of affirmation.

Candidates whose applications created a less favourable first impression were treated with greater coolness, detachment and challenge by the interviewers, leading to candidates' behaviours becoming less warm, less confident and more protective. This, in turn, produced even less positive signalling by the interviewer and so on.

Doom loops and death spirals

You can no doubt see in the preceding example a negative spiral dynamic emerging – one that builds and reinforces with each additional interaction. This is called a 'doom loop' or 'death spiral'.

To illustrate how a negative spiral dynamic works in a leadership setting lets continue with an example from earlier in this chapter. Remember my description of your new CEO in the imagined scenario of your first morning in a new job, and how you witnessed this CEO perhaps having a really bad day (or perhaps simply concentrating and thinking intensely about a problem)? This CEO showed up as a cold and disconnected leader, which you would no doubt interpret as hostility. This means that even though this might not be the CEO's normal way of leading, your brain now holds an impression of the CEO as an arrogant, selfish jerk. In your assessment, this leader can't be trusted, and you don't feel safe around them. Your reptilian survival brain is now whispering, 'It's not safe around your new boss. I guarantee you that if you take any risks with him, it will not end well!' What happens from this point forward will be a consequence of the prophecy your brain has told you.

So, you decide to hold back on doing anything at all that might earn you a rebuke or criticism. Your CEO then interprets your silence and reluctance to speak up as a character flaw. You are passive, weak and incompetent in their estimation. You certainly can't be trusted with important tasks, so instead of giving them to you, your boss does them personally or only gives them to you if they can micromanage every aspect of the work you do.

As a result of these controlling, mistrusting behaviours, you feel further maligned and mistreated, justifying your initial assessment that your leader is an arrogant jerk, causing your further withdrawal – which, of course, further cements the CEO's assessment of you. And so it goes on, in an ever-worsening relationship doom loop, possibly only ending its downward spiral when either you leave or your boss finds a way of removing you from the team.

What is revealed in this example is the potential for just one bad experience to seed impressions that ultimately limit your success as a leader, not just on that day, but potentially over a much longer time. These first impressions also can have awful effects on your team members' workplace experience and engagement over the longer team. And being the leader in this situation is not much fun either!

Growth cycles and generative spirals

Of course, it is important to note that an IEE can also create a positive cycle, one in which your positive first impressions of a leader can result in a productive or generative upwards spiral, and enable the relationship between leader and other to create value.

For example, if your initial experience of your new CEO is warm instead of cold, you form an impression they are a nice person. If you initially experience the CEO as curious, empathetic and attentive, you may conclude that they are more likely to be a trustworthy leader who seems to value you and your contribution. Your reptilian survival brain says to your modern conscious brain, 'This is a good person. We can trust them. You should feel free to speak up and get involved!' You may, therefore, be more willing to offer up suggestions and take the initiative.

Your CEO's observations of your proactive and industrious efforts then cause them to view you as a diligent and intelligent team member. So, in turn, they offer you greater opportunities, which you respond to with even more effort and application. In this instance, you have produced a cycle that generates positive feelings and outcomes for both you and your leader.

SPIRAL DYNAMICS: PULL UP! PULL UP!

It's a classic scene from many war movies. The hero, a daring and courageous pilot, is trapped in his smoking, damaged plane as it performs a death spiral, twisting and snaking its way uncontrollably towards the ground. His comrades watching implore him to 'Pull up! Pull up!', knowing in their hearts that his chances of survival are near zero.

The feeling can be similar when we observe our own relationships caught in a doom loop, spiralling their way to an inevitably destructive conclusion. We know we are in a death spiral, yet we feel powerless to change its trajectory.

Even when we suspect that our first impressions may be contributing to the mess we are now in, why can we still struggle to overcome the prevailing dynamics? The following sections provide a few reasons.

An impression of being a bastard lasts longer

Reversing a negative impression of strength is much easier than reversing a negative impression of warmth. While a failure can be seen as a signal of low strength and competence, subsequent successes and evidence of competence can go some way to reversing those initial assessments. For example, if I tanked when making a presentation but followed up with a brilliant one later, I will likely be perceived as more competent than I was after the initial presentation.

However, reversing a negative warmth judgement is a lot harder, once a person is suspected of lacking warmth owing to an initial act of hostility – for example, an angry outburst or taking advantage of someone else.[13] In other words, initial negative information looms larger in our warmth assessments than any subsequent positive information.

This explains a dynamic that you may have experienced yourself. Imagine you are in some sort of relationship with someone that hasn't started off well. You know you got off on the wrong foot and you are now each making negative interpretations of each other's intent. You think that the other person is mostly to blame but you also know that your behaviour is not helping – you are contributing to the mess too. So, you decide to try a different tack and introduce some warmth into the relationship. You try to be friendly, conciliatory and collaborative, but the other person just doesn't respond. They remain negative, blaming, guarded or whatever version of disconnection you are observing. Having failed to change the other person's behaviour, after one or two attempts you give up, telling yourself, 'I tried. Clearly they're the problem!'

What you're likely failing to acknowledge, though, is that the other person will probably need more than one or two experiences of you as warm and connecting for their initial impressions to change, and before they begin to start to trust you.

Reversing public declarations is embarrassing

Let's now imagine that you've told everyone else about your assessment of someone you've just met – 'She's a jerk', or 'He's a nice person'. Imagine that after making that public declaration, you then start to notice signals that your assessment may have been wrong. Having to now backtrack on your previous assertions and declare your initial assessment was wrong might be embarrassing – especially if you have declared it publicly to our co-workers or colleagues. By doing so, you might feel you're also admitting you are in some way incompetent or prone to errors in judgement, something many people struggle to acknowledge publicly, let alone in private to themselves.

Many of us lack the courage to own our role in the mess publicly and acknowledge that we were wrong. The truth is we would rather go down with the relationship than acknowledge we were, in fact, not so good at reading other people after all.

Untangling interconnected beliefs

Removing a belief about someone else can be difficult when it's been woven into a wider web of beliefs, and it's especially hard when doing so might cause the whole lot to come tumbling down. It's like the classic game Jenga, in which players are challenged to remove pieces from a tower made of wooden blocks, one block at a time, without disturbing the structure and causing it collapse. The game always reaches a point where certain blocks can't be removed without a collapse being guaranteed.

Here's a typical example of beliefs being similarly connected that I see often in my work. Let's imagine I've made an assessment of my boss as a selfish jerk, which, in my mind, perfectly explains why I don't get the career opportunities I desire. This is consistent with a broader set of beliefs I have that all bosses are selfish jerks, authority can't be trusted, and getting somewhere in a company is based on who you know, not merit.

Now imagine, however, that my belief is challenged by new data that suggests my boss is, in fact, not a jerk, and that he can be trusted to make fair, merit-based decisions. This, of course, would require me to re-examine the reasons I am not being favoured for new and interesting assignments. It may even require me to contemplate the idea that at least part of the reason I am often overlooked is because of my effort, my attitude or my competence. In other words, I would need to acknowledge my role in the mess.

The psychological work involved in doing so, however, may be too disturbing for me. The work involved in dismantling an integrated set of beliefs may create too much cognitive dissonance or disturbance for me to be willing to get started. In which case, I (consciously or unconsciously) decide I'm probably better off discarding the new data that suggests my existing belief is untrue or only partly true.

Reflection

As you can see, first impressions are very powerful forces in shaping others' perceptions of us as leaders, and can be quite resistant to change. Those initial impressions create helpful or unhelpful relationship dynamics that can have long-term consequences for your leadership success.

By considering these insights into first impressions, you can start to think about the often-unconscious dynamics that quickly form between you and those you seek to lead. You can also start to discern ways in which the dance you do may be helpful or unhelpful to what you are trying to achieve as a leader.

How conscious are you of how you are showing up in those initial moments of any interaction?

Are you likely to be creating first impressions that are both warm *and* strong, or something different?

How can you become more aware of those first few moves in your leadership dance?

7

Looking down from the balcony: How to start a movement

A few years ago, a wonderful short leadership video was doing the rounds in social media. It showed a daytime outdoor festival held in a green public park with hundreds of partygoers present. The music is pumping but, at first, no-one appeared to be dancing. Then suddenly a young man runs into the open grassed area and starts to dance wildly to the music, all by himself, seemingly unconcerned about how he looks or what others think about his dancing. After a short while, he is joined by another person who also dances madly. Before too long a few more people join in. Then, all of a sudden, a tipping point seems to be reached and a flood of people rush to the area to join in the dance. The video ends at that point, with the once empty grassed area now a heaving mass of dancers.

This video, entitled 'How to start a movement' is a great leadership discussion primer. It shows how one person's behaviour can influence and affect others.

GETTING ON THE BALCONY

The leadership dance isn't always about staying among the action and other dancers. To see the dance we do as leaders and discern the impact our behaviour has on others, we also need to get off the dance floor and up on to the balcony.

This is an idea I first heard at Harvard University from Marty Linsky and Ron Heifetz, both teachers of leadership. Ron is a psychiatrist as well as a gifted Juilliard-trained violinist. As result, he and Marty use the analogy of music and dancing to explore leadership concepts and practices. One of my favourites is this notion of the dance floor versus balcony, which they (along with co-author Alexander Grashow) describe in *The Practice of Adaptive Leadership*.

When you are in the act of leading, influencing and mobilising others, you are on the dance floor. This is where most of your work is done; however, similar to being on a nightclub dance floor, you may struggle to see very well beyond your own dancing, past the heaving masses, or through the strobing haze produced by the lights and smoke machine. You don't know how your leadership looks to others and you can't see the impact it is having beyond the immediate moment.

You need to occasionally get up on to the metaphorical balcony to look down on the dance floor and see the dance you are doing as a leader, and the impact you are having on others. Does your dance encourage and mobilise more people onto the dance floor? Or are some people staying seated on the sidelines, passively watching? When you step on to the dance floor, does it encourage more people to do the same, or do people leave the dance floor instead? What is the effect of your dance on others, and how are you responding to them?

These are extremely useful questions to ask and answer from the balcony, before you decide what you might need to do differently on the dance floor.

OBSERVING THE DANCE BETWEEN LEADER AND TEAM MEMBER

I regularly invite my clients in workshops and coaching sessions to get up on the balcony and examine how they're dancing with their team members.

I use my Xtraordinary Leadership Model (X Model, introduced in chapter 5 and shown again in the following figure) as a tool for examining these behavioural dynamics. The model provides a shared framework for observing, describing and categorising behaviour.

The Xtraordinary Leadership Model

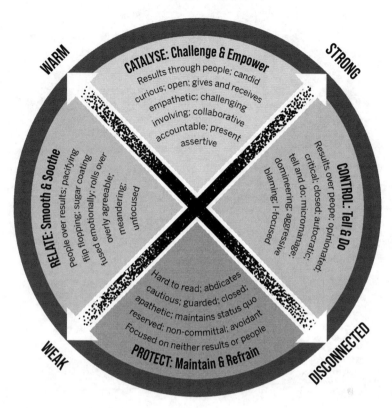

In this activity, I ask participants to consider each of the four leadership patterns and describe the behaviours that they see others demonstrate in response in real life – in their workplaces. They then share whatever words they feel best describes team member responses.

I also challenge participants to think about the common and typical responses they might see from a team member or direct report in response to each pattern of leadership behaviour. In other words, if a leader shows up in a particular way, I ask them to consider which very human ways a subordinate will likely respond to them, remembering that they are driven as much by emotions and non-conscious survival reflexes as they might be by logical, considered, and well-thought-out rational responses.

What thousands of leaders have observed

The following table outlines what thousands of my clients have told me they typically see in their workplaces in response to each pattern of leadership behaviour.

If a leaders behaviour pattern is …	The most typical behavioural response of subordinates will be …
Control: Tell & Do (for example, micromanaging, demanding, dictating, over-controlling and telling without asking)	Overtly agree and acquiesce (Relate) Show little response to avoid conflict (Protect) Resist, push back and argue (Control)
Relate: Smooth & Soothe (for example, appeasing, sugar-coating, lacking focus, over-talking and meandering)	Show frustration and take charge (Control) Give up and withdraw in frustration (Protect) Go along with it to maintain harmony (Relate)
Protect: Maintain & Refrain (for example, non-committal, resistant to change and innovation, gives little away and non-responsive to others)	Initial frustration with inertia and take charge (Control) Eventually giving up and withdrawing (Protect) Anger at being ignored leading to passive-aggression (Control/Protect)
Catalyse: Challenge & Empower (for example, involving others, teaching through questions, recognises contributions, holds others accountable, and open to feedback and ideas)	Step up to the challenge (Catalyse) Provide input and contribution (Catalyse) Take accountability (Catalyse)

Perhaps not surprisingly, a quick scan of the preceding table shows that the only leadership behavioural pattern that produces a response that is similar in nature is the Catalyse: Challenge and Empower pattern. As you can see, the Catalyst leadership behaviour produces similarly strong and warm behaviours in team members. All of the other leadership behaviours produce responses that reflect a larger range of less productive patterns.

But what about the dance between leader and team member when it involves someone who doesn't report directly to you, where you don't have the formal power and authority in the relationship?

LEADING WITHOUT AUTHORITY

Leadership is not a one-directional act, exercised only downwards with those who report to you. You have to exercise leadership in all directions, especially with others over whom you have no or limited authority – such as peers, bosses, and even customers and suppliers. Leadership is, therefore, *omni-directional*, and you need to examine the impact of your leader behaviour on these other important groups too, as shown in the following example.

Influencing without authority

James had just been promoted to the CEO role of the biggest division of a highly regarded Australian public company. The company chairman had referred James for coaching, concerned he might struggle with getting the best out of his executive team – James and another executive had been peers before his promotion, and had clashed dramatically on several issues previously. The chairman was worried their relationship would get worse now that James had been promoted over his peer. The company couldn't afford to lose the unique skills and experience of the other executive, so James needed to find a way to make it work.

James realised that if he tried to use his absolute authority to demand compliance from his former peer, it would not create the best outcomes. His peer could easily choose not to recognise James's new authority, resist his directions, or even leave the business. James's ability to lead and engage successfully would instead depend on his ability to leverage his peer's engagement, motivation and commitment. He understood he would need to show up differently if he was to build a more connected and trusting relationship.

Courageously, James accepted that despite being the CEO, he had more to learn about leadership and set about building trust and rapport with his colleague through a series of candid conversations and new approaches. Fortunately, his colleague responded well, and they were able to establish a productive and agreeable relationship that produced great business results. When James was later elevated to the managing director role of the group, he even promoted his colleague into his former CEO role.

When compliance can't be demanded

Leading without authority is a difficult act. Without positional authority, you don't have the fallback of simply demanding that someone do what you tell them. They can choose to say no or do the opposite of what you expect because you have few sanctions to impose on them that they might care about.

You also may lead teams where some of the members don't recognise your positional authority to start with. For example, I often hear of the challenge younger and less-experienced leaders have in trying to direct and guide older, more-experienced or even better-qualified team members. A similar challenge occurs when leaders are responsible for motivating members of cross-functional project teams where the team members report to someone else. In these situations, positional authority may not be enough so all a leader is left to work with is their leadership style and approach.

In situations such as these, where you're hoping to generate productive responses in those over whom you have no authority, identifying which pattern of leadership behaviour is more likely to be effective is even more important.

Control: Tell and Do

Typically, this pattern of behaviour has little positive impact on others if a lack of authority exists. Simply being told what to do by someone whom you have no obligation to comply with is unlikely to generate your agreement and commitment. In fact, if you also possess a need for autonomy or independence yourself, you are likely to react negatively to being controlled and micromanaged by someone whose authority you don't recognise. The result? You either push back with your own power and seek to dominate them instead (Control response) or ignore the commands and demands because the situation is not worth you expending energy on it (Protect response).

Relate: Smooth and Soothe

This pattern of leadership behaviour trades on the relationships and goodwill that it generates through connecting with people. Being warm, attentive and agreeable provides some assistance when it comes to asking peers and bosses for support or resources, provided what you are asking them to do is within their means and is relatively easy to oblige.

The challenge for those in the Relate leadership pattern shows up in response to its lack of directness and candour. These leaders can often be so vague and take so long to get to 'the ask' of what they really want that others do not know how to support them. This same lack of focus and agency can frustrate others higher up the chain, because they are generally time-poor and don't have the time to beat around the bush and engage with unfocused, poorly planned and vaguely described initiatives – which are some of the hallmarks of Relate behaviour. This can lead to a frustrated Control response from others.

Likewise, Relate behaviour is unlikely to assert its views sufficiently to be listened to by others who respect strength, instead encouraging them to quickly make negative assessments of what is being proposed and cut short the conversation.

Protect: Maintain and Refrain

If one pattern of leadership behaviour is most likely to frustrate and trigger peers and more senior leaders, it is the unresponsive nature of the Protect pattern. The lack of engagement with either the person or the task can easily incite a dominance response from the peer or senior leader. Further unresponsiveness is usually met with an ever-increasing dialling up of strength and a simultaneous reduction in any warmth, a clear shift towards the outer ranges of the Control zone.

If the behaviour remains avoidant and protective, the person in this pattern is likely to be taken out of the picture through firing, redundancy or moving them elsewhere. In other cases, a sustained avoidant and unresponsive pattern can cause the peer or boss to eventually give up and adopt a 'harm minimisation' strategy, in which they will limit their exposure to the protective behaviour through marginalisation and avoidance. I have seen this happen frequently in workplaces where leaders are unable or reluctant to have tough conversations or fire team members, such as in highly protected unionised environments or cultures where moving people sideways is easier than moving them on.

Catalyse: Challenge and Empower

Catalyst leadership is sufficiently assertive to be impactful with peers and superiors who value strength. At the same time, because leaders in this pattern always seek to connect to the needs of others and use that to mobilise action, Catalyst leadership is more likely to result in voluntary support and engagement.

This leadership pattern occupies the productive space created when you refuse to pursue only your own interests or only others' interests. Instead, you seek to pursue both by using the genius of *and* to explore and find mutually beneficial reasons for superiors and peers to engage. Catalyst behaviour means leaders in this pattern are also more likely to prepare for the interaction, knowing they have a limited amount of time and goodwill to be influential. Their focused businesslike behaviours also generate favourable responses from those who are busy and time-poor.

Again, it's easy to see how the only leadership pattern that generates a productive response from potential followers, even when unaccompanied by positional authority, is Catalyst: Challenge and Empower.

The long shadow of leadership

While working with a large company, I kept hearing the same leader's name over and over, and I realise this member of the global leadership team cast a frightful shadow over the business.

His apparently aggressive, almost brutal 'take-no-prisoners' approach seemed to have scarred many people during his frequent visits to Australia. I could even feel the discernible rise in anxiety and tension among the local leadership group in the weeks before his next visit, with all the warmth and agency being sucked out of the organisation. It was if the whole organisation was going into a protective 'cover-your-ass' mode and nothing mattered other than survival.

(For more on the concept of the leadership shadow, see chapter 8.)

IT'S HOW YOU MAKE THEM FEEL

Few would argue that American poet, singer and civil rights activist Maya Angelou was a wise woman. She was invited to speak at the inauguration of US President Bill Clinton and was awarded the 2010 Presidential Medal of Freedom by Barack Obama.

I have found, however, that Maya is perhaps best known for this often-repeated – and misattributed – quote: 'I've learned that people will forget what you said, people will forget what you did, but people will never forget how you made them feel'. (Carl W Buehner should actually be credited with this adage.)

Our brains don't forget pain

Whatever its source, some scientific truth exists in that statement. People don't forget how you make them feel, and especially the negative emotional responses you may promote in them through your actions and behaviours.

Anthropologists believe that remembering negative or painful experiences evolved as an important survival mechanism in the brain to help us avoid experiencing them in the future. If we weren't wired that way, we would be like Homer Simpson, repeatedly touching a hot plate and experiencing a painful sensation. D'oh!

The same is true for bad leaders. We are likely to remember the sensations, feelings and emotions that accompany the negative experiences caused by these bad leaders much more easily and readily than the positive ones. Indeed, in the best-selling book *Buddha's Brain*, psychologist and author Rick Hanson states that our minds are like Velcro for painful experiences. Thus leaders especially stick in our memory when they are the cause of negative and painful experiences.

How people remember you

The implication for your leadership is that people are not only responding to you in the moment. They are often also responding to the memory of you, and the feelings and thoughts that come instantly into their minds and bodies when they think about you.

This will affect their stance towards you in any meeting or interaction they have with you, as well as in any approach by you – such as a meeting request, email or text message. Will they be open and engaged, or closed and cautious? Will they be getting ready to fight, or to flee from what they perceive will be an unpleasant or unproductive encounter?

Relying on what you represent

Sometimes, people aren't even responding to you personally. For example, when you meet people for the first time, they have only very limited and superficial data on you personally. So, what does their brain rely on to decide how to respond to you? It relies on your initial behaviour, and more specifically what your particular combination of strength and warmth represents in their brain, producing certain feelings and automatic instantaneous responses, so deeply embedded that others may not even conscious of their existence.

And, as I outline in chapter 6, people make these assessments super-quick. When they encounter you, in less than one-tenth of a second, their brain is already activating those powerful non-conscious associations in its neural networks, which then influence what thoughts and feelings appear in their conscious stream of thought, shaping their actual reactions and responses to you.

As discussed, the mechanism by which non-conscious cognition shapes and determines what we think consciously is a product of our brain architecture. This thinking that goes on before we actually become aware of it is known as 'pre-conscious cognition'.

Using pre-conscious cognition

This is the thinking that your brain does before you become aware of it, sifting and sorting information before presenting it to your conscious mind (as outlined by Tilmann Betsch and Susanne Haberstroh in *The Routines of Decision Making*). Sometimes we call this kind of processing of information – when we instantly just know something, or find an answer to a question that we didn't have to think about – 'intuition' or 'gut feeling'. The thought or answer just appears in our conscious stream of thought.

Harvard psychology professor Timothy Wilson provides a simple example of pre-conscious cognition in *Stranger to Ourselves: Discovering the Adaptive Unconscious*, where he asks the reader to consider a description of a person and then identify their most likely occupation. It goes something like this:

> *John is a shy, timid and retiring type of fellow, preferring solitude and the quiet company of his own thoughts. Is John more likely to be a librarian or a farmer?*

Most people when asked this question respond almost instantly that John must be a librarian. They are sure of it. This is despite, firstly, that statistically many more male farmers are in the world than male librarians and, therefore, farmer is a more likely outcome and, secondly, possibly many more opportunities exist for quiet contemplation on a tractor than do in a library frequented by other people.

So why did their brains assume John would be a librarian? Because they have already been pre-programmed by popular culture to hold strong associations between the personality traits described and what we hold to be the stereotypical librarian.

Your non-conscious mind relies on these kinds of strong associations to produce pre-conscious cognition that then generates a conscious 'knowing'.

Conscious and compelling

This knowing can be powerful too, capable of compelling us to immediate action. Psychologist Gary Klein reported on a group of firefighters who entered a burning building where the kitchen was on fire. Standing on the ground floor hosing down the kitchen, the commander heard himself shouting to everybody to get out, without knowing why. The team had just exited the building when it collapsed. Afterwards the commander remembered that he had noticed the fire was unusually quiet and that his ears felt unusually hot. These impressions prompted what he called a 'sixth sense' of danger. He had no idea what was wrong, but he just knew that something was. It turned out the heart of the fire had been raging in the basement, beneath the floor the firefighters were standing on. The commander couldn't explain why he felt danger, but his non-conscious mind recognised that quiet fire plus hot ears meant that the fire was underneath them.

Automatic thinking

Much of this non-conscious thinking is automatic too. It's always on, beyond our awareness, until it picks up something we should be paying conscious attention to.

You're likely familiar with the experience of being in a busy social setting where you hear your name used by someone in a different conversation to the one you are in. How did hear your name being used when you weren't focused on that conversation? Well, your brain is processing all of the auditory signals received by your ears, kind of like a big radar, looking for important signals or patterns that it thinks you should be paying attention to. Your non-conscious brain hears your name, and quickly taps on the shoulder of your conscious mind, saying, 'Hey you! Listen to this. Someone over there just said your name in their conversation. It could be good or bad so you better listen in.' All of a sudden, you know that someone has said your name and that you should be paying attention over there!

Emerging into our consciousness

Here's a further example on non-conscious thought emerging into your conscious thinking. Imagine you're driving on a freeway and notice at the edges of your peripheral vision the slightly erratic movements of a nearby vehicle. These tell you straightaway that the driver is a danger to your safety. Immediately, you start to track the vehicle with your eyes, grip the steering wheel a little tighter and prepare for evasive action if necessary. Your pre-conscious thinking generated the feeling of danger, using a pre-existing set of rules that said something like:

Erratic driving = danger = become alert and feel apprehensive.

What followed milliseconds after your non-conscious had done its important work was the appearance of the conscious thought, *That driver is driving erratically*, accompanied by a feeling of apprehension and alertness.

All these examples – the librarian stereotype, the firefighter's 'gut instinct' and the instantaneous alert caused by the erratic driver – along with many other daily examples, highlight that your conscious mind is merely an observer to, or is simply responding to, what your non-conscious has already decided.

STRENGTH AND WARMTH PRE-COGNITION

The examples from this chapter and from earlier in this book establish clearly that your non-conscious mind is always active and processing sense data, determining what you pay attention to and how you think and feel about it. Now let's examine how strength and warmth produce pre-conscious cognitions that affect how we feel and act towards others.

Some nifty psychological research in this area has helped reveal the more common feelings produced by our non-conscious when exposed to each of the four combinations of strength and warmth. These responses are shown in the following figure.

Bias responses to the four combinations
of strength and warmth

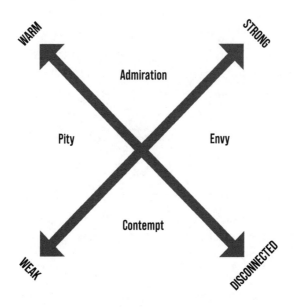

Adapted from the BIAS Map: Behaviors From Intergroup Affect and Stereotypes,
Journal of Personality and Social Psychology, 2007, Vol. 92, No. 4, 631–648

These pre-conscious influences are termed 'bias responses' because they are the result of our pre-conscious cognition weighting our conscious thoughts and feelings in a particular direction. In summary, the research shows the following:

- We are pre-disposed to feel jealousy or resentment towards someone who is strong and competent although not very likeable, because their resulting success feels self-serving and may come at our expense.
- On the other hand, we feel pity towards those we perceive to be warm and likeable but weak. We might think something like, *Nice person but poor them; not very competent are they?*
- The news is even worse for those we experience as weak and disconnected, with contempt and even disgust emerging from our non-conscious into our conscious thinking to shape our stream of thought and feeling.

- When both warmth and strength are present, however, we are more likely to feel admiration. Why? Because the person's connection and concern for us makes them likeable, influencing us to judge that their strength and associated success is well deserved.

The implications of this are significant for leadership and raise important questions:

- How likely is it that you will be able to successfully engage someone when their brain is biased towards feeling envy, jealousy, pity or contempt should you lead without strength, or warmth, or both?

- How much more likely is that they would be willing to engage with and support you if they admire you instead?

WARMTH AND STRENGTH AND WILLINGNESS TO FOLLOW

Even more exciting research emerged in the last decade to help us understand the impact of leader behaviour on others' willingness to follow. This includes the work of social psychologist and Harvard lecturer Amy Cuddy and her colleagues Peter Glick and Susan Fiske, who together studied the response of followers to different leadership styles, focusing especially on the effect of strength and warmth on the engagement of others. Their line of enquiry specifically studied the effect that each combination of strength and warmth had on enlisting others' support

Their research findings can be plotted on an engagement continuum, anchored at one end by followers responding with *active engagement*. This occurs when followers will not only go along with your leadership agenda, but also help you realise it. At the other end of the continuum is *active harm*, which is characterised by followers actively resisting and even harassing and sabotaging your leadership agenda. In the middle is *passive harm*, which occurs if others simply neglect your leadership agenda, and *passive support*, with others cooperating with your leadership agenda only when convenient.

This continuum, and how engagement relates to leadership patterns of behaviour, is shown in the following figure.

Effect of leader behaviour on others' support

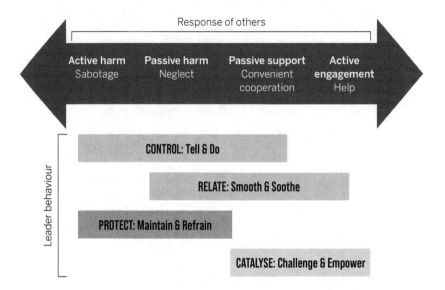

Adapted from Susan T. Fiske, Amy J.C. Cuddy and Peter Glick, Universal Dimensions of Social Cognition, Warmth and Competence, *Trends in Cognitive Sciences*, Vol. 11, No. 2, 77–83

This continuum connects with the four leadership patterns in the following ways:

- **Control: Tell and Do:** You can see that while a high-strength and low-warmth pattern generates passive support and compliance, it also has the potential to cultivate active harm. In other words, followers will go out of their way to sabotage or derail your agenda. This is the psychological phenomenon behind the tendency of Australians to 'cut down tall poppies', a reference to their dislike of successful people who become arrogant and egotistical, losing their humility and warmth along the way.

  I saw this response in operation recently when a strong, successful but aloof and competitive divisional CEO I was coaching shared that he felt terribly hurt by a whistle-blower complaint about his alleged involvement in corruption.

The allegations, eventually proven to be false, exposed him to a long, stressful and personally intrusive investigation. He shared with me that what caused him to feel most aggrieved and disappointed was that neither his boss nor any of his peers checked on his wellbeing during that time. He couldn't understand why, until I familiarised him with the research included through this book. He then realised that his meteoric rise to the top, at the cost of showing any warmth to others, probably cultivated resentment, jealousy and envy among those around him. These were hardly the conditions to engender support.

- **Relate: Smooth and Soothe:** Warmth without strength, on the other hand, can cultivate active engagement and support, but it can just as likely result in passive harm or neglect. While you might be inclined to support the leadership agenda of someone you like, you may just as equally feel frustrated or concerned with their lack of strength or competence. Should their plan be poorly thought out, unfocused or badly resourced, you may not feel inclined to support it or them. Although their likeability and warmth will probably result in you simply being passive and ambivalent about their agenda as opposed to actively sabotaging it.

- **Protect: Maintain and Refrain:** The combination of low strength and low warmth at best generates passive support for the leader but can also result in active harm, through a wilful working against their agenda and seeking to undermine their authority. This is where white-anting and deliberate sabotage of a leader and their agenda can occur.

We were able to see a very public example of this following the Deepwater Horizon disaster in the Gulf of Mexico. Even though 11 people died on the BP-owned oil rig and billions of litres of oil were released into the environment, the public behaviours of then CEO Tony Hayward created the perception that he was not interested in exercising his competence to solve the terrible problem, and nor did he appear interested in anything beyond his own interests. He was perceived to be attempting to deflect blame and avoid personal accountability, which created powerful feelings of resentment, contempt and disgust in the public – President Obama even said at the time that Tony Hayward would be have been fired if he was working for him. The contempt and resentment that others felt towards Hayward's protective, low-warmth and low-strength behaviour, many of whom had only ever seen him in television news conferences, led to him being subject to a widespread call for him to be fired. He was fired, being then replaced on the ground by a much more empathetic and responsive leader in Bob Dudley.

- **Catalyse: Challenge and Empower:** The research by Cuddy, Fiske and Glick clearly shows that a leadership pattern that combines strength and warmth generates a positive follower response, resulting in active engagement and willingness to help advance the leader's agenda or, at a minimum, cooperation when convenient.

Another term I have for this support for others who show warmth and strength together is the 'Hugh Jackman effect'. In Australia, people love the actor and producer Hugh Jackman. He is a very successful Hollywood star and businessman, but his fellow citizens are not inclined to cut this tall poppy down like they typically do because he is warm, modest, humble and likeable at the same time as being highly competent and successful. His warmth and strength combined result in us feeling admiration for him, wishing him continued success, and flocking to attend his theatre shows and watch his films.

The state of disengagement

The leader–other engagement dynamic also helps explain the significant disengagement many people report experiencing at work. For example, in a Gallup *State of the American Workplace* report, researchers found that only 30 per cent of employees in the United States reported being engaged and inspired at work, while a further 20 per cent of people reported feeling actively disengaged, going out of their way to resist and sabotage the efforts of their leaders.[1]

This state of affairs is not restricted to the United States. A further Gallup study of 142 countries suggests that engagement may be worse elsewhere, with only 13 per cent of employees in the study actively engaged and 24 per cent actively disengaged.[2]

We know that leadership, by far, is the number one factor that influences how engaged employees are at work. A 2015 *Harvard Business Review* article reported that leaders account for as much as a 70 per cent variance in employee engagement scores.[3] So it's reasonable to assume that the blame for this widespread disengagement must lay heavily with the poor-quality leadership behaviour that people are experiencing. Even in the US military, where high levels of motivation and commitment in its 'employees' are essential to success, a 2009–10 survey showed at least 20 per cent of the 22,000 soldiers surveyed reported they were serving under a toxic leader.[4]

Performance requires engagement from followers

The importance of these findings and those of other researchers can't be overstated. If the commitment and discretionary effort of followers is the key indicator of effective leadership, those leaders who can mobilise greater engagement among others will naturally be more successful.

Here's a small sampling of the evidence why:

- Engaged teams and their organisations produce better performance more sustainably, with the global consultancy Aon Hewitt reporting that companies with the top 25 per cent of engagement scores have 50 per cent higher shareholder return.

- Insync Surveys, a leading research and measurement firm, found that engaged employees have 18 per cent higher productivity and 60 per cent higher quality than disengaged employees.

- Highly engaged employees score up to 34 per cent higher in customer satisfaction ratings.[5]

- Among Fortune 100 companies, a whopping 1,000 per cent decrease in errors was seen among engaged versus disengaged employees.[6]

Employee engagement is such a critical issue to organisational success that virtually all leading companies measure and track it in some way. And so serious are some that they report the results at board level, and leaders from the CEO down are compensated partly on these results. They know that engaged and committed people are an essential ingredient of high-performance cultures.

In the next chapter we extend our exploration of the impact of Xtraordinary leadership beyond engagement, into culture and performance. Before reading on, take a moment to complete the Reflection below.

Reflection

Your leadership behaviour has an enormous impact on the engagement and support you receive from others.

What can you see from the balcony, looking down at the dance of leadership between yourself and your team?

What aspects of your leadership behaviour are likely to cultivate engagement and support from others?

What elements of your leadership behaviour may limit the engagement and support of others?

8

Culture and performance: The way we do things

When Ian McLeod took over the reins at Coles Supermarkets in 2008, he was walking into a mess. The $43 billion dollar retailing giant was worn out and, in some places, completely broken. Ian's mission was to turn the company around and recover its fortunes. The plan that he took to shareholders and investors focused on the most critical aspects – customers, food quality, efficiency, and especially culture and leadership.

Ian understood that without the right leadership, the culture would remain unresponsive and conservative. He also knew that they would only succeed if they created an innovative, challenging and responsive culture.

In Ian's mind the key leverage point for the culture change was leadership. To make it patently clear to everyone – investors and employees alike – Ian crafted a five-year plan that showed the key priorities in each of three major phases of the turnaround. The very first priority in all three stages was 'leadership and culture'. From that moment, every time that Ian briefed team members or analysts, he never strayed from that order of importance. To him, nothing else was possible without the right leadership and culture.

For the next five years, Ian and an ever-increasing community of like-minded leaders successfully transformed the business funda- mentally by reshaping its leadership and culture, executing what is generally regarded as the most successful corporate turnaround in Australian corporate history, and at the time the biggest turnaround in food retailing in the world.

WHAT IS CULTURE?

Culture, simply put, is 'the way we do things around here'. More specifically, the Oxford Dictionary defines culture as the attitudes and behaviour characteristics of a particular social group. Every team, organisation, club, community or social group forms its own system of ideas, customs and social behaviours that become reinforced. They become cultural norms – that is, the ways of doing things that are considered 'normal'. Indeed, they come to be considered not only normal, but also desirable and acceptable. So much so, that new and existing members of the social system must adopt and demonstrate these ways of doing things, or risk being punished, marginalised or rejected.

A powerful hidden force

Just how quickly new members of a group learn to fit in is always surprising to me. Even if their behaviour before joining that social system was not in alignment with it, within months, if not weeks or days, the powerful forces of group belonging and social acceptance will bring them into alignment. Although, I probably shouldn't be surprised because I am fully aware of just how powerful group dynamics can be ...

In primary school, I was the target of bullying behaviour for much of my time there and, as a result, I don't have fond memories of my early schooling. I didn't fit either of the two main ethnic groups, and I was too uncoordinated to have any sporting ability – a necessary ingredient to build social capital in Australian primary schools back then. I was also socially immature (I started a year early) and small. This all made me the perfect target as the outsider. I remember often feeling sad that I wasn't part of any 'in group'.

Fortunately, I grew and puberty took hold. By the time I transitioned to secondary school, I was becoming as strong and quick as anyone.

This brought new confidence, and I suppose the way I carried myself suggested I was no longer an easy target. Despite this, I very much still craved to be accepted and belong, and over time remade myself in a way that allowed me to fit in, adopting the teenage behaviours, language, dress and attitudes typical of the time.

I was nonetheless surprised to find myself in my third year at secondary school smack bang in the middle of a heaving mass of pubescent boys on the school oval, facing off against another boy as the crowd chanted, 'Fight! Fight! Fight!'

The other boy's name was Andrew and he didn't deserve to be there. He had committed no affront any greater than being different: quirky and gentle. This was enough, though, for him to become the target of bullying, and I was a perpetrator. I had fallen in with the 'tough' gang and had found my tribe. I was accepted and valued, as long as I met the expectations and norms of the group. I suppose it was inevitable that I would have to eventually prove my worth by beating up someone weaker.

I can recall with perfect clarity the look on Andrew's face as we stood in the circle. It showed the same bewilderment, confusion and fear that I had experienced in primary school. I saw myself in him. In that moment, I realised I had become that which I despised. I was the bully.

To Andrew's surprise, and the great disappointment of the blood-thirsty crowd, I turned and pushed my way through the group, walking away from the jeering and booing. Thereafter, I was known as a wimp, but that was okay because I actually felt stronger and more powerful than I had been before – I now understood just how much of a hold those group forces had had on me, and I was now genuinely free to make an independent and conscious choice.

Group dynamics are powerful

The power of group dynamics and social forces has been well documented since the 1950s, when social psychologists started to research and report on the tendency in social animals to change their behaviour to fit in to the group.

The Asch Experiments from the 1950s were just one series of ground-breaking investigations into just how powerful these forces are, with test subjects completely inverting what they said or thought just to fit into the group. In one version of the experiment, a test subject is unwittingly placed into a group of peers, who are secretly co-conspirators with the researchers. The test subject is shown some lines drawn on a page and asked to answer a simple question, as shown in the following figure.

**Which line on the right (A, B or C) is an identical
length to the example line on the left?**

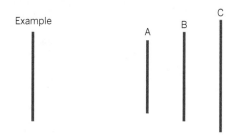

The answer seems easy. It's B. A is too short, C is too long. B is just right.

Each test subject in the group is then asked to tell the researcher which line they believe matches. A, B or C. The test subject reports B, the correct answer. To that person's surprise, though, the other members of the group, one at a time, all indicate that C is the correct answer. The test subject looks incredulous and confused. What the …?!

The researchers then repeat the process with a new set of lines. Again, the rest of the group have been secretly instructed beforehand to give the same incorrect answer. Again, the test subject is confused about what is going on. He or she becomes uncertain and wary. As the experiment proceeds, they start to delay responding to the researchers until they have heard the other group members give their answer. They then give the same answer as the rest of the group, even when they do not believe it is the right answer. They have learned to fit in.

'Smile, you're on *Candid Camera.*'

The popular television prank show from the 1960s *Candid Camera* reproduced the phenomenon revealed by the Asch Experiments when they secretly filmed a sole office worker entering an elevator that was already full of other people, all of them actors who were in on the prank. At the beginning, everyone is facing the elevator doors. As the doors close, the actors all turn in unison to the left to face the side wall of the elevator. The poor unsuspecting office worker at first looks confused and bewildered, but says nothing. Within seconds, they also turn to the left to face the wall. The show performed this trick repeatedly and showed the same result over and over. In one hilarious instance, the actors turned to the left four times in less than ten seconds, with an unsuspecting office worker following along dutifully and obediently.

CULTURE AND LEADERSHIP

So, to summarise, culture is the product of the operation of group social forces. These forces define what is normal, acceptable and correct in the social system the person is in. These norms and expectations shape patterns of observable behaviours, which we then call our organisational culture – or, simply, how we do things around here.

But who decides 'how we do things around here' to start with? Of the many people we are exposed to in our organisations, who do we especially pay attention to when learning the rules? Leaders, of course, because they play a particularly important role in shaping and reinforcing cultural patterns

The leadership shadow

Today, BHP is a global mining giant that prioritises the safety of the people who work there. Every meeting starts with a safety discussion and every person is empowered to challenge others on their safety behaviours. However, this was not always the case. At times in its long history, safety was not the priority and people paid the price – with injuries and fatalities.

The turning point for the company came during a period in the 1990s when it was grappling with significant headwinds and struggling financially. Paul Anderson, an experienced US businessman, was appointed to the CEO role to lead a turnaround effort. Paul quickly assembled a team and got to work restructuring the company and transforming its culture, making good headway in all measures except safety and injuries.

Frustrated by the lack of positive change in safety results and the mounting human cost, Paul called in his most senior safety manager and put pressure on him to provide the answers on what was causing the safety problem. The manager seemed to avoid giving a straight answer, skirting the real issue. So Paul dialled up the pressure until finally the manager broke. 'It's you. You're the problem,' he said to Paul. The manager then went on to explain that Paul was often seen riding his motorcycle without a helmet (contrary to local laws), drove his car out of the head office garage much faster than the posted speed limit, often failed to hold the hand rails or wear safety glasses at sites, and never asked about safety first when discussing results, instead prioritising cost, reliability and output. He often spoke about safety, but his personal actions spoke much louder than his words.

Confronted by such frank feedback, Paul responded admirably. He got the message and did something about it. From that moment forward, he changed all of his personal behaviours. Not only did injury and fatality rates begin to fall immediately, but the ripples of his changes still flow through the organisation decades later. Today their head office is one of the only places I have visited where every single person holds the handrails when using stairs, where junior people call out more senior leaders for not following the correct safety procedures, and every meeting starts with a discussion about safety because it is the number one priority. Even today Paul Anderson's leadership is considered to be the catalyst for the remaking of BHP into the successful modern company it is now.

Had Paul not been helped to see the negative impact of his everyday behaviours on the many thousands of people who worked there, the outcome could have been very different for the BHP of today.

The shadow you cast

The term 'leadership shadow' is now commonly understood to refer to the metaphorical shadow that leaders cast over the organisation.

Your leadership shadow can be an asset or a liability. When your words and actions consistently tell the same story about what you truly believe and value, and when they reflect what you wish to project into your world, it can be a tremendous asset.

Paul Anderson eventually brought his words and actions into alignment to send a consistent message into BHP – one of 'I value safety above all else. You should too.' By doing so, he removed any confusion in others' minds about what really was valued, and what would be tolerated at BHP.

The more senior you are, the bigger your influence ...

In social hierarchies, newer or more junior members in the social system look to the more experienced or senior members for guidance on what is acceptable and unacceptable behaviour. The more senior you are, the more closely others watch you for cues on 'how we do things around here'. The behaviours of the leader, magnified by the power and authority of the positions they occupy, has enormous impact on those lower down.

For example, a senior leader who bullies and overly dominates will create followers who comply, cringe and nod yes. Paradoxically, this may also breed more bullying behaviour lower down – many studies have shown that bullying is inter-generational and inter-hierarchical. These patterns of behaviour can become institutionalised and form the culture of the organisation.

Even a new team leader or supervisor casts a shadow over the rest of their team. In those first few days, weeks and months of taking up a new position, others are watching carefully them for the clues and cues to 'how things will get done around here'.

... And the more contagious you are

Recent research by emotional intelligence guru Daniel Goleman, psychology professor Richard Boyatzis and fellow academic Annie McKee has shown just how contagious a leader's style can be, transmitted through the organisation as if it were electricity.

Their research involved thousands of executives, especially CEOs and senior leaders, and showed in their words that,

> The leader's mood and behaviors drive the moods and behaviors
> of everyone else. A cranky and ruthless boss creates a toxic

organization filled with negative underachievers who ignore
opportunities; an inspirational, inclusive leader spawns acolytes for
whom any challenge is surmountable.[1]

THE LEADERSHIP LEVER

Leadership at its very best creates and reinforces productive cultures, as well as disrupting and reshaping previously dysfunctional cultures.

At its worst, leadership creates, entrenches and feeds harmful, dysfunctional and unproductive team and organisational cultures.

Over 30 years of leading, consulting and teaching, I've seen shareholder value, employee pride, and leaders' fortunes fall or rise on the back of cultural waves created by the ordinary and extraordinary patterns of leadership discussed throughout this book. I've been able to observe up close the results of leaders shaping cultures for better or worse.

The best of these results have included successful turnarounds of broken corporate behemoths such as Coles and Treasury Wine Estates, along with small players successfully taking on giant duopolies, and inspiring examples of completely reimagined and reborn traditional businesses.

The worst have included the collapse of titans into bankruptcy through arrogance and hubris, as well as the inevitable extinction of previous market leaders such as Ansett airlines, the giant insurer HIH and the once dominant Pacific Magazines, which were unable to adapt, pivot and innovate.

The following example details some of what I have seen.

The primacy of leadership when facing cultural challenges

In March 2014 I found myself standing in the light-filled atrium of the global head office of Treasury Wine Estates, one of the largest wine companies in the world. Along with thousands of others I was there to hear from the new CEO Michael Clarke (no relation to the cricketer!) on his very first day on the job. Bad bets on wine trends and massive write-downs had left the share price reeling for the company and the former CEO sacked. Like everyone else, I was hopeful that Mike had some idea about how the profits and morale of this ailing business, the once proud owner of many iconic wine labels such as Penfolds Grange, could be turned around.

Having met with many leaders across the business in the weeks prior, I had some insight into some of the cultural challenges Mike would have to deal with – including entrenched infighting and low levels of trust between the different departments that really should have been working together for the good of the business. This lack of co-operation in a vertically integrated business was destroying value right through the value chain and it needed to stop.

When Mike stepped up to speak with the many employees in the room, as well as those watching around the world via live stream, this is part of what he said:

'What you should know about me is that I am open, straightforward and collaborative. I love getting teams to win and deliver results. Nothing pleases me more than a team going from the bottom of the ladder to the top by delivering and winning. To do that, though, you need trust in the team. There are two experiences I have had in my life that have taught me this.

'Six years ago I was part of a team that took on a non-stop charity bike ride from London to Paris. That's about 500 kilometres, which is a long way for a group of overweight, unfit and poorly trained business leaders. It was a lot of hard work to get there but we supported each other and pushed each other to keep going.

'You can't imagine how sweet it was to cycle up the Champs-Élysées with your teammates and have a well-deserved beer at the end. It was only because we had committed to each other as a team that we got there.

'More recently, this same group committed to climb Mount Kilimanjaro. None of us are climbers or had any climbing experience, but we knew from our Paris ride that together we could do it.

'We met in Amsterdam and flew on to Tanzania together to start the climb, and climb we did, with headaches from the altitude, blisters and sore legs, right to the top. That feeling you

get, when you get to the top and the headaches go and you look across the plains is incredible. When you take on a challenge there is always pain and hardship, but when you achieve it …

'There is going to be some hard work to turn our business around. It is going to be challenging, especially in the early stages, but we will get there. We will find that sweet spot, and we will enjoy it. You will enjoy it.'

In that moment, I knew that Mike understood exactly what was needed to turn the business around, and that it started with the leadership culture. He was signalling in no uncertain terms to his executive group that infighting, blaming others and a lack of cooperation had no place in the business, and that genuine teamwork and accountability was needed. He knew that if he could shift the culture of the senior leadership group, it would cultivate a more collaborative culture across the business units, and therefore create more value through the integrated business model. This was a key part of how they would compete and win.

Which they did! Staying focused on teamwork and accountability helped them improve their share price, almost quadrupling over the following three years, a clear sign Treasury had rebuilt its reputation as a highly respected wine business.

LEADERSHIP, CULTURE AND RESULTS

Leadership and culture is increasingly being recognised as a key ingredient for organisational success – and also the reason for many huge organisational failures over the past decades, such as Enron, General Motors, Kodak and Blockbuster.

Extraordinary leaders know a simple truth: Leadership shapes culture, and culture creates results.

Leadership shapes culture

Michael Clarke at Treasury Wine Estates understood that leadership is the single biggest influence on culture. So too did Paul Anderson at BHP and Ian McLeod at Coles.

The bottom line is that if you are to execute a winning business strategy, you must address leadership and culture directly. If you are to cultivate sustainable performance, you must first cultivate the right kind of leadership and culture.

Culture creates results

'Culture eats strategy for breakfast' is a saying well known to management consultants and business analysts who understand that even the most brilliant business plans and strategies will wallow and fail if the organisational culture is dysfunctional or misaligned.

In fact, a failure to address culture is at the core of the often-quoted research findings that more than 70 per cent of business transformations will fail.

Many researchers have inspected and verified the positive relationship between organisation culture and corporate performance.[2] Having observed the rise and fall of many organisations over the last 30 years, I also have no doubt that leadership culture and performance are inextricably linked, as the following example shows.

A leader-led business transformation

This $35 billion company was broken. Once a highly regarded retailer, its stores were tired, and so too were the hundreds of thousands of managers and employees who worked there. To turn around this ailing business, its owners installed a new leadership team to drive a winning turnaround strategy.

I knew first-hand how broken the company was, and the immense task the leadership team had in front of them, because I had been asked to review and report on their cultural readiness to execute the transformation strategy. It was clear that without a major change in culture, especially among the operational leadership ranks, the transformation would fail.

When I was invited to lead a major leadership development and culture change program that would start at the top and eventually engage every single leader, I knew the challenges were not insignificant. In many pockets of the organisation, leaders had lost their drive for results, and also the trust of others, resulting in low levels of action, poor customer focus, no innovation and mistrust between people – a guaranteed combination for mediocre performance. Encouraging them to change the way they were leading would be difficult but essential.

The multi-day residential program they participated in was purposely designed to help leaders learn how to engage, influence and mobilise their teams and each other, and generate greater commitment and contribution in doing so. New skills and techniques were shared, as well as a confronting 360-degree feedback process, all engineered to bring real awareness and real learning.

The program was a challenging experience that the vast majority of leaders took up courageously, applying the learnings with disciplined execution back on the job and with the tremendous support of their own leaders. Through their collective leadership, they began transforming the company from broken to something extraordinary.

In the months and years in which the program rolled out, the business reported extraordinary improvement in results, outperforming their main competitor in all measures. Employees experienced significant shifts in culture, and industry analysts and the business media noted clear evidence of a healthier and higher performing organisation. The business became the main contributor to its parent company's superior share price performance and is considered one of the most extraordinary comeback stories in Australian corporate history.

INSIGHT FROM LEADERS

The leaders I've worked with also back up the research in this area of the importance of leadership and culture on results. For many years I've been using the Xtraordinary Leadership Model (introduced in chapter 5 and shown again in the following figure) to test the relationship between leadership, culture and performance against the real-world views and insights of the thousands of leaders who come to my workshops. I have conducted hundreds of exercises with these leaders that reveal their lived experience of the relationship between each pattern of leadership, and the culture and performance they generate.

The Xtraordinary Leadership Model

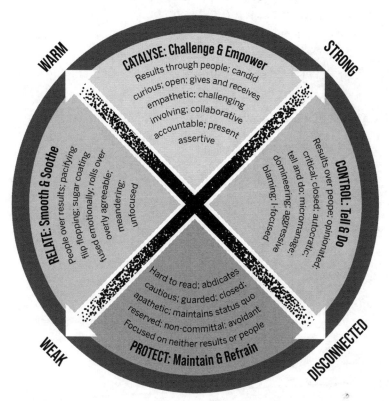

WARM

STRONG

CATALYSE: Challenge & Empower
Results through people; candid
curious; open; gives and receives
empathetic; challenging
involving; collaborative
accountable; present
assertive

CONTROL: Tell & Do
Results over people; opinionated;
critical; closed; autocratic;
tell and do; micromanage;
domineering; aggressive
blaming; I-focused

RELATE: Smooth & Soothe
People over results; pacifying
flip flopping; sugar coating
fused emotionally; rolls over
overly agreeable;
meandering;
unfocused

Hard to read; abdicates
cautious; guarded; closed;
apathetic; maintains status quo
reserved; non-committal; avoidant
Focused on neither results or people
PROTECT: Maintain & Refrain

WEAK

DISCONNECTED

Regardless of the industry they come from, these leaders have told me unequivocally that the four leadership patterns influence culture in the following ways:

- **Control: Tell and Do:** This leadership pattern creates cultures that produce results but – and this is a big 'but' – these results are usually short term and require enormous amounts of effort from the leaders to maintain momentum. The process is exhausting and normally reaches a natural limit when the leader has nothing left to give, even though the team has not yet given all it is capable of.

- **Relate: Smooth and Soothe:** This leadership pattern can create positive and optimistic cultures where employees commit to what matters to the collective. A lack of focus or performance tension and accountability, however, can generate less than optimal outcomes.

- **Protect: Maintain and Refrain:** Here, the leadership pattern creates conservative cultures that are stable and predictable over time. The dark side of this, however, is resistance to change and a lack of innovation from team members, which may render them unresponsive to changes in the external environment and poorly adapted over time.

- **Catalyse: Challenge and Empower:** This leadership pattern creates cultures that generate better results sustainably and over the long term. Results are sustainable because they are generated from the engagement and commitment of the followers, not just the leaders. The role of the leaders is to catalyse the release of energy from their followers through challenging and empowering them.

Leader–follower–culture dynamics

Leaders clearly have a strong influence over the culture within their organisation, and their influence increases the more senior they are. In turn, each of the four leadership patterns examined through this book sets up specific dynamics with followers that become reinforced over time as the prevailing culture. In addition to the insights already shared from the leaders I've worked with, the following sections outline how each leadership pattern works in with followers and culture in more detail.

Control: Tell and Do

The ways the Control leadership pattern influences followers and culture include:

- The quality of problem-analysis and decision-making by others can be limited because the leader typically doesn't invite their insights or perspectives.

- As a result of their lack of opportunity to participate with their views or ideas, commitment from others to decisions and plans formulated by the Control leader are often minimised. In other words, because others can't weigh in, they can't buy in.

- Also as a result of not being able to fully contribute or influence decisions, the motivation of direct reports can wane. Feeling that their boss doesn't trust them or doesn't have a high expectation of their competence or potential, their motivation usually trends downwards.

- Team members will often do or say whatever is necessary to be seen positively by the boss (because otherwise they get punished) but not much more than that. In this way, compliance cultures are built and this has some advantages; however, the dark side is a lack of willingness to innovate and experiment.

- Some team members do respond to the Control leadership pattern with high levels of effort, making many sacrifices and heroic efforts to please the boss. This is, of course, unsustainable over the medium to long term and can result in burnout, a costly and harmful outcome for the individual and the organisation.

- Subordinates may also be fearful of disappointing the leader and being punished in some way. I saw this during the first few months of COVID-19, with a general manager unwilling to acknowledge publicly the short- to mid-term hit to revenue. This was because his CEO was so demanding that he refused to accept any bad news and would punish those who delivered it.

- Of course, the brightest and most innovative team members will not stay under this pattern of leadership for long. Attrition or turnover among direct reports can consequently be high; however, a paradoxical effect is that Control leadership over the long term can also reduce turnover. Employees lose self-confidence over time as they are exposed to regular signals that they are not competent, valued or trusted. Over time, self-esteem is battered and the direct report may choose to stay based on their lack of confidence they would be attractive to other employers.

- Those who don't quit and choose to stay can become preoccupied with protecting themselves from their boss and do whatever they can to avoid the outbursts, attacks and criticisms. New ideas are not offered, risks are not taken, and real growth and learning is constrained.

- As studies have shown, those who have been at the receiving end of Control behaviour from their bosses are also more likely to adopt the same behaviour with their own direct reports, creating a broader cultural pattern in the organisation. If widespread, this pattern can significantly limit cross-functional collaboration, cultivate protective silos, and inevitably harm the organisation's productivity and health.

- The doom loop or negative spiral (as covered in chapter 6) is now being reinforced as more people do just what they are told and become cautious of trying anything new or different. The boss now perceives that he or she is the only person willing or capable enough to show initiative or take on the toughest and most challenging jobs.

- The pernicious effect of all of this is twofold. First, direct reports fail to learn and grow, reinforcing the cycle. Second, the boss is more burdened with work that otherwise should have been delegated and consequently experiences more pressure and higher stress. The emotional and psychological stress leads to a highly activated fight–flight reflex. This results in impairment of the leader's decision-making and emotional regulation as they become more prone to irrational emotional outbursts. This creates an even more fearful and risky environment for the team if they were to now speak up or challenge the leader's thinking so instead they continue to hunker down, say nothing and just do what they are told.

Relate: Smooth and Soothe

Here's how the Relate leadership pattern influences followers and culture:

- This pattern of leadership behaviour avoids tension and conflict. As a result, poor performance is rarely addressed directly and so performance is never fully optimised. A reluctance to engage in conflict, even when it could be productive, means that disagreements are swept under the rug. Rather than being dealt with openly, they instead produce an undercurrent of mistrust because everyone knows something is not being said.

- Leaders in the Relate pattern often say yes to demands and requests without carefully evaluating whether they are aligned with key objectives, or able to be properly resourced. This means that resources may be over-allocated to less-productive activities, harming performance.

- As these leaders rarely plan robustly, trusting that everything will be okay and people will be able to work it out, little visibility exists when resources have been over-allocated and too much has been committed to. This means work is often completed inefficiently and deadlines and commitments are often missed. This can be frustrating to others who are relying on timely delivery. Team members can also become burned out because of the tendency of their boss to overcommit.

- Addressing thorny issues or potential problems related to people is not a strong suit of the Relate leadership pattern. As a result, these issues need to become critical and immediate before they are finally addressed (if even then). In turn, frequent crisis management results – a lack of planning and attention to potential problems early generally leads to a crisis later on. The panicked crisis response simply adds to the observation of unfocused and disorganised behaviours.

- Because the Relate leaders does not like giving critical feedback, sharing dissenting views or having tough conversations, people are often unclear as to where the leader sits on important issues. Because these leaders appear to stand for everything and everyone, others find the lack of direction and clarity from the leader is confusing and ambiguous. This makes it difficult for others to make difficult trade-off decisions as required or push forward with some certainty on tough issues.

- Perhaps not surprisingly, employee engagement scores can be high under Relate leadership, even if lots of inefficiency and constrained productivity exists at the same time. As a result, typical engagement and culture surveys' comments under this pattern of leadership are along the lines of, 'It's a nice place to work but it's frustrating that poor performance doesn't get addressed.'

- Ultimately too much optimism, love and warmth without adequate challenge, feedback or robust planning leads to suboptimal business results and creates major problems when the prevailing winds turn against the organisation.

Protect: Maintain and Refrain

The Protect leadership pattern influences followers and culture in these ways:

- Procrastination and inaction are the signature moves in teams and groups where this leadership prevails. If a situation or problem is charged, challenging or out of the routine, decisions are often delayed so that the risk of making a wrong decision is avoided. This means that decisions are often delayed until forced by someone with more authority, or never made at all.

- While the Protect pattern promotes predictability and adherence to routine, it also fails to encourage innovation, change or stretching of potential. Instead, it promotes compliance with what is known and proven. It will even build lots of policies and procedures over time to encourage compliance and discourage deviation from the prescribed way of doing things.

- Likewise, as change is viewed suspiciously, new ideas or ways of doing things are regarded negatively and, if possible, ignored. 'That's not the way we do things here' or 'We tried that once and it didn't work' are frequent responses to fresh ideas and suggestions for change. The protect leadership pattern rewards maintaining the status quo and, in doing so, fails to respond to changes inside the organisation or outside, resulting in missed opportunities and failure to adapt to new realities.

- At first, team members and others may become frustrated when confronted with this leadership behaviour. After a while, motivation levels are reduced as their ideas for change and innovation are ignored. If they do not quit, their own behaviour over time will likely begin to reflect that of the leader – that is, passive, fatalistic, negative and resistant. They learn to do only what is prescribed.

- Of course, all of these cultural aspects limit the results that the business achieves at the same time as limiting the adaptive capacity of the organisation to respond to new and different circumstances. Inevitably, the steadily declining performance will eventually trigger the need for a major organisational transformation, at which time the passive and resistant culture that has been allowed to thrive becomes the major barrier to transformation. Paradoxically, the change and disruption that everyone so diligently sought to avoid becomes an avalanche as painful retrenchments and restructuring occur en masse.

Catalyse: Challenging and Empowering

Finally, here's how the Catalyst leadership pattern can influence culture and followers, and optimise results:

- Leaders in this pattern challenge themselves and others to make progress on important issues, while providing the necessary trust, support and interaction for collective efforts to generate better and more sustainable outcomes.

- Importantly, this kind of challenging and empowering leadership is not democratic, and nor is it management by consensus. These leaders can be very assertive, focused and single-minded about achieving a certain goal or objective; however, they are also able to establish how to involve others in a way that maximises their commitment and ensures the best outcome is achieved, in a way that is sustainable.

- Two of the key consequences of Catalyst leadership are better decisions and better execution. By pooling resources and seeking contributions, a larger collective intelligence is accessed to make better decisions, and a larger group of people are committed to successful implementation.

- Challenging and empowering leadership also pushes problems downwards in the organisation so that issues and problems are solved at the lowest feasible level. This not only frees up capacity in the organisation, but also naturally stimulates growth and initiative; people know they're expected to think for themselves, and so they do. Taking accountability and solving problems enhances the competence and confidence of the workforce, which in turn translates into even more future progress.

- Team members whose views have been sought, and whose contributions have been integrated also experience greater satisfaction and engagement. Their potential is challenged, and they are stretched.

- Because Catalyst leadership is open and candid, it doesn't unnecessarily protect others from harsh reality or tough messages. While they are empathetic to the challenges people face, these leaders also make sure that others have an accurate and truthful understanding of challenging situations so they can make properly informed decisions or make the necessary adaptations to adjust to new circumstances.

- As highlighted in chapter 5 and using the language of Jim Collins, author of *Good to Great*, this pattern of leadership looks out the window when things go well but looks in the mirror when they are not. In other words, leaders in this pattern are more likely to recognise the contributions and efforts of others when success is achieved but, when things are not going well, they are more likely to take personal accountability. By seeing and accepting their role in the mess, leaders in this pattern can then take action but, even more importantly, also signal something important about taking accountability into the organisation. When your leader takes accountability, you also learn to do the right thing, even when it's hard.

- Make no mistake, working in cultures where leaders regularly engage in Catalyse: Challenge and Empower leadership can be challenging. You are expected to bring the best you are capable of. Because of that, however, working in this culture is also extremely rewarding.

- More is achieved as people are compelled to acquire and develop capabilities that may have otherwise remained untapped and unrealised. This has the consequence of creating high levels of loyalty and engagement, and improves succession and retention with much deeper pools of talent to draw from.

- The cultures that are produced are more responsive, performance-oriented, collaborative, change-agile and sustainable.

EXTRAORDINARY CULTURES PRODUCE EXTRAORDINARY RESULTS

With this understanding of how leadership patterns influence culture and results, we can now properly answer the question, 'Why Catalyst leadership?' Why does this more extraordinary pattern of behaviour make such a difference?

It's simple: *Catalyst leadership shapes extraordinary cultures that produce extraordinary results.*

Sustainable and superior performance is a function of cultures that innovate and perform by harnessing the highest potential contribution of every person involved. Extraordinary leadership is the catalyst that activates and releases that potential.

Numerous studies support the proposition that strong and warm catalyst leadership behaviours produce superior organisational performance. The following sections outline a few examples.

Example 1: Catalyst leadership is transformational leadership

The rapid pace of disruption and innovation that has characterised competitive markets over the last few decades has required organisations to become more agile, capable of constantly improving themselves, and leveraging the efforts of teams. This has required a style of leadership that researchers call 'transformational'.[3]

In essence, transformational leadership involves motivating and guiding team members by painting a compelling vision of the future, connecting team members' efforts to a meaningful purpose, setting challenging objectives, and guiding their actions by promoting a shared set of ideal values. Teams are given a significant degree of latitude and empowerment to make the necessary decisions to realise the vision and objectives.

Transformational leadership is often contrasted to both autocratic command-and-control leadership that dictates to subordinates, aka the Control leadership pattern, and the more democratic style of the Relate leadership pattern. Control leadership emphasises the leader's competence at the expense of warmth, whereas the democratic style of the Relate pattern emphasise a leader's warmth, often at the expense of competence.[4] Transformational leadership instead represents the combination of competence with warmth.[5]

Successful transformational leadership depends on challenge and empower behaviours, the hallmark of Catalyst leaders, with numerous studies now having shown these behaviours generate superior contributions to organisational performance outcomes,[6] with especially pronounced effects seen in private companies.[7]

Example 2: Catalyst leadership motivates universally

Recent and compelling research into human motivation has revealed that we all share certain powerful motivations, and that a particular way of leading will tap into these motivations, releasing greater energy and commitment from team members and others.

I examine this contemporary research, known as 'self-determination theory', in more detail in chapter 11 (which covers energising and motivating others), so won't outline the common motivations here. What is important to note at this point is that the leadership behaviours that activate and leverage these motivations[8] are the same behaviours found in the Catalyst skill set, including:

- encouraging self-initiation
- enquiring genuinely
- listening and showing empathy
- offering choice
- seeking perspective
- using open communication and sharing perspective.

The chapters in the following part outline this skill set, or habits, of Catalyst leaders in much more detail.

Research also shows conclusively[9] that organisations with leaders who adopt these behaviours can access superior outcomes in terms of:

- changing workplace behaviours
- cultivating positive attitudes towards work among employees
- facilitating greater psychological health and wellbeing
- increasing job satisfaction levels

- producing effective performance, especially in tasks requiring creativity

- promoting organisational citizenship behaviours.

Example 3: Catalyst leadership is 'Level 5 Leadership'

When management guru Jim Collins published the seminal book *Good to Great* in 2001, he reported on the results of a five-year examination of over 1000 public companies to reveal what had enabled just 11 of them to become truly great. His measure of greatness was the ultimate measure of company performance – stock market valuation and return to shareholders over the long term.

Notably, the 11 companies he categorised as great performers generated several times better stock market returns over the long term when compared to their peers, companies that were, in their own right, successful and profitable businesses. Hence, the question became what allowed these few companies to transcend good, and become truly extraordinary?

In *Good to Great*, Collins outlines a number of characteristics that these great companies all possessed and which made them unique when compared to the 'good' cohort. One of these characteristics was the quality of leadership at the top.

Collins reported that these unique leaders possessed a seemingly paradoxical combination of humility and fierce resolve, which, in Collins' eyes, produced something quite extraordinary, certainly a level of leadership above the ordinary. Naming this unique leadership 'Level 5 Leadership', Collins described the paradoxical combination of humility and fierce resolve as a 'triumph'. In this context of this book, however, we can now see it for what it is: the quintessence of warmth combined with strength.

Collins highlights that the warm, humble behaviours of these leaders means they attribute success to others but take personal accountability for failures, never assume that they have all the answers and, above all else, show unassuming modesty and humbleness. They are never demanding or need to be the smartest or most important person in the room, and instead prefer the spotlight to be on others doing the hard work.

And these leaders' strength-originated fierce resolve results in them never accepting that the status quo is good enough, making hard tough decisions, courageously pursuing their convictions and challenging their teams to reach higher and stretch further.

In *Good to Great*, Collins has, in effect, found living, breathing examples of the extraordinary impact of Catalyst: Challenge and Empower leadership.

Example 4: Catalyst leadership involves mastery of leadership

Mastering Leadership (published in 2016) is a book written by Bob Anderson and Bill Adams, who are respectively the founder and CEO of the Leadership Circle organisation, headquartered in Atlanta with coaches and offices around the world.

The organisation developed a very comprehensive and robust framework for understanding leadership development, which has been translated into an online diagnostic tool for assessing leader behaviour and underlying patterns of thought. This assessment has now been completed by millions of leaders worldwide, providing an enormous database of information on leadership behaviour, its effectiveness and the impact on business results.

Mining the data shows that achieving results (strength), with and through others (warmth) are behind the leadership competencies most highly correlated with leadership effectiveness and with business results in six metrics, including revenue growth, market share, profitability, product and service quality, innovation and overall performance.

Anderson and Adams also examined the relationship between leadership effectiveness and business results, and the patterns of behaviour that involve trading off strength for warmth or warmth for strength, reporting strong negative correlations for both.

Example 5: Catalyst leadership changes business trajectories

Bill Torbert is a highly respected academic from Yale University and Boston College (now retired), and business leader who has studied and shared his findings on leadership for decades. Along with David

Rooke, in 1998 Torbert authored the seminal article 'Organisational transformation as a function of CEOs' developmental stage'. This then led to them authoring the 2005 article 'Seven Transformations of leadership', one of the most-downloaded leadership articles in the *Harvard Business Review* of all time.

The core of their original investigation involved taking a random sample of experienced CEOs who were then clustered into two equally sized groups. The first group was recognisable by their demonstration of leadership behaviours consistent with those described in the Catalyst pattern. The other group was made up of leaders whose behaviours reflected those found across the other three patterns.

Their business records were then examined, along with historical performance of the companies they had led. Torbert and Rooke were specifically interested in counting the number of successful organisational transformations or company turnarounds that each CEO had led.

Why did they focus on transformations and turnarounds? Because a successful and sustainable transformation of a company and its performance requires a higher level of leadership skill and effectiveness than does maintaining the momentum of an already successful company.

When Torbert and Rooke tallied the results, the outcome was striking. Of the leaders who demonstrated Catalyst-type behaviours, each had led on average three successful organisational transformations. And how many successful transformations had the non-catalyst leadership group led? Exactly zero.

A final word

Respected British businessman Archie Norman was knighted for his contribution to business leadership in the UK. The former McKinsey partner and leader of Marks and Spencer, iTV and Royal Mail was dubbed the 'turnaround king' by the business press for his golden touch in leading large-scale turnarounds.

Sir Archie also came to an interesting conclusion about the role of Catalyst leadership behaviours. A former colleague of mine once spoke with him about the type of leadership needed to create a sustainable high-performance organisation. He responded by saying that you certainly don't want any leaders who behave in ways consistent with the Protect or Relate leadership patterns. He also noted you might tolerate a bit of the Control pattern (because at least it gets things done). However, he argued what you really want is a whole of lot of strong and warm leadership – that is, Catalyst: Challenge and Empower leadership.

SO WHAT?

So, what can we conclude from all of this? Essentially, leaders who are able to grow into the Catalyst pattern and lead from strength and warmth are more likely to:

- produce superior business results in almost any metric you can think of
- build cultures that perform better and are more sustainable
- generate higher levels of engagement and commitment from others
- be seen as more successful as leaders
- grow more leaders around them, multiplying their impact exponentially.

So what now?

The question I suspect you now have is, 'How do I do it?' How can you make progress from ordinary towards extraordinary?

For sure, knowing what extraordinary looks like is one thing; it's another thing altogether to show up as extraordinary in everyday life, using the behaviours, skills, strategies, techniques as well as the mind sets and beliefs of an extraordinary leader.

The chapters in the following part, which outline the habits of Xtraordinary leaders, help you begin this important work.

Reflection

Using the Xtraordinary Leadership Model, how would you describe the culture of your team and organisation?

What aspects of the team or organisational culture around you would you like to change?

In what ways might your current behaviour be shaping or reinforcing the culture around you?

PART III

The habits of Xtraordinary leaders

My experience of developing thousands of leaders in Australia and abroad has taught me that the warm and strong behaviours of the Catalyst leader can be learned – provided you are motivated to do the work of experimenting with new approaches and persistent practising.

The role of experimentation and persistence can't be overstated. A willingness to try new and different approaches while remaining open to the results of these experiments radically enhances the rate and depth of learning. 'Practise, practise, practise' is a helpful mantra.

Andrew Mackenzie, former long-serving CEO of global top-50 company BHP, was asked how he developed his leadership. He replied that he would choose one leadership best practice at a time, and then focus on it and practise it until it became a habit. Only then would he choose another best practice to work on.

After some time, Andrew discovered something quite remarkable had happened. He'd turned a whole bunch of leadership best practices into daily routines and behaviours. They had now become the habits of an extraordinary leader.

In the following chapters, you will find an in-depth description of eight habits of the Catalyst leader, any of which you can learn, practise and turn into a powerful leadership habit. These habits are:

1. **Be intentional:** Choosing how you can show up more helpfully.
2. **Manage impressions:** Cultivating the right conditions for those initial moments.
3. **Release energy:** Tapping into the powerful motivations within other people.
4. **Curiously enquire:** Asking questions to engage, challenge and empower.
5. **Listen deeply:** Surfacing new perspectives and ideas that otherwise remain hidden.
6. **Connect emotionally:** Connecting emotionally at the right level for the moment.
7. **Share perspective:** Influencing through courageous advocacy.
8. **Regulate heat:** Getting comfortable with the heat of productive conflict.

9

Be intentional

In *The Child's Theory of Mind*, psychologist Henry Wellman argues that, before you reached four years of age, you would have developed a mind-reading capacity that by adulthood had turned into a full-blown talent. Even though you can't actually see other people's thoughts, your brain compulsively tries to predict what other people might be thinking and what they will do next. In other words, you're predicting others' intentions. Psychologists call this mind-reading capacity the 'theory of mind' mechanism, or ToMM.[1]

MEET ToMM

ToMM is always on, constantly looking to attribute an intent to others' actions, often based on quite limited data. If I see someone running down the footpath towards the bottom a hill, I will quickly develop a hypothesis of why. 'He must be late for something; maybe he's running to catch the bus,' I might assume. If I were also to observe a look of fear on his face, and notice him looking backwards repeatedly as he ran, my ToMM would generate a different hypothesis. 'He's not running towards something; he's running away from something! He's afraid!!'

ToMM is essential for social interactions and relationships because often we have to deduce what other people are thinking and feeling if we are to relate to them properly. This happens from early in life with our parents – 'Daddy looks upset with what I'm doing, the foot is about to come down, I'd best behave' – through to our adulthood – 'My boss looks upset with my arguing with her, she's about to put her foot down, I'd better toe the line and just agree'. It even determines how we interpret someone's intent – what they are actually thinking – when their words or actions are somewhat ambiguous or open to different interpretations.

The problem is that most people think they are good at reading others' minds, given they have been doing it their entire lives. Yet empirical research and our own lived experience tell us that ToMM is quite prone to error. Otherwise, how else would we explain the plethora of misunderstandings and conflicts that arise in day-to-day life, usually accompanied by statements along the lines of, 'I didn't mean that' or 'You've misunderstood me' and 'That's not what I intended'.

Trading off speed and accuracy

One reason ToMM is often inaccurate is the necessary trade-off between speed and accuracy. To be helpful in survival situations, ToMM has to work rapidly, and forsakes accuracy for speed to do so.

An example might be assessing someone else's intent as hostile – 'He's upset and I'm about to get sacked' – based on limited data present at the beginning of a meeting, such as a lack of eye contact and no warmth in the greeting. Of course, the behaviour may be due to some other reason but it's safe for our survival brain to assume the worst.

Sometimes the assessment may occur even before any interaction, with the wording of a short and abrupt email, or perhaps the absence of emojis in a text message, being enough to send warning signals through our primitive reptilian brain.

Mixed messages

ToMM is especially sensitive to mixed and conflicting signals. This is because one of the dangers that human beings have always had to contend with is deception by others – where they might try to take advantage of us through lies and falsehoods. As a result, your brain is especially on the lookout for conflicts between words and body language, eye contact and verbal delivery and so on. When discrepancies are spotted, such as a lack of eye contact from someone making an earnest statement, ToMM will generate a negative prediction of the other person's mental state such as, 'She doesn't mean what she says. She means to take advantage of me.'

Unfortunately, mixed signals are not just the result of an intended deception. The lack of eye contact from the leader, for example, could be the result of her being distracted by a text message from her partner, who is home ill, flashing up on her phone just as she uttered the words, 'Your opinion on this really matters to me'. Unfortunately, however, ToMM has now produced an unhelpful and inaccurate inference of the leader's state of mind.

'He means to win', 'She doesn't care about my feelings', 'He isn't serious', 'They want the best for me' – these are all examples of predictions from ToMM that have significant implications for the quality of interactions others will have with you as their leader.

When others make a more generous interpretation of your intent, your interactions are more likely to generate a positive relationship spiral, and others will support your leadership agenda. If they instead make a hostile interpretation of your intent, the quality of the ongoing interaction, indeed even the starting point, is likely to be sub-optimal and unhelpful to your leadership goals and aspirations.

Therefore, thinking carefully about what your actual intentions are becomes incredibly important, as does then paying careful attention to how you signal and communicate these intentions through your words and actions. And, as Buddhist scholar and neuroscience researcher Dawa Tarchin Phillips notes, 'Your intentions walk into the room before you do.'

XTRAORDINARY INTENTIONS

Intentions that are both warm and strong are the hallmarks of extraordinary leaders. A concern for progress, goal achievement and organisational success, while also being as equally concerned for others' contribution, satisfaction and personal success are the cornerstone intentions of the Catalyst: Challenge and Empower behaviours.

Part of the process of adopting the habits of these remarkable leaders is believing that it is your role to contribute to the success of those you lead, thereby ensuring the success of the team, division or enterprise. Your intention for every meeting and every interaction needs to be to help others make their best contribution.

A terrific example of this was demonstrated by Steve Kerr, who has enjoyed a stellar career as head coach of the Golden State Warriors basketball team in the NBA. In one particular instance, he had a conversation with his star player Steph Curry, who had become disconsolate after missing an overly optimistic shot from 20 metres away. Rather than focus on what Curry did wrong, he instead encouraged him to get his head back in the game and bring his best by telling him, 'You're doing great stuff out there. The tempo is so different when you're in the game. Everything you generate is so positive. You're doing great. Carry on, my son.'[2]

Remarkable leaders don't fix people

Kerr's comments stand in stark contrast to a typical manager in a modern organisation, who is more likely to have the intent of fixing people, and resolving their deviation from what is acceptable or perfect. This is an unfortunate product of the kind of management thinking that arose from the industrial revolution, whereby we expect that once organisational processes are perfectly designed, the manager's job is to look for deviation from design or, simply put, to look for errors. These errors must be jumped on and remediated quickly. This includes people, who when not performing perfectly need to be fixed.

The unfortunate side effect of this remedial thinking is that it creates premeditations for both the leader and the employee that are likely to encourage negative predictions by ToMM. The leader doesn't really want to have the conversation about potential problems because it is not a pleasant one and they assume the team member won't respond well. The employee, on the other hand, doesn't want to be 'fixed' and assumes that the manager's intent is to control and punish. Most of what they signal to each other in the lead-up to the conversation says that neither are looking forward to it, and nor do they trust the other person's intent. These are hardly the conditions for a generative or constructive conversation.

However, if the leader approaches the conversation with the intention to help the employee be more successful and satisfied in their work – even if this involves introducing some necessary tension or discomfort – the signalling is positive and is more likely to generate positive ToMM predictions as a result. The leader will be more motivated and keener to approach the conversation because their intentions are good, and the employee is much more likely to engage productively, even if in a difficult conversation, because the leader's intentions are perceived as being good.

TWO BRAINS, TWO INTENTIONS

A significant challenge in turning up with the right intentions, however, arises from having two brains – not in the physical sense (as in the movie starring Steve Martin about a man who actually had two brains), but more so in the sense that it is possible – and frequently common – that we have two different systems operating in our brain that can produce contradictory intentions.

Basically, humans have two thinking systems. The first is a fast, automatic, survival-oriented system that operates below our consciousness. Sometimes called the reptilian brain, it is responsible for the instinctive flight-flight-freeze response and other kinds of responses discussed in the previous parts in this book. This thinking system is predominantly oriented around the more primitive neural structures located in the rear brain. Its central function is to protect us and keep us safe – physically and psychologically.

The second thinking system is a slower, intentional, choiceful one that we use to consciously make decisions. Called the 'executive brain', it is responsible for our logical decision-making and planning, and for regulating our less helpful impulses. Largely oriented around the modern, more recently evolved frontal brain region, it is capable of taking calculated risks in order to expand our boundaries and create the world that we would like to live in tomorrow.

Your reptilian brain makes you want to yell at a colleague who seems to have wilfully and completely ignored your input and concerns when putting together a project that would affect your area. Your modern brain is what tells you calming down and attempting to have an assertive but calm conversation about your concerns may be better for your future relationship, and make it more likely that you can influence a better outcome.

These two brains can sometimes be in competition with each other for control of your actions.

Competing intentions

This competition for control happens when the two thinking systems simultaneously produce competing intentions.[3] Here's an experience I had that illustrates this dynamic.

Not so long ago I attended a masterclass in professional public speaking, along with a number of other people. As the workshop approached, I decided that I would adopt a 'learner's mind', be receptive to everything, and be prepared to try new things in the workshop even if I might not succeed in applying them masterfully. Nonetheless, it was during a reflective moment on the first day that I recognised a familiar and uncomfortable feeling in the pit of my stomach. 'Butterflies' are what some people call them. I know the feeling signals I am feeling nervous, something that I usually associate with mild performance anxiety. 'What could I be feeling nervous about?' I asked myself. Then it struck me. Although I was consciously committed to being a learner, part of me, at a non-conscious level, was also committed to showing up in this room of peers as appearing competent and capable. This was my survival brain's attempt to protect me – to maintain my sense of worth and ego. If I were to heed its call, I was at risk of showing up as someone who acts as if they have all the answers, rather than being a learner with nothing but questions. In that moment of awareness, I was given the opportunity to choose one intention – to be a learner or be an expert.

Each of us is similarly capable of possessing and being driven by non-conscious intentions that conflict with our conscious intentions. When this happens, it's as if we have one foot on the accelerator while holding the other foot down hard on the brake.[4]

The following table outlines some common leadership-related examples of conscious intentions being sabotaged by a competing intention.

Conscious intention	Competing intention
I want to empower others ...	but, I want it done the right way (my way).
I want to challenge my team members ...	although, I don't want them to dislike me.
I want to innovate and experiment ...	but I don't want to be seen to fail.
I want to be open and vulnerable ...	although, I don't want to feel unsafe and at risk.
I want to collaborate ...	but I also want to win.
I want others to learn ...	but I don't want them to make costly mistakes.

The risk for you as a leader is that unless you are aware of these competing intentions, you may signal conflicting intentions to others, generating doubt and negativity in the other person's mind, leading to negative ToMM predictions, and ultimately producing a less-productive dance with the other person.

The challenge for you as you move towards being an extraordinary leader is to be self-aware and vigilant enough to know you will often be subject to competing intentions, courageous enough to surface them, and purposeful enough to choose the intentions that will serve our leadership aspirations best. This is an ongoing process, and one that needs to be practised daily.

CONSCIOUSLY INTENTIONAL PRACTICES

You can do several practical things immediately to show up with more consciously aligned and intentionally warm and strong. These include:

- **Before any key meeting or interaction, take a quiet moment to reflect honestly on your intentions:** Ask yourself: what do I really want from this conversation? What do I wish for the other person from this conversation? What would be a strong and warm intention that I can pursue?

- **Signal positive intentions in advance:** Use language and tone in emails, texts or meeting invitations that make your warm and strong intentions clear. Meeting titles such as 'Success planning session' or 'Collaboration meeting' can signal positive intent. So too can giving the other person notice of what you'd like to achieve and flagging what preparation they could do in advance.

- **Commence meetings with a strong and warm purpose statement:** Within the first minute of the meeting, state the purpose of the meeting in clear and unambiguous terms that blend a concern for action with a concern for the person. For example, 'My intention in this meeting is to support you in developing a plan for successfully meeting your targets' or 'I'd like us to use this discussion to help you make progress with a challenge you seem to be struggling with'. Even if you are flagging a difficult topic, a warm and strong purpose statement is much more likely to generate higher levels of interest and receptivity from the other person.

- **Be clear about the type of conversation you want to have:** If you wish to have a conversation that allows you to co-create and collaborate with someone, let them know that up front. Likewise, if you only need an information download from them at this time, be up front with that as well. Even better, flag these intentions in advance so that the other person can align their contribution and their expectations before the conversation.

Reflection

How conscious are you of your intentions when interacting with others?

How often might you be caught by competing intentions?

How clearly do you declare your intentions to the other person in a way that signals strength (getting important things done) and warmth (with, through and for the benefit of them/us)?

10

Manage impressions

Early in my career I had the opportunity to interview David, a senior leader from a global financial services company. He managed a large back-office operation, where thousands of employees worked in a huge nondescript office building tucked away in an industrial suburb. I asked David what skills or attributes he believed were most important to be able to do his role well. 'Projecting,' he said. I had no idea what he meant so I asked him to elaborate.

'I'm the most senior person here,' he said. 'People pay a lot of attention to me. What I say, what I pay attention to, generally how I show up. I've realised that I play a big role in setting the mood of this place. So, from the moment I walk in of a morning, I'm very conscious about what I'm projecting. Even if I'm having a crappy day … no, especially if I'm having a crappy day, I will sit in my car in the car park for a little while before I walk in and get my head straight. I'll get in the mood I want to see around me. For me it's 'showtime' because those first few minutes I walk through the building each day have an enormous impact on how others respond to me for the rest of the day. If I walk in all shitty, head down, closed off, I can leave my office door open for the rest of the day, but I guarantee hardly anyone will want to walk through it. If I walk in and say hello to everyone, keep my head up, stop for a brief chat here and there, well, people will come through my office door all day long – which is good, because it shows they feel they can ask for help, speak up about things concerning them and so on. If they can't do that with me, well, we're in real trouble because in a closed-shop environment like this, when people don't speak about stuff that's on their mind, it tends to ferment and build into something much worse'.

To my typed notes from that conversation, which I have kept all these years, I added a handwritten comment: *How we show up, especially in the first few moments that people see us, has an enormous effect on our leadership impact!*

WHEN INITIAL IMPRESSIONS MATTER

Being able to quickly build others' trust in your intentions and your competence is a hallmark of more extraordinary leadership. It allows you to get and hold others' attention, and create the conditions in which they are more willing to engage with you, listen to you and be influenced by you. Initial impressions play a critical part in leading successfully.

What situations especially depend on creating a positive initial impression of your leadership warmth and strength? Here are just a few examples:

- coaching a team member
- commencing a performance conversation
- influencing more broadly to gain support for your idea or plan
- networking for opportunities and talent
- presenting online
- reaching out to peers on a shared challenge or opportunity
- recruiting and hiring talent
- seeking to establish productive partnerships with potential partners
- seeking to win hearts and minds in town halls or large meetings.

The opportunities for creating positive initial impressions of your leadership are both frequent and important. For David, they happened every day, all day long. How you show up matters. Should you fail to initially project warmth or strength in the initial moments of an important interaction, you're likely to be experienced as weak, disconnected or even both – which, of course, are associated with the three ordinary leadership patterns of Control, Relate and Protect. As the first two parts of this book have already established, showing up with these patterns of behaviour is unhelpful to your chances of engaging others.

This means deliberately projecting the Catalyst leader combination of warmth and strength in the initial impressions you make on others helps your goal of gaining attention, trust and engagement. Indeed, more effective and Xtraordinary leaders pay disproportionate attention to how they initially show up because they understand the importance of creating a positive dynamic in the interaction and avoiding a negative spiral or doom loop.

Practically, though, how do you do that? How do you convey warmth and strength clearly in those first moments of any interaction? The rest of this chapter provides some ideas.

OUR SENSES ARE NOT EQUAL

To understand impression formation, we need first to make sense of sensing. While the importance of the senses of touch,[1] taste[2] and smell[3] has been explored by social science researchers, it's generally agreed that sight and sound are the two most important senses we use for perceiving other people.

Which is more influential, though – how we sound or how we appear? If you conduct an internet search on communication effectiveness, you will likely find a frequently quoted set of figures from a famous experiment in the 1960s that found 7 per cent of our communication comes through our words, 38 per cent from the way we speak, and a whopping 55 per cent from our non-verbal behaviours such as facial expressions.

While possibly being the most frequently quoted statistics in the topic of communication effectiveness, they are also potentially the most misquoted and misrepresented.

The real story

Professor Albert Mehrabian's original 1967 studies[4] at UCLA weren't even concerned with communication effectiveness. He was actually studying the relative influence of different communication cues on how we interpret the feelings or mental state of another person.

Mehrabian was attempting to answer the question, 'Do words, tone or facial expressions carry equal weight in conveying how a person is feeling?' This has an especially important consequence when we receive conflicting signals from the other person's behaviour. For example, your supervisor says earnestly, 'I am interested in your ideas,' while simultaneously appearing distracted as they swipe their phone screen. Or a new colleague mumbles, 'Pleased to meet you' while shifting uncomfortably in their seat, unwilling to make anything more than fleeting eye contact.

In the previous chapter, I introduce the 'theory of mind' mechanism (ToMM). So what does ToMM likely cause you to assume to be their true mental state and their intentions? Does the supervisor genuinely value you, or are they just using a throwaway line to hide their lack of interest? Is the new colleague actually pleased to meet you or have they already decided they aren't really that interested in making a new connection? Which of these conflicting sound and sight cues will ToMM cause you to take more notice of when assessing this person's intentions towards you?

Sight is primary

Mehrabian's research suggested that when we attempt to make predictions of what others are really feeling and meaning, we are influenced principally by cues from what we see of their facial expressions (55 per cent), then what we hear from their tone and inflection (38 per cent) as well as their words (7 per cent).

The bottom line is that you may *sound* warm, but if you simultaneously appear hostile, cold or disconnected, your words won't matter too much. In other words, what others *see* has primacy in the formation of their first impressions of your warmth.

The research that followed on from Mehrabian's landmark study also shows overwhelming evidence that initial impressions stem largely, if not exclusively, from physical appearances[5] – that is, what people see of us.

FACES FIGURE PROMINENTLY

Doctor Nicole Nelson, from the School of Psychology at the University of Queensland, studies how other people's visual cues such as facial expressions affect our judgements about them. Nelson argues, 'When we are interacting with other people, we look at their faces about 80 per cent of the time'.[6]

In fact, faces are so important to us that a dedicated area of the brain has evolved that appears to be exclusively used for processing information about other people's faces. The fusiform face area is intimately involved in helping us make warmth and strength assessments, and in determining whether we adopt a high-trust approach strategy with a stranger, or a lower-trust avoidance strategy.

But why are faces so central to the formation of initial impressions? Largely because they are readily available when we encounter a stranger at closer range, and what we see on their faces is highly suggestive of their mental state. As their state of mind and emotional experience have enormous implications for their intentions towards us, we are tuned to watch faces closely for telltale signs of emotions such as happiness, contentment and curiosity, or fear, anger and rage.

For many people, the mask-wearing requirement during the COVID-19 pandemic illustrated just how important being able to see other's faces really is. In my hometown, we were required to wear face masks outside our homes from early on, especially when in public places and when shopping. Many friends reported that being unable to see the lower half of strangers' faces created greater apprehension or anxiety, in much the same way as when we encounter someone whose face is in the shadows or hidden beneath the folds of a hood.

The leap to video conferencing, especially if many faces were on screen, was also draining, as this quote from Kyle, a strategic account manager, during the pandemic shows:

I just feel so tired from all these video meetings. When there's more than a few people on the call, and their faces are just small tiles on your computer screen, it's so hard to work out what they're thinking and feeling. It's near impossible to read their faces.

PREDICTIVE IMPRESSIONS FROM FACES

The impressions that we form from people's faces are extremely predictive too, accurately foretelling a range of outcomes including voting patterns in elections (as discussed in chapter 6), popularity on social media, and even success in gig economy businesses such as Airbnb – more trustworthy looking Airbnb hosts have higher rental incomes. Impressions from faces even predict death penalty decisions in the United States.[7]

So how can you use your facial expressions to manage people's impressions of you, and ensure you are conveying warmth and strength? The following sections provide some pointers, starting with that all-important smile.

Smiling

Smiling is probably the single most important cue to trustworthiness. You can pretty much make yourself look extremely trustworthy by just having a genuine smile.[8]

Importantly, though, your smile can't look posed or artificial. One of the markers of a genuine smile is that it extends up to the eyes, making them turn up and crinkle in the corners. This combination of smiling with your mouth and your eyes is called the 'Duchenne smile', a smile which reflects feelings of happiness and wellbeing.[9]

Smiling is also contagious – people instinctively smile when looking at a smiling face.[10] So, if you flash a Duchenne smile, you also elicit positive emotions in others, such as pleasure and empathy.[11]

The added bonus is that smiling also positively affects your own mood and state. Forcing yourself to smile activates a mechanism called 'facial feedback', which causes you to actually feel happier as a result.[12]

The 'shit-eating smile'

Despite conveying many social benefits, smiling is problematic when it comes to simultaneously signalling strength *and* warmth.

While some studies show that smiling when meeting others signals strength through confidence and social dominance, other studies have shown the opposite – that smiles can elicit impressions of lower social dominance,[13] submission or weakness. In other words, smiles can minimise projections of strength.

Smiling can be perceived as an ingratiating and pacifying behaviour, and one intended to curry favour, avoid confrontation and convey the impression that you are not here to make trouble for the other person – aka the Relate: Smooth and Soothe pattern. Have you noticed in wildlife documentaries the teeth-baring smile-like submissive expressions of chimps lower in the hierarchy? Another name for this, which one of my clients uses, is the 'shit-eating smile'. He describes this type of smile as the big expansive grin you give to someone more powerful and higher up than you, even though you are being asked to do something distasteful or uncomfortable. It's the 'Sure, no worries, I'd do anything for you' kind of smile, accompanied by the hope that this act of willing subservience will be met by their approval.

The strong smile

The antidote to this conundrum of smiling potentially being seen as submissive or weak is what is known as the 'strong smile': a warm upper face in which you allow your eyes to crinkle up at the edges as you tighten and lift your cheek muscles, but without allowing your mouth to form the shape of a full smile. This is helped by hardening your jawline and tightening your lips, forming your lower face into a squarish shape – a feature typically associated with higher dominance. Given that tight set lips and a hard jawline also signal determination and strength, this combination of a warm upper face with a strong lower face is able to convey warmth and strength simultaneously. (If you want to see it done well, watch Clint Eastwood in the comedy-action movie *Any Which Way but Loose*, one of his earliest forays into playing characters who were not just tough, but also warm.)

Eye contact

Humans typically look at whatever it is they are concentrating on. When you make eye contact with others, you are signalling that you are focusing on them.

Eye contact is important for projecting both warmth and strength. Looking at someone else's eyes signals our intent to connect with them (warmth). Have you ever tried intensely staring into a relative stranger's eyes for more than a few seconds? I ask leaders to do this with each other very early in my workshops, just to illustrate how powerful it is in creating connection.

Eye contact also signals dominance and confidence (strength). In many social species such as primates and dogs, making eye contact with another individual signals that you are at least equal if not higher in the hierarchy. Even as humans, by making eye contact through a confident and unconstrained gaze we are signalling something important about our status and competence. This reflects an observation I made a number of years ago after watching thousands of video snippets of real leaders – the powerful and dominant leaders look wherever they wish. Those who are more submissive avert their gaze.

A lack of eye contact may not only signal submissiveness, though; it can also set off warning signals in others' brains about a possible deception. If I notice you looking away, unable to maintain eye contact, my brain will instantaneously try to attribute an intent to your behaviour – is it because you are extremely uncomfortable? Is that discomfort because your words and your real intentions don't match? Are you trying to deceive me? Shifty eyes are considered a marker of inauthenticity and deception.

Of course, too intense a level of eye contact for too long can similarly create a different interpretation of intent. Intense eye contact can be a signal of confrontation and challenge. Notice how intensely boxers get right into each other's faces just before a match, staring ferociously into their opponent's eyes.

Too intense eye contact can simply just make others uncomfortable too. I worked with a brilliant and very high achieving academic who was told at some stage that she lacked interpersonal skills. Taking that feedback to heart, she mastered the art of eye contact almost too well. She never looked away and almost never blinked, appearing as if she were from some alien reptilian species. Others noticed and commented on this too, reporting mild discomfort at their experience.

The goal with eye contact is to be focused but relaxed at the same time.

Don't forget the neck

While your neck is technically not part of your face, what you do with it can change the perception that others have of your strength and warmth. It does this directly on its own, and also in how it alters the way that your head and face is positioned to an observer's eyes.

The neck itself

A straight neck, extended upwards to continue the projection of a straight spine, is well accepted as creating a strong, confident and dominant stance.

Conversely, retracting your neck and raising your shoulders is perceived as withdrawing, and being submissive and protective in much the same way that a turtle might draw its head back into its shell when threatened.

Stooping or bending your neck forward and downwards conveys a sense of tiredness, fatigue, submission and generally having given up. These are low-strength signals.

Forward-backward head positions

Your neck also plays a supportive role for your head, and can change its position and that of your face in relation to an observer, changing the impression they may form of your intentions.

By tilting your head forward while maintaining a stiff neck, you are presenting your forehead and top of your skull to the observer. This is the hardest region of your head and most impervious to damage. It is often presented forward in many other species as a precursor to a physical challenge – think of animals that butt heads to assert dominance. If you tilt your head forward while also trying to maintain eye contact, your eyes appear hooded by your overhanging eyebrows – a strong but also potentially hostile expression.

On the other hand, tilting your head backwards can convey an imperious, superior or arrogant impression, creating by the perception that you are looking down your nose at the other person. While this signals strength, it also signals indifference and apathy, not an endearing impression for a leader to project.

Sideways

Tilting your head to the side can make you appear quizzical and possibly flirtatious, generally an appealing and inviting expression – just look at the many videos available online of cute, human-like dogs responding to their owners by tilting their heads to the side. Be careful, though, not to use this kind of head tilt habitually – a too frequent projection of curiosity may also be perceived as being caused by a lack of knowledge or competence.

WARMTH BELOW THE NECK: THE IMPORTANCE OF BODY LANGUAGE

One of the challenges I experienced during the COVID pandemic related to body language. For the 30 years previously, I had taught, facilitated and coached face to face with people, and so had enjoyed unrestricted and immediate access to what their bodies were telling me. I had become so attuned to reading body language that I was doing it automatically and habitually, without conscious processing or deliberate thought. It was just part of the rich stream of information being conveyed by the other person and had become a source of my professional skill, reading the room or the individual so well that I could pick up cues and subtext to what people were really thinking or feeling that would then guide my actions and interventions.

For almost 12 months from the beginning of the pandemic, however, all of my meetings were virtual, where I could no longer see movement below the neck, and was dealing instead with disembodied faces. At first, I couldn't explain why I would feel tense or anxious following some of those initial online workshops and coaching sessions. Objectively, I could assess myself as having done a good job under the circumstances, and clients were telling me that the sessions had gone well, but intuitively I felt I was missing something important. It took me a few weeks to work out that the discomfort I was feeling was created by the greater ambiguity and uncertainty present in those personal interactions, caused by being unable to access and process body language signals. Part of my brain was wondering whether I had really understood what was going on for the other person.

The experience reminded me that the role our bodies play in signalling strength and warmth cannot be overstated. While we look principally at other people's faces most of the time, our bodies are also creating impressions, providing important information about our intent and competence, both overtly and subtly.

Open, interested and relaxed posture

Warm body language is universally beneficial when building productive relationships with others. People who exhibit warm non-verbal behaviours (NVBs), both female and male, are perceived as friendlier and more likeable than those who do not.[14]

Warmth is largely conveyed through NVBs that indicate you are positively interested in the other person and engaged. This includes leaning forward in your chair or across the table, turning your body towards the other person so you are facing them squarely or thereabouts, and nodding your head as you actively listen to what they have to say.

Conversely, leaning backwards and orientating your body away from the other person signals coldness. Researchers have found that doing so can cause others to reciprocate with less engagement, perform less effectively on a task, and perceive the person with whom they are interacting as less friendly.[15]

Your arms and shoulders also play an important role in signalling warmth. Crossing your arms across your chest is perceived as protective, signalling 'I don't trust you', whereas relaxed arms and shoulders convey a more trustworthy position. As a general rule, a trustworthy posture is one in which the arms are down and your body is relaxed, neutral and comfortable as well as not too big and expansive.

If seated, your hands should be visible, not hidden under the table or some other object such as a coat you removed earlier, or even in your pockets. This is a practice I was taught when working with the management consulting firm Bain & Company. The reason is that if you wanted to do physical harm to someone else using a handheld weapon, your best strategy would be to keep it hidden out of view until you were able to surprise the other person at close range. By keeping your hands visible, you minimise the risk of setting off the instinctual warning systems in the other person and convey the position that you have nothing to hide.

Pay attention to what your hands are doing too. Making fists,[16] holding them stiff and flat like you are about to perform a karate chop, or pointing with your forefinger as if shooting a metaphorical gun are all gestures that will be perceived as aggressive and intrusive. If you need to point or gesture at someone or something, either use your thumb as if holding an invisible wand (like Harry Potter or Hermione Granger), or gesture with a relaxed, curved hand.

If you're not sure what to do with your hands, place them in a relaxed position on the table, on your lap, or let them hang loosely by your sides. John Neffinger and Matthew Kohut observe that a relaxed hand is one in which the fingers are not stiff, and are held with a gentle curl and spacing between them.[17]

... Then strength

Strength is also important to project in your body language if you wish others to judge you as worth paying attention to. How you hold yourself, how you move, and where you position yourself in relation to others all has an impact.

Amy Cuddy is a professor and researcher from Harvard Business School. Her TEDx presentation on 'power poses' – or standing like Wonder Woman or Superman – brought the public's attention to our posture and body language, and how it can not only signal strength to others but also change our own internal psychology and body chemistry so that we feel more competent and powerful.

Dr Cuddy explained how standing up with your back and neck straight and erect, with your legs at shoulder width and our hands planted firmly on your hips can increase your confidence, allowing you to project more competently, and in turn create a positive feedback loop with your audience – they see you as competent, you see their positive affirming reactions, and subsequently feel more confident and competent.

What Dr Cuddy shared was the culmination of research findings generated by many scientists over several decades that showed how your NVBs can positively or negatively affect others' perceptions of your strength as well as influencing your own confidence, competence and agency.

Open and expansive posture = strength

Certain body postures and stances convey strength characteristics such as dominance, power and confidence. They are more expansive and open, and usually take up more space – such as when standing with a broader stance, sitting with your legs spread more widely or standing with your hands on your hips. They also involve keeping your limbs open and extended, such as sitting back with your arms behind your head or lifting and extending your arms into the space around us.[18]

You might have already noticed that people with higher status or more power are more likely to adopt these open and expansive postures, whereas lower status and more submissive people adopt contracted and closed postures – such as a hunched neck and shoulders, a stooped or slouched back, as well as crossed arms and legs.[19]

Other people's judgements and inferences of your strength and competence are influenced by what is conveyed by your posture. When you display higher-power, more expansive and open body posture, you're seen to be more skilful, capable and competent.[20] In other words, when you adopt strong, open and expansive body postures, others will judge that you are worth paying attention to. Again, it is important to not overdo it, however, because 'manspreading' (or similarly taking up too much space) can appear arrogant and invasive of others' personal space.

Strength and the body–brain link

More expansive and open NVBs can also reflect your internal mental state. This phenomenon was first reported by American psychologists Glenn Weisfeld and Jody Beresford back in the 1980s, when they noted college students' postures became more erect when they received a higher grade on an exam.[21] I noticed this same phenomenon when coaching my daughter's basketball team. Whenever I called out and praised a specific team member's effort during a game, they lifted their head and stood taller afterwards.

However, the brain–body link is not just a one-way connection. What you do with your body can also influence your mental state, similar to the positive effect that smiling can have in lifting your mood. By adopting open and expansive body postures, similar to the power poses discussed earlier in this chapter, you can create feelings of being more powerful and having more agency.[22]

Try changing your posture yourself the next time you want to dial up your feelings of confidence and competence. Simply stand with your feet shoulder-width apart and place your hands on your hips. Straighten your back and lift your chin so it is horizontal and you are facing forward. Do this for two minutes. Based on the findings of several studies, you are likely to feel more powerful, and more willing to take action and even perform better in abstract thinking tasks.[23]

Reflection

How much attention do you pay to the signals you send through your face, voice and body?

Have you ever recorded yourself in an interaction (such as a zoom meeting), to see how you're experienced by others?

What specific behaviours could you become more conscious of to dial up your perceived warmth? What about strength?

11

Release energy

In the early months of 2020, the COVID-19 pandemic had reached Australian shores, and case numbers were rising daily as hospitals scrambled to implement new hygiene practices and prepare for an expected tidal wave of emergency admissions.

Nurses and doctors were praised for their selfless commitment at the frontline. Less visible were the efforts of others at the hospitals, with some truly heroic examples going unnoticed.

Jack Hung was a cleaning supervisor at St Vincent's Hospital in Sydney, leading a cleaning crew who were at high risk of becoming sick themselves as they disinfected emergency rooms and other clinical areas of the hospital. Many of the cleaners were especially at risk because they came from more vulnerable health categories (such as being smokers or living with diabetes). Despite this, they chose to continue to work demanding shifts in risky environments, even though they were given the option not to.

Jack said about his team:

They saw that they were making a contribution in a really crucial time. Let's be honest: a cleaner in the hospital social scale is at the bottom of the ladder. Before COVID, some of my staff would say, 'I'm just a cleaner.' That's how they saw themselves. I'd say to them, 'No! You're not just a cleaner! You are doing something great. You are part of the whole system of care! And for that system to work, everyone has to pull together.' They came to see that even though they weren't doctors directly treating patients, they were making a huge contribution.[1]

EXTRAORDINARY LEADERS ARE CATALYSTS

The essence of leading others is to tap in to and release their energy and commitment to make the required effort and do the work well. To lead well is to be a catalyst.

As already discussed, Catalyst leadership triggers a reaction in others, one that releases their energy and transforms their relationship with the work, without the leader themselves being consumed in the process. This gives you as the leader the ability to continue to catalyse across more people and situations.

Why extraordinary leadership catalyses

Extraordinary leaders catalyse in two ways:

1. **Their behaviour releases energy and motivates:** The way in which extraordinary leaders communicate, act and generally show up cultivates greater effort, commitment and satisfaction from a greater proportion of people exposed to their leadership.

2. **They prefer to tap into 'Type I' energy and motivations:** They are masterful at tapping into the more powerful and sustainable internal motivators of each individual they have to personally lead and influence, such as direct reports, peers, other stakeholders and even their own bosses.

Understanding human motivation is, therefore, central to understanding the effectiveness of these catalysing, extraordinary leaders as they release the energy of others.

THE FOUNDATIONS OF MOTIVATIONAL THEORY

Managers have always been fascinated by what motivates people, even if for the simple reason that if we can motivate people to work harder and with greater commitment, we can produce better results.

The first credible, evidence-based theories around human motivation started emerging around the 1950s, backed by the work of researchers in the areas of psychological sciences and management. Harry Harlow, Abraham Maslow and Edward Deci are just a few names you may encounter in courses at university or business school.

Douglas McGregor's theory, developed during the 1940s and '50s while working at the MIT Sloan School of Management, is worth calling out. He identified a critical schism in how we think about leadership and motivation, and proposed a manager can hold two vastly different mindsets about people. These are mindset A and mindset B:

1. Mindset A assumes people are generally lazy, avoid responsibility, work principally to earn income or some other self-serving need, and generally lack self-motivation. This mindset is accompanied by a management style heavy on direction and control that uses rewards and punishments to motivate. This is effectively a low-trust style.

2. Mindset B assumes people are self-motivated, enjoy their jobs, want to better themselves, and will generally do the right thing if given the right information and support. This mindset is accompanied by a management style that provides empowerment and autonomy and appeals to people's internal motivation to perform quality work. This is a high-trust style.

Professor McGregor didn't proclaim which version was more helpful to leadership, and instead left that for researchers to determine decades later. He did, however, provide a peek at two different sources of motivational energy – external and internal – with the first being consistent with the 'carrot and stick' approach that was being used extensively in workplaces at the time.

Once there was a donkey, a carrot and a stick ...

You're no doubt familiar with the analogy of the 'carrot and stick' approach to motivation, which assumes that people are just like donkeys and other beasts of burden. Dangle a carrot or other external reward in front of the animal, and you get them to move forwards – or the behaviour you want. Use the stick to keep them moving forwards and stop them going backwards – or to punish and discourage the behaviour you don't want.

The donkey wasn't chosen for the analogy by accident. Donkeys are generally considered stupid and stubborn, and often have to be dealt with forcibly. And working out whether mindset A or B is in play here isn't difficult.

In the workplace, 'carrots' include salary and bonuses, awards, praise and promotions. The 'stick' includes sanctions and punishments such as reduced hours, lower bonuses, criticism, yelling, abuse, poor ratings at performance review time, poor reputation, lack of access to interesting work and, ultimately, being fired.

These are all examples of classic 'Type E' motivations.

Type E motivational energy

These are motivations that are:

- **Externally generated:** Our behaviour produces an outcome that originates external to us but has the effect of encouraging or discouraging our actions (such as a carrot, or a stick).

- **Externally controlled:** Our access to the reward or punishment is regulated by someone or something outside our direct control, such as our manager or the performance management system. In other words, the reward or punishment is determined by others.

- **Effective immediately:** Type E motivators can be fast-acting. For example, I can get you to do something pretty quickly if I offer you a large wad of money to do it. Likewise, I can motivate you to stop doing something immediately if I wave a gun in your face. Of course, these strategies can also produce other undesirable effects.

- **Exhaustible:** Type E motivations, while fast-acting, are also short lived. Their efficacy in motivating behaviour reduces over time, as anyone who has ever received a bonus or salary increase can attest. We acclimatise pretty quickly to the reward and need bigger and bigger doses to get the same motivational high. What's more, each dose consumes limited resources, such as a manager's time, money from the business or available positions to be promoted into. The reality is the number of carrots available is limited.

- **Expectation-based:** Type E motivations also produce thoughts and feelings that 'I have to' do something – for example, *I have to* hit my sales target to get my bonus, or *I have* to adhere to this policy or I will get in to trouble. Type E motivations generally produce a sense of pressure and sometimes even reluctance, which then requires a lot of willpower to mobilise ourselves into action.

Type E motivations are still very commonly used to mobilise behaviour in many workplaces, and by many average leaders, even though they have been proven generally to produce less energy, commitment and satisfaction over the long run. The other, more effective, option is Type I motivations.

TYPE I MOTIVATIONAL ENERGY

Over time, management thinkers and psychological researchers became aware of a different type of motivational drive that appeared to produce higher levels of energy, effort, commitment, creativity and engagement than Type E motivational sources – especially over the long term. They were originally distinguishable from Type E motivations in that their origin did not appear to be *external* to the person. Instead, they came from within the individual and seemed to be an *intrinsic* part of the person's make-up, seemingly interwoven into their identity and psychology.

These are Type I motivations, and they include the following factors:

- **Intrinsically satisfying:** The very action or behaviour itself produces a pleasurable or satisfying experience within the individual, and one that is sufficient to motivate them to continue or repeat the action. It may even induce a 'flow' state where actions seem effortless. For example, scientists and engineers are naturally motivated to solve challenging problems and will spend long periods in a state of effortless concentration, often forgoing breaks or food.

- **Internally regulated:** The access to the benefits of the behaviour or action are provided from within the self, not from an external controller. In other words, the extent to which they are satisfying is controlled by the self or self-determined. I access the motivational effects through pre-action thought (*I'll do it because it makes me feel satisfied*) and post-action reflection (*I did it and now I feel satisfied*).

- **Identity related:** Many Type I motivations are powerful because they reflect a deep-seated desire to be, or become, a particular version of ourselves. For example, John is a nurse motivated to perform even unpleasant and menial tasks for patients because doing so reflects how he sees himself and what a good nurse does – being warm and caring. Likewise, Tam is an accountant working on complex and detailed financial reports over the weekend because doing so reflects how she sees herself and what a good accountant does – being diligent and conscientious.

- **Infinite:** Type I energy is renewable and long-lasting, similar to solar power from the sun. (In this analogy, Type E motivational energy is more like power that comes from fossil fuels.)

Type I motivations are more commonly leveraged by extraordinary leaders, and by extraordinary organisations, because they consistently produce higher levels of performance, commitment and satisfaction, even if they take a greater level of thought and skill to leverage across individuals and teams.

Researchers were particularly astounded to discover that applying 'carrot and stick', or Type E motivators, can actually extinguish Type I energy. A range of studies involving adults and children measured motivation levels and performance in a range of tasks that the subjects were naturally interested in – that is, where Type I motivations were in operation. When the subjects were then told that they would also receive a monetary or other external reward matched to their level of performance, researchers found that both motivation and performance in the subsequent tasks were reduced. However, when the reward contingency was not announced before the task and was only offered as a surprise after the task was completed, they found that motivation and satisfaction levels did not reduce, and in some instances actually went up.

The key learning that evolved from this research was that Type E motivators can induce a sense of the subject being 'controlled', and so reduce the positive effect of spontaneously occurring, self-determined Type I motivators. This led to the formulation of self-determination motivational theory.

The ultimate Type I energy sources

Self-determination theory evolved through the 1970s and '80s, and is a highly validated view on motivation that provides further insight into Type I energy, producing a definitive list of the three most common and powerful motivational energy sources shared by adults.

The following table shows these three areas, and what's involved in meeting their needs.

Motivational need	What's involved
Autonomy	Ability to choose our actions
	Some control and independence over what we do, or how and when we do it
	Not being over-controlled or forced
Mastery	Ability to master an action or task
	Successfully accomplish something or have the confidence that we can make progress towards what we set out to achieve
Relatedness	Knowing where we belong
	Understanding how our efforts fit in relation to others, and even how they fit into the whole and answer the question, 'What's bigger purpose of this?'

You can put this theory to the test yourself. Think about a time in your life when you were highly motivated to do something difficult over a longer period of time. I'm sure you will be able to identify the role that one or more of these motivations played in driving your persistence and success.

Writing this book is a good case in point for me. It has taken a few years of serious effort to create it. Days, weeks and months of my life have been willingly invested in it; however, this wasn't always the case. At first, I contemplated writing a book because other people I respected told me that I should. Others told me it would be good for business. To be frank, fulfilling others' expectations, or making more money, weren't good enough reasons to catalyse my effort, and my early attempts were half-hearted and unconvincing.

When I connected the importance of writing a book to my needs, my purpose and my drives, however, I started to release the level of energy and commitment necessary to make progress.

That moment came when I realised that no matter how many workshops or executive coaching sessions I ran, the number of people I could properly help would always be limited. A book was the only way I could help more people with the knowledge and experience I had accrued, short of cloning myself.

While writing this book, I have thrived because I have control over the topic, the content and the process – it has all been my choice. I have had the satisfaction of mastering new skills and abilities as I've learnt how to write a book and even found leadership research I hadn't known existed. Finally, I have had to expand the group of people I trust and rely on to contribute to, edit, design, publish and promote this book, all for the driving purpose of helping more leaders become extraordinary.

Conversely, if you wish to *demotivate* someone, the best way is to remove their ability to satisfy one or more of these three needs. At the extremes, imprisonment or isolation in a jail or a detention centre shows just how detrimental to the human spirit and psychological wellbeing a loss of choice, control or belonging can be. Indeed, in my hometown of Melbourne, Australia, the second round of lockdowns in response to the COVID-19 pandemic also illustrated just how hard it can be for people to deal with not having a choice or losing control, not knowing or having the answers, and being isolated from others.

Tapping into Type I energy produces better outcomes

The big question for many is, 'Which source of motivational energy produces better results in organisational settings?' Does 'carrot and stick' work better or worse than using Type I energy sources in a typical company, department or team setting?

The answer is that Type I energy sources, when effectively tapped and cultivated, produce a superior result: When the three Type I needs of autonomy, mastery and relatedness are met through the leadership and climate provided, research shows conclusively[2] that organisations access superior outcomes. These outcomes are seen in terms of:

- changing workplace behaviours
- cultivating positive attitudes towards work among employees
- facilitating greater psychological health and wellbeing
- increasing the amount of job satisfaction
- producing effective performance, especially in tasks requiring creativity
- promoting organisational citizenship behaviours.

A PRACTICAL COMPARISON OF TYPE E AND TYPE I MOTIVATIONS

So, now you're up to date with the key information you need to know about human motivation, the following table provides a summary of the practical issues of relying on Type E or Type I motivations and energy when leading.

Type E motivations	Type I motivations
Require constant/frequent supervision – may not be effective when the leader is not present	In operation even when the leader is not present
Consume finite organisational resources – money, time, attention	Consume a relatively infinite supply of energy resources from within the individual

Type E motivations	Type I motivations
Produce effects that diminish quickly over time – leaders have to keep upping the ante	Effects are long lasting
Require more self-discipline and effort to self-regulate – consume more willpower than may be available	Much more effortless, especially when in 'flow' states
Usually require authority and power to exercise – which you may not have, especially when motivating peers and superiors	Not dependent on power or hierarchy, so can be used to motivate others when you do not have authority
Produce lower levels of behaviour change, performance, job satisfaction, positive work-related attitudes, organisational citizenship behaviours and wellbeing	Produce higher levels of behaviour change, performance, job satisfaction, positive work-related attitudes, organisational citizenship behaviours and wellbeing

Challenging and empowering works best with Type I energy

Probably unsurprisingly, the leadership pattern best suited to meeting the common Type I motivational needs of autonomy, competence/mastery and relatedness for employees is the Catalyst: Challenging and Empowering pattern.

Overwhelmingly, the research to date[3] reveals the most important leadership behaviours for leveraging this powerful source of Type I energy include those that are part of the Catalyst pattern – for example:

- encouraging team members to self-initiate rather than pressuring them to behave in a particular way
- acknowledging team members' perspectives
- offering choice in what, how or when work gets done
- sharing information openly and not manipulatively.

These behaviours are all products of leadership that is strong and warm, challenging and empowering.

The following section now examines how Xtraordinary leaders accomplish the first item from the preceding list – encouraging team members to self-initiate and exercise a productive choice, rather than pressuring them or acting coercively. I cover the remaining three energy-promoting behaviours in later sections of this chapter.

WHEN BEGRUDGING COMPLIANCE IS INSUFFICIENT

'But why can't I pressure and coerce people into doing what they're told? Why can't I just tell people what to do? It would surely be more efficient!' These are the kinds of questions often asked by leaders who might like to rely on a 'tell and do' style of leadership. In truth, you can pressure and coerce your team members. It is your choice. It is just that it comes with consequences and limitations.

Firstly, the consequences: as already established in earlier chapters, a consistent pattern of telling and demanding provides compliance. And this may be all that you get – provided you have the authority to demand it. Passive support and compliance is often the most positive outcome, with resentment just as likely a partner. This can then lead to sabotage and active resistance to your leadership.

Secondly, the limitations relate to situations where you need to motivate and influence others under conditions in which you have no authority over them. Influencing peers in other functions, guiding members of virtual teams who don't report to you, and motivating your boss to support your agenda and plans are just a few of the many situations where you simply do not have the authority to demand compliance.

The good news is that there is one essential leadership skill that works without authority and is powerful in motivating others when mastered – and this skill does not rely solely on you having control and authority.

As Stephen Covey teaches us in *The 7 Habits of Highly Effective People*, even if you can't control something, you may still be able to influence it.

The art of influence

Dwight Eisenhower, the former US President and Supreme Commander of the Allied forces in Europe in World War II, possessed an ability to mobilise people around shared goals and objectives that is still considered extraordinary today. As he noted, 'The art of influence is getting others to do what needs to be done because they want to do it.' Take, for example, his role in leading the Allied forces during the daring and successful D-Day landings in 1944 (codenamed 'Operation Overlord'). This pivotal point in the war required the American General to gain the full commitment and buy-in of strongminded senior military leaders from other countries, each with their own views, opinions and ideas. Imagine if he had only been able to gain their begrudging commitment and had sent this communication to President Roosevelt on the eve of the battle:

> *Message begins – Mr President, good news. Operation Overlord is proceeding. Allied commanders have reluctantly agreed. Begrudging compliance will be forthcoming. Wish us luck. Gen. DE – end message.*

Tapping into individual motivations to influence

Xtraordinary leaders such as Eisenhower understand the most important questions to answer are, What motivates this person? What do they want and need? What will compel them to do what needs to be done? The answers allow you to flex and tailor your approaches to motivating individuals who possess a diverse and unique range of needs and wants.

The failing of ordinary leaders is that they assume everyone else is motivated by the same things that they are, they are quite happy to tell others what to do and hope they will get compliance, or they don't really care enough to put in the effort to motivate and influence properly. All of these approaches help to explain their ordinary, 'ho-hum' leadership performance, results and relationships.

As an extraordinary leader, Eisenhower pointed us towards the role of motivation in mobilising others to *want* to do the work, even if it is difficult and challenging. By connecting an individual to a compelling reason to act and perform, you as the leader catalyse the release of personal energy and sustained discretionary effort towards meaningful and important work goals. When you make this connection, you produce effort from the person you are leading.

Not surprisingly, the business turnaround king Sir Archie Norman also recognises the primacy of energising others when he leads large-scale business transformation – one of the most challenging scenarios for a leader who must mobilise thousands of tired, jaded and often reluctant people. 'My interest is in transforming the way organisations work,' he says. 'I am not a mercenary and I'm much more interested in people and motivation than in financial engineering.'[4]

Remember – if you don't know what dreams and aspirations draw a person forward, or what fears and anxieties hold them back, you are powerless to move them.

Identifying what motivates individuals

You can determine what motivates an individual in two ways: conversation and observation. Here's how they both work:

- **Conversation:** This involves engaging in genuine inquiry about what motivates an individual. You can use direct questions around what do they like doing and why, and what do they dislike doing, and why. You can also use less direct lines of inquiry, such as asking about their dreams, goals and aspirations, and what their fears, anxieties and concerns might be. You can also enquire based on past experiences, such as when they found their motivation or energy highest at work, and when it was less energised.

  One of the problems of this approach is that many people are not that self-aware or candid enough to be able to give you a completely accurate picture. The other major problem is you may not feel comfortable asking these questions of certain people, or might not feel you have the opportunity to do so, such as asking your boss or a peer. In this case, relying on observation is best.

- **Observation:** Assuming that a person will act in ways that satisfy their motivational needs is logical. This means the behaviours you observe of the person can indicate what is actually motivating them at the time.

For example, if someone has a need for autonomy and control, they will often seek to exert their independence and choice, and will resist attempts that others make to limit their autonomy. The same goes for mastery and competence – perhaps you have noticed that some people regularly let you know that they have the best insights, ideas and answers by how frequently they share their views and often fail to hear others' views? Relatedness needs are also signalled by behaviours that facilitate greater connections and intimacy, such as small talk and enquiries into how you are feeling.

The realisation that your observations of other people and their behaviour may yield useful information about their motivations opens up a range of insights that you may have not realised you had access to before. Simply by watching and observing people you need to influence and lead, you can be accumulating critical insights into what they need and want.

NAVIGATING MOTIVATIONS AND RELEASING ENERGY USING THE X MODEL

Once you have sufficient observational data about another person's behaviour, you can use a variation of the Xtraordinary Leadership Model as a ready reckoner to provide some clues to what motivations might be driving that behaviour. The following figure shows this variation of the model, building upon several different motivational frameworks, including self-determination theory, to highlight the most common motivational needs that drive each pattern of behaviour.

By observing others' behaviour over time, and discerning patterns in response to different situations and people, this model can then help you develop a reasonable hypothesis of what is motivating each person. You can then use this insight to energise their efforts by connecting their future action to outcomes that will meet their motivational needs. The following sections show you how.

Motivational needs of each pattern of behaviour

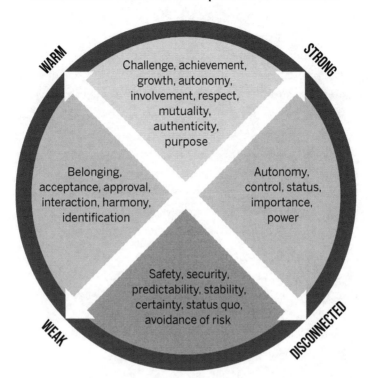

Connecting action to benefits

Once you feel you have a reasonable understanding of what motivates an individual, the key is to then help them evaluate how choosing to do or not do something will meet their own motivational needs.

This is the essence of Catalyse: Challenge and Empower leadership – helping an individual meet their own needs (warmth) by connecting them to the work to be done (strength).

For example, if I wish to influence a senior leader with controlling tendencies to take a particular action – such as endorse a plan, provide support or sign off an investment – I might wish to point out how taking that action could help them maintain their independence, exercise control over something critical or be recognised as having played an important part. The key here, though, is to give them the choice and respect their autonomy needs. The moment they feel they are being forced into something, they are unlikely to acquiesce and will most likely become obstructive and defiant. Perhaps use a questioning approach – such as, 'You want to get there first. Which option that we presented do you want us to pursue?'

If you wanted to influence a peer with protective behaviours to agree to support a key project, you need to show them how their involvement or support could reduce risk or uncertainty for them. You could say, for example, 'With your support and expert guidance, we can reduce the risks associated with this unavoidable change.'

Likewise, if you want to influence a warm but not so strong team member to take up an important but challenging assignment, you need to highlight how it will meet their needs for belonging and approval by saying something like, 'I think your teammates would be most appreciative of you taking up this critical task.'

Finally, if you wanted to encourage a team member with catalyst behaviours to take up a challenging assignment, you could appeal to their desire to grow and develop, or their sense of making a contribution to the greater good.

This motivational technique is incredibly powerful because you are helping the individual connect their decision to do what needs to be done to a reason that is compelling enough for them to want to do it. In doing so, you're tapping in to the powerful and sustainable motivational sources of Type I energy that each person possesses.

Choice, not coercion

A few words of warning here. You must be genuinely interested in meeting the other person's needs, not just in getting the work done. Otherwise, you're still using coercion and manipulation.

Secondly, you need to provide genuine choice. If they feel they can't say no or express their concerns, they don't really have a choice. The truth is that if they do say no, you probably haven't accurately identified what they truly care about or need.

Finally, asking a question can be more helpful than simply telling them the benefits. For example, you might ask, 'If you were to do this, how do you think the team would feel about it?' or 'How would this help you show what you're capable of to senior management?'

Questions genuinely provide autonomy and choice, which increases motivation and commitment.

Issues and concerns

Here are some the more common questions that leaders ask about using behaviours and needs when motivating others, with some thoughts in response:

- **Isn't it manipulative?** Where a leader's intent is generally perceived as purely self-serving, attempts to motivate through using benefits may be experienced as manipulative. For example, I once worked with a senior leader who tried to motivate me by appealing to my desire to make lots of money – a motivation he had but I didn't share. As a result, I felt misunderstood and manipulated.

  Where a leader's intent is generally perceived to be of service to the individual and their needs, benefits will most likely be experienced as genuine.

- **What if no benefits *per se* exist?** Even if you can't help them connect their action to a specific upside or benefit, you may be able to highlight the negative consequences avoided through their actions. For example, avoiding being seen as selfish, minimising loss of control or mitigating risk.

- **What about Type E motivators?** Can I use them? Yes, you can. Nothing is wrong with using carrot and stick motivations if you are unable to find or connect the individuals' actions to Type I motivations. As long as you recognise Type E motivators have limitations, and they make your leadership less effective if you use them as your default motivational strategy. The general rule here is to appeal to Type I motivations before Type E motivations wherever possible. This is neatly summed up in the phrase, 'In the word *motivate*, i comes before e.'

Reflection

What is your normal approach to influencing others? How likely are you to appeal to what motivates you, rather than what motivates them?

What do you know about the real motivations of those you need to mobilise? Are these unreliable and untested assumptions or do you have good data to support them?

How effective are you at making the connection explicit between what's in it for them and them doing the work?

12

Curiously enquire

WHEN LEADERS 'TELL' AS THE DEFAULT

I'm an observer. I notice people's behaviour. This means that whenever I find myself in a cafe in the city between meetings, I find myself listening to and watching the comings and goings of other people. I'll often see a manager and a team member sit down and have a coffee as they meet. Even if I cannot hear the conversation, I can see the behaviours, and observe that many leaders are addicted to telling – speaking first and often. During any of these leader–team member interactions I typically see a ratio of at least 3:1 of the leader doing the talking compared to the team member. This is also consistent with what I have seen across thousands of formal leadership assessments.

Leaders need to talk and to tell for many good reasons – to share information, for example, give directions, coach, give an opinion and provide feedback. However, negative consequences also arise when you fall into the habit of talking first and telling often, rather than asking and listening. The following fable illustrates some of these negative consequences.

The Scotty who knew too much

In this fable by James Thurber, a Scottish Terrier visits a house in the country. The dog in the house describes how all the farm dogs are scared of another animal with a white stripe down its back. The Scotty quickly decides all the farms dogs are cowards:

'You are a pussycat and I can lick you,' the Scotty said to the farm dog who lived in the house where the Scotty was visiting. 'I can lick the little animal with the white stripe too. Show him to me.'

'Don't you want to ask any questions?'

'Nah,' said the Scotty. 'You ask the questions.'

So the farm dog took the Scotty into the woods and showed him the white-striped animal and the Scotty closed in on him, growling and slashing. It was all over in a moment and the Scotty lay on his back.

When he came to, the farm dog said, 'What happened?'

'He threw vitriol,'* said the Scotty, 'but he never laid a glove on me.'

The Scotty then decides he can take on another strange animal all the farm dogs are scared of. Again, he refuses to ask any questions about the animal, sure he can easily win. Again, he ends up flat on his back, this time with quills sticking out of him. The Scotty claims the other animal pulled a knife on him and, furious, rounds on the farm dog, certain he now knows how the creatures fight out in the country:

So he closed in on the farm dog, holding his nose with one front paw to ward off the vitriol and covering his eyes with the other front paw to keep out the knives. The Scotty couldn't see his opponent and he couldn't smell his opponent and he was so badly beaten that he had to be taken back to the city and put in a nursing home.

Thurber's moral for the story? It is better to ask some of the questions than to know all the answers.

* Vitriol is sulfuric acid.

More specifically, the negative consequences of doing more talking and telling than listening and asking include:

- **Missing or failing to uncover critical information the other person has:** It would have been helpful for the Scotty to know he was dealing with a skunk or a hedgehog.
- **Signalling you have more interest in your own views than the other person's:** That's why the farm dog ending up beating Scotty up so badly. He thought he was an arrogant jerk.

- **Minimising involvement and engagement, reducing buy-in and commitment from others:** The computer chip company Intel has a saying for this – 'If you can't weigh in, you can't buy-in'.
- **Doing the heavy lifting on the thinking:** This creates a dance of dependency where others learn it is not their responsibility to solve problems because you as the leader will tell them the answer whether they ask for it or not.
- **Promoting submissive behaviours:** You end up creating a situation where people just do what they are told, or nod and agree even though they are not aligned with your view.
- **Cultivating group think through the one dominant voice:** This takes up all the oxygen and limits alternate views.
- **Leading to stress, fatigue and burnout for the leader:** You're doing most of the heavy lifting, and this inevitably leads to burnout.

FINDING A BALANCE

Unlike a typical or average leader, extraordinary leaders are particularly curious and listen at least as much as they talk, so that the ratio of talking to listening is at least 1:1. Sometimes it's 1:2, with the other person doing more talking than the leader. As one of my successful clients who runs a multibillion-dollar business told me, 'We have two ears and one mouth. That should tell you something about how much listening to talking we should do.'

Not surprisingly, curiosity plays a big role in the practice of Xtraordinary leadership.

Curiosity through questioning and listening

Curiosity in leadership involves asking questions and listening carefully to the answers. It ranks high among the behaviours that signal warmth and strength simultaneously. Curiosity signals warmth because the act of asking others the right questions and showing you are paying attention to what they are telling you is a strong signal that their views and opinions are invited and are considered valuable.

Research also shows that we prefer leaders who ask us more questions,[1] liking them more than those that ask us fewer questions.

Strength is also signalled when the questions you ask are focused on the issue, problem or opportunity you are seeking to make progress with. I have seen leaders pose a single provocative and powerful question to a large group and unleash way more movement or energy than a long speech could ever have achieved. What's more, insightful and relevant questions also create a sense with others that you know what you are doing.

These are not the only benefits of curiosity, though. In his *Harvard Business Review* article 'Why curious people are destined for the C-Suite', author Warren Berger showed how curiosity is behind many of the better-known leadership successes of market leaders and disrupters such as Disney, Netflix, Google and Airbnb.

Indeed, Edgar Schein, the highly regarded MIT professor and author of *Humble Inquiry: The Gentle Art of Asking Instead of Telling*, also argues that curiosity is perhaps the most important leadership capability in this modern age.

Curiosity and enquiry

Curiosity is operationalised through genuine enquiry, which itself is dependent upon three Catalyst beliefs:

1. *I don't have all the answers; in a complex and rapidly evolving world, my range of knowing and understanding will be limited, and I can't possibly know everything I need to in order to be able to make the best decisions or choose the best actions.*

2. *When in conversation with someone else, I know they have something to contribute, and that through the contributions of others we can better analyse, problem-solve and make progress with opportunities and challenges.*

3. *The person I am conversing with is a human being, and consequently needs to feel heard; otherwise, they are less likely to engage and commit to whatever it is that needs to be done. I will get the best from others when they feel involved.*

You have probably already realised that these Catalyst mindsets are the product of both warm and strong tendencies. They are based on a belief that other people matter and have something to offer, and that by engaging with the other person rather than just telling them what to do you are much more likely to generate higher levels of effectiveness and commitment and, therefore, more sustainable superior outcomes.

Curiosity creates the Catalyst effect

When leaders show curiosity and enquire through questions, they are not just collecting information. The 'ask don't tell' approach has been proven to have a significantly greater impact than just improving the quality of the information collected by the leader. When used deliberately and consciously to catalyse a transformative reaction in others, curiosity and enquiry can also:

- **Give back the work:** When you ask questions as a leader, the other person needs to do the work. Instead of just telling, micromanaging and over-controlling, you can use questions such as, 'How will you fix this issue?' or 'What is your plan for taking advantage of this opportunity?' to hold the other person accountable for making progress with the problems or opportunities being discussed.

- **Build capability and capacity:** When you challenge and support employees and followers to think through their problems using careful questioning, they build the self-confidence and capability that allows them solve problems and take action faster and often more successfully. You can also start to learn just what employees are and aren't yet capable of, and start to teach employees the helpful thinking patterns that allow them to solve problems and make progress with opportunities. As a leader, a key responsibility for you is to teach and coach others through thoughtful questioning and careful listening.

- **Invite collaboration and build commitment:** Many of our modern-day problems are too complex for any one individual to have all the answers or be able to solve completely independently. Enquiry allows you to tap into diverse observations and perspectives from a range of stakeholders to help build a better picture of what is really going on. By involving others, you also build commitment to the solutions or actions that result.

- **Manage unproductive behaviours:** Questions can also help manage unhelpful behaviours and tendencies in others. For example, meandering and unfocused explanations can be crystallised through the use of tightly targeted questions. Likewise, the esteem and ego needs of others can be satisfied through the use of a few respectful questions up front.

Other benefits of curiosity

Several other compelling cultural and performance benefits come from adopting a curious stance in your leadership:

- **Curiosity creates open cultures:** Many modern human-caused tragedies and disasters (such as airline crashes, mine collapses, space shuttle explosions and disastrous oil spills) have occurred in cultures where team members were reluctant to share a dissenting view or option with their superiors. In many of these cases, information was available that, if shared with the leader, would have averted or minimised the crisis. You may be tempted to declare, 'That wouldn't happen in our organisation', but keep in mind that while many leaders declare they are open to new information and others' views, their tendency to tell and not ask sends a very different signal into their teams and organisations.

- **Curiosity cultivates innovation and change:** The hallmark of innovative cultures and individuals is a questioning and curious tendency that enquires into the limitation of the status quo and explores new and alternative approaches that could deliver better outcomes. In a rapidly evolving world of technological, environmental and social upheaval, the innovators will thrive, leaving those unable to change stuck in progressively more challenging survival strategies.

- **Curiosity creates agile cultures:** Where curiosity from leaders results in team members becoming more capable and empowered, they are more likely to see and solve problems at the local level rather than waiting for a slow, cumbersome and often too-late response from leaders higher up. Furthermore, employees start to try small changes and continuous improvements at the local level that generate helpful learnings. Provided the organisation also has the ability to share these insights across the organisation, teams can learn from each other and leaders can learn from employees.

• **Curiosity is highly predictive of leadership promotion and success:** Curious leaders are more likely to be seen as capable of learning, more intelligent and more adaptable than those who are not curious. They are, therefore, more likely to be promoted into more senior roles.

To be effective, however, at bringing curiosity to life in your leadership, you need to first master the skill of enquiry.

ENQUIRY HELPS YOU ENGAGE

Enquiry is the act of asking questions. Questions allow you to work on the practical aspects of the situation, opportunity or problem. They allow you to gather facts and fill in the gaps in your understanding. That leads to better diagnosis, which then helps you prescribe more effective solutions. In other words, questioning allows you to avoid a similar fate as 'the Scotty who knew too much'.

A second and just as important reason to ask questions is to meet the personal needs in the interaction. It helps you connect with and engage others. We know that people feel more valued and better understood when we enquire into what they know, think and feel about things. This leads to higher levels of involvement, engagement and commitment to the solutions or next steps.

But there's no time!

Many years ago, I facilitated a leadership workshop for the IT department of a major bank. My workshop partner was Jake, a former senior sergeant from the tactical response group of the state police force.

I was leading a discussion on the importance of asking team members for input when I noticed an angry red colour creep its way up a participant's face at the same time as he started to appear more agitated and upset. I asked him what was on his mind, which he obliged me with immediately. 'This is bull$#@%,' he blurted out. 'Most of the time you don't have the time. I look after the platform that 38,000 employees use to do their work and when that system goes down and I start getting calls from the CEO's personal assistant telling me that she can't see his calendar or his emails, I just have to start telling people what to do. There's no time for two-way conversation.' He then gestured to my colleague, Jake, who was standing quietly in the corner of the room. 'You know what I mean. When the bullets start flying, you don't get the SWAT team together to share stories and sing camp songs!'

Jake, who had been leaning against the back wall of the room, slowly and casually wandered down the side of the room. 'Yep, you're right. When it's time for action, it may be time to stop talking. In those short seconds when you enter a building to pursue your objective, you expect your team to do what they are told and follow orders. But let's not forget all of the two-way conversations that go on before that moment as we travel together to the incident site and try to make sense of what we know and what we don't know. Even as we ready ourselves to execute our plan, I always ask my deputy if there is anything we have missed. During the operation, I also have to trust that my team will report new, unexpected or even contradictory information to me as it unfolds. Afterwards, we spend a large amount of time debriefing, asking questions, sharing perspectives. So, sure – there are a few critical moments when you need to tell and not ask, but it's all the asking and listening that you do before and afterwards that give you the permission and the right to do that and still have the commitment and trust of your team.'

Why we don't enquire as much as we should

Here are some reasons many leaders develop a tendency to tell a lot more than ask:

- **They are 'busyness' people:** Unfortunately, most leaders often feel too busy to ask questions. Gathering a bare understanding of the facts and then giving an answer, direction or solution takes less time and feels more efficient. Of course, acting in this way can be counterproductive in the long run because you usually spend more time afterwards fixing a poorly diagnosed problem, or struggle to engage the team members who feel your original dealings with them were cursory, unhelpful or dissatisfying.

- **They are trained from childhood to give answers:** Most of our training and preparation for the world of work happens at school, where we are taught that having the answers is what is valued. It gets you the passing grades and garners praise and recognition and other things that feed our self-esteem. Not having the answers suggests you are dumb or incompetent – aka unworthy. Asking more than one question in a classroom for most children is, therefore, akin to stating loudly, 'I am dumb; I don't get it.' No wonder when we enter the world of work and take up our first leadership role, we are already primed to give the answers rather than ask questions.

- **They were promoted for their expertise and knowing:** A typical first-level leader is usually given their supervisory role because they were good at doing the work as an individual contributor. Their accumulated expertise and technical knowledge allow them to supervise the work of others. In other words, the reason for promoting them is that they would have the answers to others' questions. For you as that supervisor to now ask questions means challenging the very reason you were made a supervisor in the first place.

- **They fill in the gaps with assumptions:** Leo Tolstoy once noted, 'The most difficult subjects can be explained to the most slow-witted man if he has not formed any idea of them already; but the simplest thing cannot be made clear to the most intelligent man if he is firmly persuaded that he knows already, without a shadow of doubt, what is laid before him.' Human beings often only have access to part of the story and fill in the missing gaps with their own lived experiences or knowledge. Without much further enquiry and without too much convincing, we are then sure we have a good understanding of the situation, problem or opportunity. We no longer need to ask questions; the answers are clear. This tendency to fill in the gaps and make assumptions gets in the way of asking questions, especially if they lead to answers that inconveniently disprove or conflict with our world view. In truth, we sometimes don't ask because we don't want to know.

How to enquire effectively

To make your enquiry more successful and effective, try the following:

- **Ask more than one question:** 'Double clicking' is a term used by author and corporate anthropologist Judith Glaser to describe the process of digging deeper. In *Conversational Intelligence*, she highlights the way we navigate web pages by placing our cursor on objects or topics that interest us and then double clicking with our mouse to find out more. We may do this several times to go deeper on a given topic before going back to the original landing page and choosing another topic to dig into. It is a useful analogy for the way we can enquire into a topic during a conversation, 'double clicking' – or asking more than one question – on things that are shared or raised to find out more.

- **Assume you don't know everything:** Instead of assuming that you already know everything you need to know about a given topic or issue, assume there must be things you don't know. When you assume you know everything, questions tend to be superficial, and your listening filters in evidence and information that supports your existing view, discounting potentially new and novel information. By instead assuming you only know part of the story, or that your version of events is inevitably one-sided, you can allow yourself a much more curious and less judgemental stance, helping you to recognise and integrate conflicting or unexpected information.

- **Go beyond facts:** The mostly rational world of business and management focuses on facts and figures. Yet every problem you seek to make progress with is embedded in a human system of people, replete with thoughts, opinions and feelings. When you only gather facts and figures, you remain unaware of the interpretations that others are making of the facts and figures, or even how they feel about the situations and problems you are dealing with. Remember, people engage or disengage principally because of how they feel, not what they think. By going beyond what people know, and into the realm of what they think and how they feel, as a leader you gather a much more comprehensive and accurate understanding of what is going on, and what may be needed to make progress.

- **Enquire into solutions as well:** I have worked with many leaders who have made wonderful progress in incorporating enquiry into their problem-solving conversations with others. They have grown comfortable using really effective diagnostic questions that 'double click' on facts, thoughts and feelings to understand the problem. However, once the diagnosis is complete, these leaders often revert to a 'tell don't ask' style in giving the solution, leaving the subordinate suddenly demotivated and confused at the sudden about face their leader has made – switching from being empowering and involving to a more doing and controlling style. For these leaders, the opportunity is to continue to ask questions during the solution-development stage. Examples of questions that involve the other person might include, 'So what options might we consider to fix this?' or 'What could you now do to drive this forward?' By involving the other person in the solution development, not just the problem identification, you can build on the energy and commitment that has already begun to be unleashed in the conversation. It also means that the other person does their share of the heavy lifting, as well as learning to solve problems themselves.

- **Use the right types of questions:** Thomas Kuhn was a leading American scientific thinker who coined the term 'paradigm shift'. Gifted in the art of scientific enquiry, he once said, 'The answer you get depends on the question you ask.' Albert Einstein is also reputed to have said (although unsubstantiated) that if he had an hour to work on an important problem, he would spend the first 55 minutes defining the problem through working out what the right question was, and then use the final 5 minutes to work out the answer.

- **Avoid responding to every answer:** Sometimes when asking questions, the other person provides an answer that can activate you, and so makes you want to respond. Whether you want to reject, qualify, or add to what the other person is saying, giving in to this tendency means you have effectively moved into a position of advocacy rather than enquiry – telling rather than asking. Your responsiveness here also shows that in some way you are judging the other person's answers to be acceptable or otherwise. This can have the effect of shutting down the other person's willingness to answer openly and genuinely. For this reason, asking all of your questions before responding is often more effective.

Using the right types of questions

Several different types of questions can be used for different purposes, both in terms of the type of information you're hoping to gather and your impact on the other person. The following table provides some examples.

Sounds like	Good for	Benefits	Potential downsides
Open question			
What happened? What are your thoughts? How do you feel about that? How do you think you could fix it?	Opening the conversation up	Invites participation Signals you value the other person Maximises information shared, revealing things you don't know	Using too many open questions can encourage unfocused and meandering behaviour (that is, the Relate pattern)

Sounds like	Good for	Benefits	Potential downsides
Follow up question			
Tell me more? What happened next? And so ...?	Digging deeper (double clicking)	Encourages participation Provides richer insight Gets beyond initial statements	Digging too deep into a narrow line of inquiry – losing the wider view Getting distracted by too much detail
Closed question			
How many? What time? How long?	Gathering specific information	Checks for specific facts Fills small gaps in your knowledge Helps manage unfocused and meandering behaviour	Shuts down conversation if used too early Can feel like an interrogation if used too much Can come across as the Control leadership pattern
Leading question			
Do you think it was the wrong thing to do? You'd have to agree that it's the only option?	Confirming your existing view	Signals what you think the correct answer is Helps manage unfocused and meandering behaviour	May appear to be aiming to 'trap' the other person Leaves no space for the other person to say what they really think Can come across as the Control leadership pattern

Sounds like	Good for	Benefits	Potential downsides
Summary question			
So what you're telling me is ...?	Checking for understanding	Shows you're listening	Overuse can appear patronising
So if I heard you correctly ...?		Signals you value the other person's contribution	Overuse can come across as the Relate leadership pattern
		Checks you've heard correctly	

When advocacy is dressed as enquiry

Be careful. Some questions are not genuinely curious enquiries. They are, instead, questions artfully crafted by your brain to prove your pre-existing assumptions and views. Rather than your questions being underpinned by the belief 'there is much about the topic that I don't know', you assume instead that, 'I know everything there is to know and now I am going to prove that I am right. I just need to ask the right questions to generate the answers that prove my point.' When advocacy pretends to be inquiry, it signals high strength but low warmth.

Leading questions and closed questions (refer to the preceding table) are the tools most often used for advocacy dressed as enquiry, because they can be used to generate answers that validate a pre-existing belief about what is going on. I see them used extensively by very smart, experienced and knowledgeable leaders who come to conclusions very quickly about situations, problems and people. Their questions then seek to prove their conclusions and their intelligence.

Another strong signal of advocacy dressed as enquiry is a lack of genuine listening, seen in leaders who believe they already know what answer the other person is going to give. (More about listening in the next chapter.)

A practical limitation with advocacy dressed as enquiry is that the other person usually cottons on pretty quickly that you are not genuinely interested in what they know, think or feel, and so will start to disengage or become defensive as a result. Another problem is that you as the enquirer generate no new information or novel insights that might otherwise help you make progress with the issue, or influence the other person more effectively.

Reflection

Which patterns of curiosity and enquiry do you demonstrate? Consider how the different leadership patterns approach being inquisitive, and which one applies to you:

- **Control:** Rarely asks questions, and is instead more likely to tell. When asking questions, they are often intended to prove the leader's point of view or hypothesis, or find flaws in the other person's approach so that they can win an argument or have their point of view prevail. Questions can often be abrupt and interrupting when they disagree with what they are hearing. Their questions are likely to be leading and closed, and thus experienced as combative, judgemental or interrogative.

- **Relate:** Asks questions and shows high levels of responsiveness to the answers. Leaders in this pattern are unlikely to ask questions that create any heat or might be seen as challenging. They avoid asking questions that might make the other person uncomfortable, and ask questions that generate positive responses. Questions are perceived by others as superficial or overly positive in orientation. They can also be unfocused and meandering, taking far too long to get to the point.

- **Protect:** May be reluctant to ask questions if doing so is perceived as risky. If questions are asked, leaders in this pattern are more likely to focus on facts and figures, avoiding feelings. Questions are often 'black hat' (in terms of Edward de Bono's Six Thinking Hats) and overly critical, focusing on negative possibilities and aspects of the situation. Questions are, therefore, likely to be experienced by others as signals of resistance, avoidance of risks, and protection of the status quo.

- **Catalyse:** Asks questions and shows high levels of responsiveness to answers. Questions from leaders in this pattern will range across facts, opinions and feelings, and will be used to learn new information, strengthen others' thinking and achieve better shared understanding. Follow-up questions generate greater insight and involvement. Questions are likely to be perceived as genuinely curious and collaborative. Summary questions show active listening.

13

Listen deeply

Following the terrible Port Arthur massacre in Tasmania in 1996, in which 35 people were killed by a lone shooter, heated debate about gun laws in Australia grew as politicians considered severely restricting ownership of automatic firearms. I remember watching a television interview from the time involving a senior official from the National Farmers' Federation (NFF). Farmers had been generally opposed to the idea of restrictions on automatic firearms and had mounted a concerted campaign to have the proposed laws softened. Their campaign included travelling to Canberra to meet with then Prime Minister John Howard, who had been spearheading the charge to restrict gun ownership.

The NFF spokesman was interviewed following the meeting and said he was happy with the conversation with the PM because he had been very curious, 'asking lots of questions and listening carefully to our answers. I feel that even though the PM is committed to making changes, at least he understands our position clearly. I feel that we had a fair hearing today'.

The successful changes to gun laws that John Howard was able to shepherd through a fractious and divided parliament are still considered to be one of his greatest leadership achievements, with his ability to listen deeply to oppositional views a key ingredient in his success.

LISTENING TO UNDERSTAND

The great management thinker Stephen Covey, author of *The 7 Habits of Highly Effective People*, once said that most people don't listen to understand; instead they listen to respond. By highlighting our tendency to judge what is being said and prepare our response to it even while the other person is still speaking, Covey highlighted how the mere appearance of listening is not sufficient to match the power of genuine enquiry. Something else is required – a deeper, more generous type of listening.

I once heard someone who had met US President Bill Clinton describe his experience of his deep listening. He said that although they were at busy social event in the centre of Manhattan, New York, and even while he wasn't a particularly important person, he still experienced the incredible intensity with which Bill listed to what he had to say – as if no-one else existed in the room for Bill in that moment, just the person in front of him. According to author and consultant Geoffrey Tumlin in his book *Stop Talking, Start Communicating*, Clinton's ability to listen and be fully present was a key element of his extraordinary ability to communicate and connect with people, regardless of their position, background or political interests.

Benefits of deep listening

Listening is the obvious counterparty to enquiry (covered in the previous chapter); however, it is often done poorly or superficially. A vast difference exists between just listening and actually hearing and understanding what is being said by others, and especially in terms of what your listening signals about your warmth and strength.

The way you listen can have major implications for your leadership:

* Deep and attentive listening is a characteristic of warm intentions. It signals to the other person that they matter, and what they have to say is important. When others feel listened to and understood, they are much more likely to listen to your views. They are also more likely to be willing to be influenced by what you have to say. Their trust in your intentions is increased and, as a result, even if they don't agree with your leadership decisions, they are

much more likely to actively support them or at least not mount resistance to them.

- Listening also enhances your strength through building your mastery and competence. The better you understand situations and people through the act of listening, the more complete the information you gain to make better choices and decisions.

- To be effective at influencing and mobilising others, you need to be masterful at meeting others where they are at before leading them towards where they need to go. If you don't genuinely listen to how others see the world, and learn what drives them forward and what holds them back, you are essentially powerless to meet them where they are at, and certainly incapable of helping them overcome their own challenges to getting to where you need them to go.

Psychological safety – a valuable product of deep listening

Should I feel safe around you? This is a question that every team member will ask themselves about their leader – non-consciously. We rely on our non-conscious thinking to make this critical assessment because it's fast, so we get the survival benefit of this split-second judgement. If our answer is, 'No, I don't feel safe around you', we will be on guard with this person, cautious about what we can do or say around them. We do not feel 'psychologically safe'.

Psychological safety is a condition that exists when we feel safe disclosing what we really think and feel without being negatively judged by others. The condition seems deeply implicated in the functioning of effective work relationships, and so has been the subject of intense research recently – particularly as a result of a landmark study at Google Inc.

Every year within Google, thousands of teams are formed around key projects, with the success of these projects largely dependent on the quality of teamwork. Google wanted to know what allowed teams to work at their best, so they set out to study hundreds of their own teams and examine all of the team research available outside the company.[1] They found the number one influence on effective team functioning is psychological safety – that is, teams perform at their best when team members do not feel that they need to protect themselves from each other. This allows them to feel they are free to say whatever it is they think or feel without fear of rejection or reprisal. In other words, they can be open and vulnerable with each other – they can speak up.

Safe to speak up

Organisational psychology experts Hemant Kakkar (London Business School) and Subra Tangirala (University of Maryland) reported that situational factors – rather than personality factors – lead employees to speak up.[2]

Situational factors generally boil down to leadership and culture – will my leader listen to me? Do I feel dissent is welcome? The authors argued,

> *Even people who are most inclined to raise ideas and suggestions may not do so if they fear being put down or penalized. On the flip side, encouraging and rewarding speaking up can help more people do so, even if their personality makes them more risk-averse.*

Leaders make it safe or unsafe to speak up

The role of the leader in cultivating psychological safety cannot be overstated. When a team member feels psychologically unsafe and has to protect themselves from their leader, undesirable workplace consequences can emerge. For example:

- Team members are less likely to speak up when they see a problem or issue in the workplace. Usually, the problem gets worse and has a negative impact on productivity and safety. Many documented cases show examples of a lack of psychological safety contributing to a reluctance to speak up by a team member, leading to disastrous outcomes – including plane crashes,[3] mine collapses and surgical deaths[4]. (See the breakout box 'Not safe to speak up' for more on this.)

- Team members will be reluctant to disclose when they are struggling with a task or assignment or need coaching or support from their boss. Concerned that they will be judged and criticised rather than being supported, team members are more likely to hide their lack of progress until errors or failures show up, negatively affecting results.

- Creativity and innovation are stifled because more diverse views and opinions are withheld, which otherwise may have led to breakthroughs in thinking. We know from research on inclusion that a huge upside comes from raising the volume of the lesser heard voices. Greater diversity of thought can lead to less-biased decision-making and greater collective intelligence. This has obvious implications for companies that need to develop new products, services and ways of working.

Not safe to speak up

In the air

On 6 August 1997, Korean Air flight 801 crashed at Nimitz Hill, Guam. The plane had been cleared to land but crashed into high terrain about three miles south-west of the airport. The plane was destroyed on impact.

The cause of the accident was discovered to be a malfunctioning altitude indicator on the Captain's side of the controls, which led him to descend the plane onto a ridge as it approached the airport. More tellingly, it was discovered that the First Officer's indicator had been working perfectly but that he had failed to inform his Captain that he was jeopardising the flight. Studies of the flight's voice recorder shed further light on the climate in the cockpit leading up to the crash, in which an overbearing and increasingly agitated Captain had instilled such a climate of fear that none of his subordinates dared question his decisions or raise their concerns – even in an apparent life or death situation.

During the late 1990s, Korean Air had more plane crashes than almost any other airline in the world for that period. When thinking of airline crashes, it's easy to assume old planes and badly trained pilots were to blame. This wasn't the case. What they were struggling with was a broader cultural issue where it felt unsafe for more junior team members to speak up.

In the operating theatre

Rhode Island Hospital had a reputation as a leading medical institution – and also as a place divided by internal tensions. In 2000, deep, simmering hostilities existed between nurses and physicians. 'This place can be awful; the doctors make you feel like you're worthless, like you're disposable. Like you should be thankful to pick up after them,' said one nurse.

To deal with the tensions, nurses developed a whiteboard colour-coded system, denoting which surgeons were 'jerks', and which were 'never to be contradicted because they would take your head off'. When a surgeon of the latter description insisted on proceeding with delicate brain surgery without verifying which side of the patient's skull to open, the nurse knew by the colour on the whiteboard that the unwritten rules of the culture were clear – this surgeon always wins and was never to be questioned. The surgeon proceeded, and indeed opened the wrong side of the skull. The procedure took twice as long as it should have, and the patient subsequently died.

PERSPECTIVE TAKING

Xtraordinary leaders consistently put themselves in others' place. In Harper Lee's famous novel *To Kill a Mockingbird*, the character Atticus Finch says, 'You never really understand a person until you consider things from his point of view, until you climb inside of his skin and walk around in it.'

For leaders, this means taking into account the personal experience or perspective of their employees and seeing what the world looks like from where they are. Marty Linsky from Harvard University (who I introduced in chapter 7) summarised this idea well when he said, 'You can't lead people from where *you are*. You have to first connect with them where *they are*.'

Perspective taking is especially important when you do not understand, and maybe even suspect you will disagree with, someone else's viewpoint. If you do not understand someone else's perspective, you are powerless to help them change it – unless they believe you understand where they are starting from, and why that's their starting point.

Listening leads to reciprocal listening

When the other person believes that you understand their perspective, even if you don't necessarily share it, they will be more willing to listen to your perspective and point of view. This is partly because of the role that reciprocity plays in human influence, as described by Robert Cialdini, PhD, in his bestselling book *The Psychology of Persuasion*.

When you listen generously to another's position, showing clearly that you have heard them, the law of reciprocity then allows you to say, 'Is it okay if I now share with you my perspective?' and to reasonably expect agreement in response. In other words, if you seek to understand their perspective, they will be more inclined to seek to understand yours.

By engaging in perspective taking, listening and understanding, you can also avoid the negative communication spiral that is a consequence of arguing.

Hearing a different truth

Unfortunately, understanding others' perspectives is not always easy for some leaders, because they see only one possible version of things, or one version of 'the truth'. The following story illustrates this point well.

Curse or saviour?

A manager from the Department of Agriculture visited a large country town to tell the local farmers about a wonderful plan he had to eradicate a toxic introduced plant species called *Echium plantagineum* from the environment.

The plant, known commonly as Paterson's curse, had spread rampantly across the countryside and was killing cattle and other livestock when they fed on it, especially during dry periods when the toxic plant grew prolifically.

The manager did a wonderful job explaining all the benefits to the livestock farmers of his plan and left behind some information and his contact details for farmers to follow up if they were interested in trialling the solution.

Sometime after the meeting, the manager contacted the local representative of the Farmers' Federation to find out why so few farmers had followed up on the trial. The local told him that significant resistance had emerged from some sections of the community about the trial, especially among the beekeepers.

The manager learned that the beekeepers had a different name for the plant. They called it Salvation Jane, because in hotter, drier periods and drought years, it was the only plant that would flower and provide enough nectar to keep the bee colonies flourishing. His great plan to eradicate this plant species that killed livestock would also cause losses to the apiarists, and the other farmers who relied on the bees to fertilise their fruit, vegetable and seed crops. In this case, the manager hadn't understood the two versions of truth that existed – his, and the one held by the people he needed to influence.

Realising his mistake, the manager returned to the town and engaged with the resistors to understand their concerns and gather their ideas on what would allow the trial to proceed. Following these discussions, he adjusted the proposed trial to also meet the needs of the beekeepers and food-producers. This time the trial was able to proceed successfully.

The beach ball problem

The preceding story illustrates that sometimes our arguments and misunderstandings are a product of seeing the same thing but from different vantage points or perspectives. We, therefore, end up arguing about what we see, rather than what we're seeing.

What's known as 'the beach ball problem' also illustrates this. Imagine you and a colleague are seated at a table opposite each other. On the table in front of you is a multi-coloured beach ball, with different segments or strips of colour lining the ball all the way around. You can see only stripes of blue and red, while your colleague can only see stripes of yellow and green. To you it's a blue and red ball. To your colleague, it's a yellow and green ball. You are both partially right. If you were to either rotate the ball or even better swap seats with your colleague, you would see that, yes, it is a blue and red ball, as well as being a yellow and green ball, and also an orange, purple and white ball. It is, in fact, a multicoloured beach ball.

Duck or rabbit?

Perspective taking requires you to understand not only what others see from their vantage point, but also the interpretations and meaning they make of what they see.

Even when you're looking at the same thing as another person, what you think you see – the meaning you make of it – can be very different. This is well illustrated by the following image.

Duck or rabbit?

What do you see? A duck? A rabbit? Something else altogether? When I show this well-known 100-year-old optical illusion in workshops, some people can only see the image as a duck no matter how hard they stare at it, whereas others see it only as a rabbit. They can then argue about which it is, a rabbit or a duck. Both the 'rabbit people' and the 'duck people' believe they know the truth and the others do not. Of course, both groups are correct. They are also both wrong. There is no duck or rabbit. They are simply looking at a projection of ink lines on a page that represent a duck or rabbit.

Human beings make meaning of things so quickly and automatically that we often don't question the assumptions that create the meaning. For this very reason, we often end up in pitched battles with others as to who has the right view. We have the same data and information, yet we make very different meaning of it. Then, when we feel others are incapable of understanding our view, we trust them less.

For you to be an effective leader, therefore, recognising where your determination to prosecute your version of the truth is in effect cancelling out someone else's – and destroying trust in the process – is critical.

Xtraordinary leaders are conscious of the role their own assumptions play in limiting their meaning making, and are more comfortable challenging their own assumptions, or having them challenged by the world views and perspectives of others.

DEEP LISTENING TECHNIQUES

In the following sections, I outline some techniques you can use to listen deeply and gather new perspectives through others.

Be present and focused

This is perhaps one of the hardest things for modern leaders to do. Our lives are filled with so many attention-grabbing stimuli, while our internal thoughts are distracted by worries about the future and the past. To be fully present and focused on another person is demanding, but essential if you are to avoid sending unhelpful signals to the other person.

When they perceive that your own thoughts and needs are more important to you than theirs, as evidenced by your lack of focused attention on them, they experience you as disconnected, or even cold or hostile. Taking the time before key conversations to centre yourself and bring your attention into the present moment can help.

Deep breathing is a useful tool. So too is mindfulness training, which can also help you more quickly recognise those moments where your mind has wandered from what the other person is saying and provide tools to allow yourself to bring your attention back to the present moment.

Finally, an internal affirmation that 'in this moment, with this person, I am precisely where I need to be' can help alleviate anxiety and stressful thoughts that you need to hurry up and move on to the next thing.

Maintain eye contact

Eye contact is perhaps the most useful active listening technique. Your brain focuses on what it's looking at. By paying attention to the other person's face, you can maintain greater attention to what they are saying.

Pause and use silence

Instead of immediately responding when the other person finishes talking, take a moment to quietly reflect on what they have said. Pausing and being silent for just a few seconds gives you time to process what has been said and reach a deeper level of understanding.

If you are worried that the other person may misinterpret your silence as disengagement, let them know what you are doing with a comment like, 'That's interesting. Let me think about that for a moment.'

From personal experience, I have only ever perceived the other person's appreciation for my attempts at deep listening when I have used this technique. It has also led to many insights that I am sure I would have otherwise missed.

Make notes

Note-taking forces you to pay attention to what is being said. The most important meetings we have in our lives involve notes being taken – such as with lawyers and doctors – so doing so sends a clear signal to the other person that what is being said matters to you. Unless you have perfect retention and have a perfect memory, note-taking also helps recall and reflection during and after key conversations, aiding the quality of your analysis and decision-making.

I take notes in all my meetings and usually declare upfront that I am planning to do so because what the other person has to say really matters to me and I want to capture it accurately. I let them know where appropriate that my notes are for my use only and check that they are confirmable with this.

Rarely does anyone have a concern. Indeed, I find many moments where the other person is really pleased when I am able to accurately play back exactly what they said sometime later. This shows that I was really listening and clearly understand what their point of view is.

Paraphrase

Of course, hearing what has been said and being able to play it back accurately is only a signal that you have been listening, not necessarily one that suggests you have understood what has been said. Try to 'playback' what the other person has said using your own words and not theirs. This is a terrific test of whether you truly get what they are saying. You don't have to agree with what they are saying, just show that you understand it. Starting with phrases such as, 'So what you are saying is …' or, 'Let me get this right. Your view is that …' can help.

Remain silent

A very successful business leader I know required his leadership group to run what he called 'listening sessions' – every month. These listening sessions involved leaders spending time with groups of frontline employees from a business division different from their own, and asking questions for one hour about what the employees were seeing, what was and wasn't working, and what help they needed from management. Each leader was only allowed to ask questions for that whole hour. They weren't allowed to answer, respond, argue or defend. The big boss was very clear about it: 'They are listening sessions, not answering sessions.'

Each leader then had to bring the feedback into the next management team meeting and share it candidly. The process was extremely helpful to the top team in truly understanding what was going on in the business, and allowed them to perceive opportunities and challenges that they otherwise would never have seen. They also received pretty candid feedback on the on-the-ground impacts of their strategic decisions, for better or worse. Had the leaders allowed themselves to respond, justify, or argue in the sessions, the employees would not have shared a lot of the harder-to-hear but oh-so-important feedback. Simply listening is sometimes all that is needed.

Ask, 'If that were true, what would it mean?'

This is an especially helpful technique when you hear the other person saying something that is very different from your point of view and you feel triggered into quickly responding in a 'tell and do' (or Control) kind of way. When this happens, we usually want to quickly tell the other person that they are wrong – and let loose with all the reasons why they are wrong. This is hardly helpful for signalling warmth and openness. This reaction also means that you run the risk of ignoring a version of things that may have elements you can learn from, or something that expands your knowledge beyond your current assumptions and beliefs.

To remain in a curious and open state, see if you can suspend your judgement and the need to assert your version of the truth a bit longer by saying something like, 'That's very interesting. It's quite different from what I had been thinking. If what you are saying were true, what would that mean for our situation/our problem/our choices going forward?' One of two things will happen as a consequence. You might listen to their response, decide that their version is still quite different from your point of view and let them know you disagree – but at least they will feel you gave them a very fair hearing. The other possibility is what they say shifts your view and expands your thinking in some helpful way. Either way, you will benefit from hanging out with their view just that bit longer.

Reflection

How often do you listen to judge and respond rather than listening openly and generously? What situations or people trigger this?

How intense is your listening? How often do you find yourself distracted by your own thoughts or needs?

How obvious is it to others that you are listening deeply to what they are really saying? How could you signal that through your behaviour?

14

Connect emotionally

Empathy is increasingly being seen as an essential leadership skill, and the evidence is also quite clear on the relationship between empathy and leadership effectiveness.

In one of the larger studies by the Centre for Creative Leadership, researchers asked, 'Is empathy needed to be successful in a leader's job?'[1] To answer this question, they analysed leaders' empathy based on their reported behaviour. Using a sample of 6731 leaders from 38 countries, they then asked at least three subordinates to rate the leaders on their display of empathic emotion. Each manager in the sample also had one boss rate them on three items that measured job performance. This allowed the researchers to establish if a link existed between leader empathy and job performance.

The results of the study revealed that empathy is positively related to job performance. Empathy, as rated by the leader's subordinates, positively predicted job performance ratings from the leader's boss. In other words, leaders who show more empathy toward direct reports were also rated as better performers in their job by their bosses. What's more, the findings were culturally universal, with empathy being important across all 38 countries in the study.

Empathy also has a halo effect on other people's perceptions of your leadership.[2] People rated highly on empathy are much more likely to be seen as better leaders by their peers, not just in terms of relationship management, but also in terms of task performance.

In other words, empathetic leaders are viewed by their peers as more effective in managing both relationships and results. This contrasts with leaders who instead are considered smart and knowledgeable, and might be considered more competent at leading tasks, but not at leading relationships. Therefore, being perceived as empathetic will have positive influences on others' willingness to engage with you, as well as others' perceptions of your leadership effectiveness – a useful outcome, as the following comments from Julia Gillard highlight.

Q&A episode, 13 July 2020
featuring Julia Gillard, former Australian Prime Minister, professor and Brookings Institute Senior Fellow

Audience Member: Whether it's Trump in the US, Bolsonaro in Brazil, or Johnson in the UK, the pandemic has exposed the shortfalls of … a 'strong man' style of leadership. Do you think the future of global politics sits in the style of leadership exhibited by female heads of state, like Merkel in Germany or Ardern in New Zealand, and do you think there is something to be said for the distinctly feminine style of leadership being the answer to navigating this crisis?

Julia Gillard: I'm not a believer that men and women are inherently different in their leadership styles … it's not that our brains are different, but we are socialised differently … and received differently. For a female leader to succeed, she has to balance strength and empathy. If she is too strong, people will say 'she's not very likeable', and if she's too nurturing and caring, people will say 'she hasn't got the backbone to lead'. So women leaders are already very skilled in the balance of strength and empathy and, in a time like this, people want both. They want to know that someone is getting the job done, but they also want someone to care about how they are feeling, and I think people like Jacinda Ardern, Erna Solberg in Norway have really been able to put that together.

IS EMPATHY AN IMPRECISE WORD?

However, a problem exists with empathy. It is an imprecisely understood word, which means that each of us can make quite different meaning of it. I have found this can limit people's willingness to understand what empathy truly is, develop it, or even use it in their leadership.

For example, I worked with a general manager of an infrastructure construction business who wished to develop his leadership skills. When I mentioned the word 'empathy', he literally turned up his nose and leaned back uneasily in his chair, crossing his arms in the process. When I enquired about what he thought empathy was he said, 'It's about hugging people when they're sad, crying with them too.' And when I asked him what he thought about that he said, 'What do you mean? I'm not here to counsel people, blow their noses, or give 'em therapy! My job's to get these blokes to move dirt!' In this case, empathy meant the same as psychotherapy, or having an intimate connection to his team that would require a deep emotional investment by this leader. No wonder he didn't like the sound of it.

What is empathy then?

Empathy concerns your relationship with, and responsiveness to, others' emotions. In other words, it involves your connection to how they feel.

Empathy uses the suffix '-pathy', which has Greek origins and means connection. Several other words ending in '-pathy' describe various ways that we can connect with and relate to others' emotions, some of which can be plotted on the warmth or emotional connectedness continuum – as shown in the following figure.

Continuum of emotional connectedness

TOO CONNECTED				DISCONNECTED
Emotional contagion	**Affective empathy**	**Cognitive empathy**	**Antipathy**	**Apathy**
Catching	Rescuing	Acknowledging	Denying	Ignoring

The different points in the connectedness continuum can be understood in the following ways:

- **Apathy:** At this point, I ignore your emotional expressions, or make no attempt to understand them. This may be intentional, because emotions make me feel uncomfortable and I don't know what to do with them, or I may in the small percentage of people who simply do not possess the ability to recognise others' emotional states – which can be the case with individuals on the autism spectrum, for example.

- **Antipathy:** Here, I recognise your emotional state but attempt to invalidate it by arguing with the legitimacy of how you are feeling – for example, saying you have no right to feel disappointed by something. In other words, I am in opposition to your emotional experience.

- **Cognitive empathy:** This is when I intellectually understand the emotions you are experiencing and what is causing them, even though I may feel nothing in response – for example, I could say, 'I understand the restructure is causing you to feel anxious.' This connects with the 'theory of mind' mechanism (ToMM) discussed in chapter 9, which looks at the ability to predict accurately others' mental states.

- **Affective empathy:** At this point, I understand the emotions you are feeling, experience discomfort or distress at your experience, and I want to help you, even rescue you. This is also sometimes called *sympathy*. A psychological mechanism involved here is what's been dubbed 'The Empathising SyStem', or TESS[3] for short, a capacity that starts developing in humans between the ages of one and two years of age. Affective empathy requires both ToMM (recognising emotions in others) and TESS (feeling something in response). Notably, psychopaths have a functioning ToMM and can accurately recognise the emotions others are experiencing, but do not possess a functioning TESS, and therefore feel no disturbance or distress in response. This is part of the reason they can be so effective in manipulating others.

- **Syncopathy:** Sometimes called 'emotional contagion'[4] or 'herding empathy', this is where I automatically and simultaneously experience the same emotional state you are transmitting. This instantaneous synchronisation of emotion is a herding survival response, ensuring that emotions resulting from imminent dangers are quickly transmitted through the group, inciting an immediate reaction – similar to a flock of birds or a school of fish reflexively wheeling away from a predator. It is the most primitive and compulsive version of emotional connection and was implicated in the panic-buying of toilet paper around the world as the COVID-19 pandemic emerged. This was a good example of others 'catching' FOMO and panic from others, even though no rational reason existed for their action.

Too little or too much empathy

The challenge for a leader is to have an appropriate relationship to others' emotions. Apathy and antipathy are disconnections from others' emotions, and signal intentions that are 'me' focused rather than 'other' focused, leading to distrust and decreased engagement from others.

Syncopathy and some manifestations of affective empathy create the opposite problem. The leader can become *too* emotionally connected or 'fused', resulting in the leader being unable or unwilling to take independent and objective action. This is problematic because often in leadership you need to ask others to do things that make them uncomfortable. If you are uncomfortable with their discomfort, you may back-pedal on your expectations and fail to hold them accountable. What's more, being too emotionally connected to others can produce a condition called 'unmitigated empathy', where no boundary or limit exists for how connected you are to others. This can leave a leader feeling overburdened and potentially burned out as a result of carrying the emotional weight of everyone else's negative feelings, and feeling responsible to rescue them from their distress.

The amount of empathy you need is similar to what Goldilocks is looking for in the famous fairytale. You don't want to have too little or too much of a connection – you want just the right amount.

Reviewing the three ordinary leadership patterns from part I, you can see how each of them operate outside the Goldilocks zone.

1. **Control: Tell and Do** pays little attention to others' emotions, and when it does the response is just as likely to involve telling others why they are wrong to feel a particular way.

2. **Relate: Smooth and Soothe** pays too much attention to others' emotions, at the expense of getting things done or holding people accountable for responding to their own challenges.

3. **Protect: Maintain and Refrain** shows little or no response to others' emotional states, creating a perception of uncaring apathy or even disdain.

Just right

The Catalyst or Xtraordinary pattern of leadership operates within the 'Goldilocks Zone'. In this zone, you're showing enough empathy to show others that they matter and that you care, at the same time as maintaining some objectivity about the causes of their emotional states. As a Catalyst leader, you're not so emotionally fused to others that you lose the ability to think objectively and act independently. At the same time, you can be capable of showing genuine compassion for others' experiences – but you're not always compelled to rescue them from the negative experience.

The Catalyst leader knows that sometimes people need to find their own way out of the mess, building competence and confidence in themselves in the process. A leader who always feels compelled to rescue others creates an overly dependent relationship, breeds powerlessness in others, and becomes over-burdened with the management of others' emotions beyond what is reasonable and sustainable.

Without trading off strength

Being strong and empathetic is a difficult but not impossible balancing act, as this quote from Jacinda Ardern, Prime Minister of New Zealand shows:

One of the criticisms I've faced over the years is that I'm not aggressive enough or assertive enough, or maybe somehow, because

*I'm empathetic, it means I'm weak. I totally rebel against that.
I refuse to believe that you cannot be both compassionate and strong.*

However, a significant risk for highly empathetic leaders is that they give up strength and agency in their desire to alleviate the discomfort strong leadership actions inevitably create for others. Tough love is often required, and difficult trade-offs mean that leaders often need to do things that others do not like. If as a leader you are unable to maintain a fierce resolve to make difficult things happen, because you are held hostage by the need to soothe others' discomfort and unease, your leadership will stray into the high-warmth, low-strength territory of the Relate leadership pattern.

While researching the sportspeople who become great leaders, journalist Tom Young found they embraced the genius of *and* (refer to chapter 2) when it came to showing care and empathy, while maintaining drive and agency. 'All the people I interviewed really care' he wrote. 'They might be quite competitive, they can be tough and aggressive, but there is an undercurrent of compassion and empathy.'[5]

The two forms of empathy from the connectedness continuum that allow for warmth to manifest while also maintaining strength are cognitive and affective empathy.

Leading with balance

Diana was all business. In her demanding department manager role within a luxury hotel, she was straight to the point and extremely focused in all her dealings. Her cool businesslike approach was the epitome of managerial efficiency and productivity. Diana, however, was finding the people-leadership side of things a bit more challenging.

Diana's focus on results was self-evident when we first started working together on her challenge. Her focus on people was much less evident. The way she showed up was sending messages that she was interested in outcomes, not relationships. While some team members and colleagues responded well to this, others didn't. Diana needed to learn how to project differently if she was to build trust and engagement across the entire team.

Diana's development focused on becoming more curious about the experience other people were having – how did they feel about things? – as well as other techniques for building connection and trust that could be used in the hustle and bustle of a busy hotel. Her commitment to the work and willingness to experiment allowed her to make tremendous progress even within a short time. Her relationships improved, her ability to influence became more effective, and even better results followed. Not long afterwards, in recognition of her leadership success, Diana was promoted to a new role overseeing the whole hotel.

THE BENEFITS OF APPROPRIATE EMPATHY

As a leader, your use of cognitive and affective empathy has several practical benefits:

- It provides insights into others' perspectives and helps answer key influencing questions you should be asking, such as 'Are my team positively engaged or is emotional resistance present?', 'What's holding this person back?', 'What challenges does this create for this individual?' and 'What concerns do I need to help this person address or overcome if I am to enlist their commitment?'

- Empathy also makes real two-way communication possible. Talking 'at' a person is not real communication – it is a monologue. Real conversation is sensitive to this listener at this time,[6] and empathy is a powerful way of showing sensitivity to others.

- The use of empathy builds trust and engagement with others. Empathy is a powerful manifestation of warmth and signals that your intentions towards others are positive. This builds their support for the leadership agenda that you are seeking to pursue.

- Empathy also defuses blocking emotions. Your team being caught in negative emotional states can impede their ability to think logically and rationally. When you as their leader empathise with their emotions, they feel they have been heard and validated. Often you are then able to move beyond focusing on the emotional state to focus on solving the problem that caused the emotions. Without this defusing of the negative interfering emotions, you may be held back from ever solving the practical problems that created them.

IS EMPATHY TRAINABLE?

Cognitive and affective empathy is largely trainable and learnable. While a very small percentage of adults may lack the underlying neural circuitry of ToMM for cognitive empathy or TESS for affective empathy – such as some individuals diagnosed with autism, or psychopathy – I have found that the vast majority of leaders can quickly build their emotional intelligence through two key skills. These are recognising emotions and responding appropriately to emotions.

Recognising others' emotions

The most direct route to understanding how others feel is to ask them. These can be simple questions such as, 'How do you feel about that?' or 'How would you describe your emotional response to …'

Sometimes, however, you may not have the opportunity to ask these questions, so observation and careful listening become important tools in developing a better sense of what others are emitting in the way of emotional signals.

Becoming an observer

The biggest impediment to paying attention to others' emotional states is a tendency to focus on the practical issue or task at hand, rather than the person themselves. Often, we get so caught up in getting the job done and focusing on what's at stake in a meeting, that we don't pay attention to who has a stake in the meeting and what they are experiencing.

To help leaders develop this capacity, I often set them a task of becoming the watcher in a meeting they are not personally running or leading. Rather than tracking the group's progress using the practical objectives of the meeting – such as planning, reviewing and reporting – I ask the leader to instead carefully watch the faces and body language of the meeting participants, observing how they react to each other and noting the corresponding emotions that might be signalled. Most people are amazed by what is revealed to them by this exercise; however, they may struggle to accurately label the emotions they have observed.

Developing an emotional vocabulary

Having language to describe and label what you see and hear in your team is critical; however, recognising and describing emotions is akin to wine tasting. At first, most people lack the ability to distinguish more than just a few obvious aromas or flavours, but even simple training with an aroma wheel or similar can quickly and rapidly expand the range of smells and taste sensations you can pick up.

I stumbled across a similarly useful training method for emotions, quite accidentally on a cross-country flight. My headphones stopped working just as I started watching the in-flight movie starring Jack Nicholson and Meryl Streep – both very capable actors. I only had the visual data to work with so I decided to see if I could make sense of the movie without hearing the dialogue. I discovered that as I watched I could discern their emotions and was fascinated by just how much emotional information was being conveyed through their facial expressions. Try this yourself to start building your skills in reading different emotions.

Other tools such as the Mood Meter app for your phone can then be very helpful in expanding your emotional vocabulary and sense making of different emotions. I highly recommend them.

Responding to others' emotions

As a young man, I realised that while I was capable of recognising others' emotions, I wasn't quite sure what to do when I encountered them in my team members. This is partly a result of growing up in a household that valued cool logic and emotional evenness, with relatively few memorable incidences of strong negative emotions such as rage, sorrow, apprehensiveness or depression. Having little experience in seeing what overtly displayed warmth, compassion and empathy looked like in response to these emotions, I didn't have any templates for what appropriate empathetic responses might be, and at the same time admired greatly those leaders who seemed to be able to do it with ease. I consequently did a lot of conscious and deliberate work in my twenties and thirties to develop this skill.

A simple method

In that process, I learnt that perhaps the simplest and most effective way of responding to others' emotions is to acknowledge two things about the person's experience:

1. Name the actual emotion or emotions the other person is experiencing.
2. Identify the situation or issue that is generating the emotional response.

It doesn't matter which part comes first, just that you include both. Here are a few examples:

*   'I see that you are frustrated by the change to the new process.'
*   'I hear your anger at being not listened to by the accounting team.'
*   'Winning that new contract has certainly put a smile on your face!'

Being specific

The naming of the emotion and the corresponding cause is much more powerful than general statements such as, 'I understand' or 'I get it' because you are providing proof that you do actually get it. In fact, as a leader you should be careful not to use lines such as, 'I hear you' or 'I get where you are coming from'. These statements provide little to no evidence that you have, in fact, recognised the emotional state of the other person. I have also seen average leaders use these throwaway lines too many times purely to placate the other person, with that disingenuous use being quite inflammatory to the other person. I'm sure you'll agree that nothing is more infuriating than feeling you are being patronised by someone who really isn't that interested in you.

Name it if you want to tame it

Another benefit of naming a negative emotion the other person is experiencing is that doing so can help to minimise its effect. When a team member experiences strong interfering emotions such as anger, frustration or disappointment, these emotions can get in the way of them being able to move forward. 'Name it to tame it' is a phrase coined by the psychiatrist Dan Siegel, who showed that when we name unhelpful interfering emotions, we also lessen their hold over us, allowing us to engage in more deliberate and considered actions.

Using inquiry

If you are unsure of the emotion being displayed, you can also ask a question to delve deeper; for example, 'Are you feeling anxious about learning the new rules and procedures?' or 'Are you disappointed with Brian's response?' Usually, the other person will let you know if you labelled the wrong emotion, but will be appreciative at the same time that you are attempting to understand them accurately and will be more likely to elaborate on their feelings.

Reflection

What is your level of comfort with other people's emotional expressions?

Where would you place your typical response on the continuum of emotional responsiveness?

How well developed is your emotional vocabulary and empathy?

15

Share perspective

At this point in this book, you could be forgiven for thinking that Xtraordinary leaders do a lot of asking, listening and responding, with little telling. That conclusion is understandable – I have spent considerable time explaining why you might want to do the opposite of what ordinary and average leaders do, which is to mostly tell.

However, telling, sharing and advocating do have important places in the repertoire of extraordinary leaders, and while these leaders may spend less time telling as a total proportion of the time they spend with other people, when they do speak up they are compelling and influential.

EQUAL PARTS ENQUIRY AND ADVOCACY

There are times to listen, and times to tell. I and others have found that balancing the two more effectively creates better outcomes. For example, Marcel Losada from Michigan State University found that leadership teams who engage in an equal 1:1 balance of inquiry and advocacy produce far superior results when compared to poor performing teams that demonstrated a ratio of 1:5 asking versus telling.[1]

A ratio of 1:1 is consistent with what I have observed over thousands of leadership assessments. Great leaders spend on average half their time asking and listening and the other half advocating and explaining. This clearly means that telling is as important as asking. In fact, to only ask and never tell would result in showing up as warm but not strong. Maintaining your strength means that when it comes to the moments to tell, it is just as important to be able to advocate a view convincingly, argue your point clearly and communicate compellingly.

You should ask, then tell

Throughout this book I have discussed the importance of a warmth-first approach. Given that asking and inquiring is a powerful way to show warmth through interest and curiosity in the other person and their views, it makes sense that the order in which you inquire and advocate should be ask first, then tell – not the other way around. Telling first is the less effective pattern typical of the Control leadership pattern.

Why is the Catalyst ask-then-tell approach more effective? There are several reasons:

- **Reciprocity:** Asking and listening first activates a psychological response that leads to reciprocal listening, a greater willingness to pay more attention to what you have to share. (For more on this refer to chapter 13 on listening deeply, which covers Robert Cialdini's ground-breaking research into the law of reciprocity.)

- **Efficiency:** If you have already established what your team members know, think and feel about the topic, you then only need to communicate what is necessary to fill in gaps, correct an incorrect assumption, or to reinforce a key part of their view. This approach is not scattergun like the tell-then-ask approach. When you tell first, you are unsure whether what you are sharing is already known or understood by the other person. If they, in fact, already know or agree with what you are sharing, you're wasting your breath talking. It's inefficient. Thus advocating after inquiring is more efficient, requiring less time and effort.

- **Receptivity:** When you tell someone what they already know, understand or believe, you risk creating unpleasant thoughts and feelings for the other person, leading to their behaviour moving towards unhelpful patterns. For example, I may feel annoyed and frustrated that you are telling me stuff I already get (*I'm not stupid you know!*), leading to me becoming hostile or unresponsive.

- **Influence:** As we explore soon in this chapter, influential communication occurs when you use modes of communicating and relevant content that has the most impact on the other person. Asking, listening and observing first allows you to establish the other person's preferred way of processing information and making sense of the world. When you understand the other person's needs better, you can then align your communication approach, becoming more influential in the process.

Losing your voice

It was the end of a challenging senior leadership workshop. Over the three days, I had led 20 or so executives through a deep exploration of themselves and their role as leaders, including much conversation about the need for courage and speaking up. One of the most curious, articulate and engaging leaders in the room was a senior executive named Helen – who was also the most visibly passionate about the need for people in the company to speak up to leaders above them, including herself.

In the final session, I handed over to a member of the company's top team to lead a conversation about what next – how to bring these ideas and practices to life in this company. The topic of courage was raised, and Helen was first to share a view. The senior executive then asked a provocative and challenging question back to Helen. *Here we go,* I thought to myself. *Here's Helen's moment to show courage.* However, the Helen who responded was not the same confident, strong and articulate Helen I had seen for the last three days. The challenging question was like a pinprick that deflated her, robbing her of her strength and power. Like a balloon shrinking, Helen progressively lost her volume and her words, as her body language became submissive and smaller. I could tell that the senior executive's attention and engagement had now been lost because she was no longer really listening.

ADVOCATING WITH STRENGTH AND WARMTH

Under certain conditions, some leaders struggle to advocate and communicate their view effectively. Whether it's pulling punches, softening the message or staying silent, the effect is the same – they give up their strength, and sometimes warmth as well.

The following sections highlight some techniques I teach my clients to help them share their perspective more effectively and maintain their strength and warmth.

Remember – leadership is a risky business

Most people have an incomplete understanding of leadership. It's true that at times your job as a leader is to make everything okay for other people. Sometimes, however, it's not. These are moments when your work as a leader is to make others uncomfortable by bringing their attention to an uneasy truth, challenging the status quo, speaking up and speaking out. This means you may be the cause of other people's discomfort – which can make leadership feel like it's a dangerous business. People may dislike you, even if for only a brief while, for making them uncomfortable. This is the reason many people fail to exercise courageous and challenging leadership.

Interestingly, according to some sources the word 'leader' appears to originate from the ancient Indo-European word 'leit'. These sources say the 'leit' was the flag or banner bearer of the kings and queens of old. They would march at the front of the army as they went into battle, rallying and leading the troops. Being chosen to be a leit was a great honour, which we can see even to this day when the flag-bearers of each nation march proudly into stadium during the Olympic opening ceremony. It was also a dangerous position, because the other army would want to quickly take the leit out of action.

Unfortunately, we have so sanitised leadership today that many people have forgotten that to lead well means to take risks and do what can sometimes feel dangerous. You can, however, use the techniques provided here to torque the odds in your favour of being more influential and successful when sharing your view.

Agree before you disagree

Picture this. You're in a tough conversation. You've been enquiring and listening deeply, consciously refraining from interrupting or rebutting the other person's view. You've fully exhausted your questions and you've played back to them what you've heard. They've confirmed that you understand their view correctly. Great, it's now time to share your perspective. The first words that come out of your mouth are, 'I agree with you but ...'

STOP! This is the least helpful thing you can say, even though in my experience it is the most common thing that people do.

Why is it unhelpful? Let me count the ways. First, you haven't provided any indication what it is that you agree with them on. Second, the words 'I agree with you' sound like an insincere and pacifying throwaway line, not a genuine statement. Third, the word 'but' cancels out everything that comes before it. The moment it issues from your mouth it signals that all that came before is irrelevant. Fourth, while stating your view is strong, the absence of a clear indication of what you are in agreement with them means that warmth is being lost in the process.

I recommend that leaders be very clear and precise about what they agree with the other party on before they progress to describing the areas that they disagree on. It sounds something like this:

> 'Thanks for sharing your views. I agree with you that the project
> is a challenging one. I can agree with you that the timelines are
> extremely demanding, and beyond anything we have tried to
> deliver before. I also agree that you personally have been working
> very hard to try to make this work. Your individual efforts are
> undeniable. Where I disagree with you is that the deliverables
> are impossible. Yes, I agree that they are very difficult, but I don't
> believe that they are impossible if we can increase the contributions
> of some of your team. Let me explain why I think that ...'

In negotiation, this is called 'finding common ground', an important technique to build connection and trust. It builds the psychological contract between you and the other party, resulting in them being more willing to listen with an open mind to your views where you don't agree with them.

Being precise in describing what you agree on first also helps you reduce the field of potential conflict to just what you disagree on. Too many tough conversations fail because a broad sense of overall disagreement and disconnection exists rather than a precise understanding of the specific issues or items in which there is disagreement. This can cause people to give up altogether or mount greater resistance because they sense just too big a gap exists between each party's views.

Finally, the 'agree then disagree' pattern is much easier for high-warmth oriented individuals to execute on, often being the ones who struggle to advocate their view firmly, especially when they believe that what they are saying is likely to cause conflict, or be met with disapproval.

Appeal to different ways of processing information

We usually communicate in ways that reflect how we personally process information and make sense of the world. For example, some of us use numbers, others words, and then there are those who prefer images. Some of us prefer the big picture whereas others like the detail. Then there are those who like concrete and practical, whereas others prefer theoretical and conceptual.

All of these different ways of receiving and processing information and making sense of the world represent the diversity you're likely to find across the people you are trying to influence and mobilise. If you can't communicate with them in a way that aligns with their way of taking in information and making sense of it, you are unlikely to be effective in engaging or persuading them.

You can easily work out a person's preferences by observing them over time. How do they communicate information? What do they pay attention to? Even if you don't have the opportunity to observe them, ask someone else who knows them. I often do this before presenting to a senior executive I have not worked with before, asking them, a member of their team or their executive assistant how they like to receive information. I then use that insight to shape how and what I might communicate to them.

Even without prior experience with the person, you can develop useful hypotheses to start with using what limited information you might have about them. For example, it's generally safe to assume that if I want to advocate a view convincingly to a person from a finance background, I'll want to use lots of numbers and graphs. If they're an engineer, I'll want to include good robust data and facts, perhaps in the form of process flows and system architectures. If they are from marketing, strong imagery will probably be helpful. These are all helpful means for making your point more clearly and persuasively.

Building a sustainable partnership

Craig and Al are co-founders of a fast-growing renewable energy business. While the business was flourishing, their relationship was not and was unlikely to survive another year. The problem was their leadership styles were so different that anything the other person said was received poorly. Conversations were difficult and tense, with frequent blow-ups, which left Craig and Al bruised and convinced that if they couldn't work it out, they would have to sell the business.

By having each leader adapt their style of communicating to better fit with the other's way of receiving information, Craig and Al were able to stabilise their conversations. This allowed them to connect more productively and make better progress with their shared challenges and opportunities.

Now able to reinvest the energy that was previously lost to conflict, Al and Craig have forged a stronger performing business and are enjoying working with each other much more than they previously thought possible.

Use language that resonates

The words and phrases you use are also powerful tools for connecting and influencing. Xtraordinary leaders pay particular attention to words and language for two reasons.

1. **There are 'in' and 'out' groups:** In sociology, the 'in group' is us, and the 'out group' is them. The language we use signals to others whether we are part of their in group (us) or part of an out group (them). If I want to be influential, having them

perceive me as part of their in group is helpful. This is because people who are familiar to us – those we perceive to share our values and world views – are experienced as being warmer. If I use language that sounds familiar and resonant to you, you are much more likely to perceive me as warm and believe that my intentions are good. This is a helpful condition if I want you to be receptive to what I have to say.

2. **Paying attention to words and language signifies competence:** Every social grouping in the world of work has its own language. For example, marketers speak of analytics, B2C and A/B testing. Accountants refer to cash flows, assets and liabilities. Human resource professionals refer to engagement, turnover and time to hire. Senior executives focus on ROI, ROA and bottom line. The more fluent you are in using their language, the more competent you will appear, and in turn the more influential you will be.

So, remember – mastery of the terms and phrases familiar to the person you are seeking to influence allows you to show up simultaneously as stronger and warmer.

Tell stories – often

Science shows us that when we tell stories to others, we activate more regions of their brain. If neuroscientists were to place you and I in a pair of fMRI scanners and monitor our brain activity as I told you a story, the parts of your brain that light up will be the same as the parts of my brain that are activating as I tell the story. This phenomenon where your brain waves start to synchronise with mine is termed *neural entrainment*.[2] Fundamentally, this process means I am better able to make you feel and experience things through a story than I can through a dry and dull presentation of facts and figures.

This is why extraordinary leaders such as Sheryl Sandberg of Facebook, Christine Nixon as the first female chief commissioner of Victoria Police, and Michael Clarke from Treasury Wine Estates use stories as a powerful tool to communicate their perspective. It is also why many leading organisations such as Microsoft, 3M, Procter & Gamble and NASA deliberately cultivate storytelling cultures by teaching their leaders how to tell stories well.

Give tough feedback

Perhaps one of the hardest views to share is when you are giving constructive criticism or negative feedback to somebody. No matter what you call it, you're essentially drawing that person's attention to something that you believe they could do better, or need to change.

In these instances, being met with resistance to what you are saying is quite common. This response might be accompanied by anger, denial or hurt and disappointment. It may even lead to the other person's disapproval of you, and possibly a potential breakdown in the relationship. No wonder many of us can feel reluctant to give tough feedback!

Nonetheless, extraordinary leaders will still step up to the plate and give tough feedback because they know that without it, the other person will not succeed as well as they could, or grow to their full potential.

As a leader, you also need to understand that you can't control how the other person receives your feedback or responds to it. That is not your choice to make. You can only control the quality of the feedback given.

Delivering quality feedback

To give good-quality, constructive feedback to someone, be specific, factual and clear. A good method for delivering feedback that meets these criteria is variously called STAR, SBI or SIM feedback. This kind of feedback is essentially a three-step behavioural process you can follow to deliver quality feedback that is more likely to be better understood and received by the other person.

Here are the three steps:

1. **Set the scene:** Describe the situation in which you observed the poor or ineffective behaviour.
2. **Describe the person's behaviour:** Do so in specific observable terms – tell them what they said or did, or didn't say or do in that moment.
3. **Explain the impact of the person's behaviour:** Include the impact on other people or the results. Make sure you are using

factual, observed data, and go on to explain the 'so what?' – the implications of the impact of the person's behaviour.

Here are some examples:

- **Example A:** (1) In the early stages of yesterday's team meeting I noticed that (2) you abruptly interrupted Jan several times while she was speaking (3), which resulted in her withdrawing from the conversation and remaining silent for the rest of the meeting. This meant that we didn't get the benefit of hearing her expert view on this important topic.

- **Example B:** (1) When I was reviewing the recent project updates that you shared I observed that (2) the project plan you were using didn't include contingencies for over runs and delays owing to adverse weather. (3) This meant that the recent rain delays you have been experiencing have made it much harder for you to hit your deadlines, putting enormous pressure on you and the rest of the team. I am worried that this could have implications for safety.

Use factual and specific examples

Note that the preceding examples are both factual and specific. They are factual because, unlike an opinion or feeling, an observed behaviour or impact is harder to debate or reject. And they are specific, making it easier for the other person to understand and recall, as well as being easier to accept because the tough feedback is around a specific event and behaviour, not a broad judgement or generalisation about the person's character using words such as rude, lazy or stupid. These words are inflammatory and unhelpful to having your feedback received and understood.

Being specific and factual also makes this feedback easier to deliver because you have good robust data to base it on. This allows you to be more confident and surer of what you are delivering.

Of course, no matter how well you advocate your view, the other person may still disagree and so create a sense of tension, heat or conflict. How you handle yourself in these moments can also affect the quality of your leadership and your results – and the next chapter provides more on this.

Reflection

What's your typical pattern when sharing perspective? Consider how the following leadership patterns share perspective and whether they ring true for you:

- **Control:** I share my views without regard for how they impact on the other person. I tell first and rarely seek the other person's views before mine. I share opinions and assertions without reference to facts. I make generalised statements rather than specific observations. I focus on where I disagree rather than where I agree with the other person. I give negative feedback regularly but often fail to give positive feedback.

- **Relate:** I hold back saying what I really think or feel for fear of damaging my relationships. When I do share my view, I am careful to massage the message to avoid discomfort, disagreement or conflict. I can sweep issues under the carpet to preserve harmony. I rarely give constructive and direct feedback.

- **Protect:** I can sometimes say nothing even though I have a different view or disagree with others. Unless I am absolutely certain of my facts or position, I may choose to keep my mouth shut. I focus mainly on facts and rarely share how I feel. I rarely give feedback.

- **Catalyse:** I share my views courageously, candidly, openly and respectfully. I make clear distinctions between what I know (facts), what I think (opinions) and what I feel (emotions). I build the other person's willingness to listen to me by seeking their views first. I create common ground first by identifying where we agree before working on where we disagree. I use shared language and stories to enhance my communication and impact. I regularly give both positive and constructive feedback.

16

Regulate heat

On my birthday I was given a worn and weathered but still work-ing antique fruit press by my family. It conjured delicious visions of home-made apple cider from the fruit in our old orchard.

Unfortunately, the press was missing three special metal bars used to lock the curved wooden sides in place when pressing fruit. Without them, the whole contraption would break wide open and spill the fruit and juice everywhere, so they needed replacing.

I decided to make some bars up myself from short sections of rein-forcing metal, each one about as thick as my middle finger. The end of each bar needed to be bent and shaped like a spiral (similar to a pig's tail), which I had read online could be achieved by heating the metal using a propane torch, softening the bar enough to reshape it easily.

My first two attempts were less successful, and much harder work than I thought they would be. Even after applying liberal doses of heat from the torch, I found the metal incredibly hard to bend and shape. My right arm ached so from wielding the heavy hammer!

When I got to the third and final locking bar, I decided to change my approach and heat the metal a lot more to see what would happen. I turned up the torch to its highest intensity and held the fierce blue flame to the bar, for much longer than the previous attempts, until the metal was not just red – it was glowing a bright, almost translucent, cherry red-orange colour. Lo and behold, I found the metal amazingly easy to reshape, requiring only a small amount of pressure to bend and twist it.

What was clear was that I had not originally applied enough heat, or for long enough to transform the metal from a stiff and unyielding material to something more pliable and responsive.

I was reminded in that moment that sometimes you really need to turn up the heat to achieve the change you seek.

CONFLICT AND HEAT

Being able to regulate the heat in your interactions with others is an essential capacity all extraordinary leaders must master. What do I mean by heat? It's the tension or discomfort that you and others feel when conflict exists between us. This heat is usually the result of having opposing ideas, views or needs, and usually shows up in disagreements, debates and arguments. The friction between people and ideas when they are in conflict produces the heat.

The heat can be mild or severe, depending on the amount of friction, with the most acute versions leaving us feeling afraid for ourselves, out of control, and worried that our relationships will be destroyed in the process

Conflict avoidant

Even mild levels of conflict and its associated tensions are experienced by many people as uncomfortable, especially when the heat generated by the conflict goes beyond a level they are able to tolerate.

Jeffrey Pfeffer is a professor in organisational behaviour and has been teaching at Stanford University's Graduate School of Business since 1979. He writes in *Power: Why Some People Have It and Others Don't* that most people are conflict-averse, and so they avoid difficult situations and discussions, frequently submitting to others' views and requests, and changing their positions rather than paying the emotional price of standing up for themselves and their views.

Likewise, best-selling teams author and management consultant Patrick Lencioni, author of *The Five Dysfunctions of a Team*, states that most people are afraid of engaging in even mild forms of conflict and disagreement, worried that 'it may go nuclear, destroying everyone in the process'.

Staying safe

The origins of most people's tendency to avoid conflict lie in a deeply-rooted human desire to stay safe. Conflict has the potential to result in physical violence and bodily harm, so many people pull back well before it comes close to reaching that state. Likewise, conflict can also result in us being disapproved of or disliked by others, which potentially could result in us being frozen out of relationships and groups, denied opportunities and resources essential to our survival and success, and even ostracised from the tribe or community. Deeply imprinted on our brains is an understanding that not so long ago in human history, being abandoned or exiled from the tribe would mean certain death. It's no wonder that maintaining harmony and behaving in ways that guarantee our continued acceptance and belonging are common tendencies for many of us.

Heat-averse leadership

These conflict-avoidant and heat-intolerant behaviours are what you see when a leader's behaviour moves away for strength and towards submission. They can show up as the overly agreeable and pacifying behaviours of the Relate leadership pattern. Rather than disagree and hold their ground, the leader rolls over and becomes agreeable so that they can avoid the discomfort of conflict.

This sort of behaviour can also manifest in the 'keep your head down and say nothing' behaviours of the Protect leadership style. Giving nothing away and withholding your view can feel like a safer option than engaging in open conflict with someone or their views.

Either way, the tendencies are usually the result of discomfort with open disagreement and conflict, and a reluctance to continue to experience the tension and heat associated with it. The result: a giving up or some other form of submission to the other person's views or position.

Conflict prone

For some people, the opposite is true. They not only are comfortable with the heat generated by conflict but can also use conflictual heat to take advantage of situations and people – especially when others wish to avoid it.

It stands to reason that if I am comfortable with confrontation and conflict, and know others aren't, I might be prepared to turn up the heat of conflict and its associated impressions of danger and risk so that I can intimidate you into submission.

Super Hamish

Some years ago our family included two much-loved golden labradors named Hamish and Winnie. They were brother and sister but were different in many ways. Winnie was smaller, rounder and more gentle. Hamish by contrast was taller, leaner and much more active, always up for a walk, a game or a run. They were both typical labradors with happy and joyful characters and without an aggressive bone in their bodies. Or so we thought.

Everyday Hamish and Winnie enjoyed a long walk on our local off-lead beaches. One particular day, Tamsin and my children Lally and Dash were enjoying such a walk when they noticed that Winnie had lagged behind and was a now a hundred metres or so away, being harassed by a much larger German shepherd. Hamish also noticed, and immediately sprinted down the beach and launched into such a ferocious attack that the German shepherd, a much larger dog, was immediately cowed into submission and slunk off with his tail between his legs. Lally and Dash decided from that point on that our heroic labrador would be named Super Hamish and should perhaps even wear a cape.

Sometime later I witnessed another instance where a huge rottweiler tried to dominate Hamish at the local park; however, Hamish came back at him with such a lightning-fast, loud, teeth-baring and snapping display of strength that the other dog backed down immediately, even though he was much larger and physically stronger. No blood was spilled in the encounter, but it was clear from that point on who was the boss.

Shock and awe

Shock and awe (technically known as 'rapid dominance') is a military tactic that uses overwhelming power and spectacular displays of force to paralyse the enemy's reactions, and destroy their will to fight by changing their perception of the battleground conditions.[1]

Shock and awe is also a tactic used by some leaders to create perceptions of strength and dominance that are so overwhelming that others quickly back down in a conflict and acquiesce. This is how the leader gets what they want.

I know three individuals who have perfected this approach, each in their own special way, that illustrate the shock and awe tactic:

- **Using intellect:** The first, a brilliant former rocket scientist with a brain the size of a planet, was a senior executive in a global technology company. He would shock and awe through the use of his enormous intelligence and eidetic memory, which gave him the capacity to argue and counter-argue with precise facts in such a rapid-fire manner that the other person had no time to formulate a decent response, eventually brow-beating the other person into submission with his intellect.

- **Using irrationality:** The second was a corporate litigator (lawyer) raised and trained in one of the most legally aggressive cultures in the world, the United States. Described by some as 'an attack dog', his hyperaggressive, take-no-prisoners style was often perceived as irrational and unpredictable, effectively creating greater anxiety and stress for the other party. This approach often shocked the other party into submission and made them agreeable to a settlement much earlier and at much less favourable terms than they would potentially have gotten if the matter went to court.

- **Using rage and anger:** The third person I worked with who deployed the shock and awe tactic was a client who was very powerful – both personally and professionally. He had a tendency in conflictual situations to quickly anger, turn beet red, shout and throw things and threaten the other party. More often than not, others would back down quickly and give him what he wanted.

He then needed to do little to get others' agreement in the future, because they knew what response he was capable of should they think of disagreeing with him.

Destructive heat

A conflict-prone, overly hot style of leadership, which is characteristic of more extreme versions of the Control leadership pattern, can be very damaging to other people and your relationships with them.

Your behaviour doesn't even need to be as extreme as the shock and awe approaches I describe in the previous section – even fleeting applications of too much heat can destroy trust quickly, leaving others wary and protective around you, cultivating behaviour and cultures that are risk averse, conservative and avoidant. Of course, this inevitably leads to less innovative, accountable and energised employees, limiting your results.

Longer or more regular applications of destructive heat can leave others feeling permanently diminished, afraid and taken advantage of, resulting in dramatically lower levels of engagement, commitment and motivation, as well as increasing staff turnover.

Conflict comfortable

One of the hallmarks of Catalyst leaders is their ability to engage with conflict without losing themselves in it. They are able to generate and tolerate enough heat for something transformative to happen, and at the same time regulate the heat to avoid the extreme versions of conflict, tension and discomfort that produce unnecessary collateral damage.

As discussed in chapter 4, a catalyst triggers a transformative reaction in otherwise inert substances. In the process of doing so, dormant embedded energy is released. Some of the energy may be in the form of heat.

When repairing dings and damage to my surfboards, I add a few drops of catalyst to a plastic cup full of liquid resin and mix it together. As I do so, I can feel heat being released by the chemical reaction through the thin walls of the cup as the mixture begins to transform. The heat is an inevitable part of the process and tells me that the transformation is underway. Eventually, after applying the sticky resin to the repair area, it will cool and harden, becoming a more durable material.

The Catalyst pattern of leadership is, therefore, very comfortable with heat, and willing to generate heat by challenging others because they know it is a necessary part of the process. Whether it be confronting limitations in others' thinking, candidly addressing poor performance, or openly questioning unhelpful behaviours and mindsets, the Catalyst leader expects heat at times, both intellectual and possibly also emotional. These leaders understand that without challenge and its attendant heat, others may settle for less than what they are truly capable of, falling short of expressing their true potential.

The Xtraordinary leader is also able to turn up the heat on others over time, so that something changes. The simple fact is that when people are comfortable with the status quo, they have little reason to change. As a very effective personal trainer I met was fond of saying, 'If nothing changes, nothing changes.'

The role of the Catalyst leader is to question the status quo, to turn up the heat on themselves or others and challenge people to think and behave differently so the process of innovation, adaptation and improvement is constant and continual.

PRODUCTIVE LEVELS OF HEAT AND CONFLICT

Genuine innovation, change and improvement inevitably mean that the unavoidable conflict between the old and new mindsets, attitudes and ways of working must be surfaced and examined. Holding people in this space – when they want to escape the discomfort – is a difficult skill to master; however, it is so necessary, because only through appropriately fierce debates and productive levels of conflict are new understandings forged, with the best version of the answer able to emerge.

Marty Linsky of Harvard University likes to use the analogy of cooking a stew in this context. Sufficient heat and time is needed to allow the different ingredients to meld and combine, producing something delicious. However, cooking it too long or at too high a temperature means you risk burning the stew, creating a distasteful and undesirable mess.

As the leader, you need to regulate the heat and hold people in the conflict long enough for something transformative to happen. The Catalyst pattern of leadership generates just the right amount of heat – unlike the other patterns, which produce either too little heat for any productive effect, or so much heat that it is also destructive to relationships, creativity and commitment. The following figure shows these heat options in relation to the four leadership patterns.

Leadership heat thermostat

Performance tension

Another familiar challenge that may require the application of heat is dealing with the unproductive behaviour or poor performance of a team member. Usually, as the leader, you need to actively engage with the team member to address the issue. A curious, empathetic and supportive approach is sometimes sufficient to uncover the underlying issues and allow the team member to get back on track or make the necessary adjustments to their ways of working. Many times, however, a warmth-based approach alone is insufficient, with the introduction of heat and performance tension a necessary second ingredient.

What do I mean by 'performance tension'? It is the cultivation of discomfort in the individual while the status quo prevails. It involves the establishment of a clear understanding between you as the leader and your team member that a change in behaviour or an improvement in performance is necessary, and that unless something changes, that tension and discomfort will remain, and even grow over time. Tension is the inevitable consequence of you challenging the team member to do or produce something that seems some distance away from where they currently are. Like a rubber band, tension is created when a person is stretched and challenged, with the bigger the stretch, the greater the tension.

The discomfort for the team member produced by that tension can be significant. They may not initially be prepared to respond to the challenge, or even believe that they can make the change. Often, they will signal their discomfort in overt or subtle ways to you as the leader, and even indicate their disapproval of you for making them uncomfortable. If you need to be liked as a leader, or are uncomfortable with a sense of conflict, you may then be tempted to back off the tension, letting the team member off the hook. This is unhelpful to creating the necessary change – although what is even less helpful is the leader who fails to even initially address the issue or attempt to create some tension, instead preferring to protect themselves and maintain the status quo.

Using tension productively

A Catalyst leader understands that tension is a necessary ingredient for change and learns to not take it personally when they earn others' disapproval simply for asking them to do their job to the best of their ability, which may be beyond their current efforts. They also intuitively understand that the laws of physics state that tension always seeks resolution. The tension created when they challenge others to lift their contribution or change their ways of working can be resolved in one of two ways. Either the leader conspires with the team member to release them from the tension by accepting little or no change, or they remain committed to continuing to challenge and empower the team member until they grow, adapt and perform at the level they are capable of.

Regulating the heat and tension

A key idea that has emerged from the influential theory of adaptive leadership (as taught at Harvard University by Marty Linsky and Ron Heifetz) is the idea that a leader's job is to hold others within a range of tension, heat, conflict or discomfort long enough for transformation and change to occur, allowing something productive to emerge. This includes a helpful change in attitudes, beliefs, behaviours, practices or performance. The ideal range is called the 'productive zone of disequilibrium'[2], as shown in the following figure.

The productive zone of disequilibrium

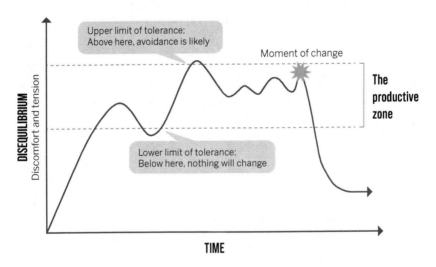

Adapted from A. Grashow, R. Heifetz and M. Linsky (2009). *The practice of adaptive leadership: Tools and tactics for changing your organisation and the world*, Harvard Business Press, Cambridge

A key feature of this theory is an understanding that too much disequilibrium will result in others avoiding the hard work of change and adaptation. At the same time, too little discomfort will mean the heat or tension is insufficient for change to actually occur. The work of the leader is, therefore, to hold people in the 'productive zone', turning the heat and tension up and down as required, and holding them there long enough for change and transformation to occur. This means a key skill for you as the leader is to regulate the heat and tension according to each individual's tolerance and the rate at which they are adapting and transforming.

Learning how to hold the heat

Brian is a friendly, warm and polite leader who headed up the Asia–Pacific region for one of the world's largest oil and gas companies, running a division that had been highly profitable for many decades. Operating for over 100 years, his company knew how to make money hand over fist; however, they were increasingly being disrupted by new players, changes in technology and a systemic shift in consumer preferences towards renewable energy. Margins were eroding and targets were getting harder to reach.

Brian's team needed to change their thinking and leading, moving from the polite and conflict-averse style that was a feature of the company's culture towards a more challenging and innovative approach. The problem was they had grown so comfortable with the status quo and polite harmony that they didn't know how to have the fierce debates necessary to generate new ideas or make the tough decisions they all knew were needed.

Brian especially struggled with holding the heat in the meetings of his senior team. It wasn't until he realised where his discomfort with conflict and tension came from – unpleasant childhood experiences of being bullied – that he understood how his Relate (soothe and smooth) conflict-avoidant leadership style was enabling his team's unproductive patterns. Brian would often turn down the heat when the tension built up, or when people started looking uncomfortable. He was afraid that if he allowed the heat to damage people or relationships, or indeed if he challenged others' views or perspectives to the point of them feeling uncomfortable, he would be seen as the enabler or the actual perpetrator – a bully, the very thing he despised.

Unable to embrace the tension to generate fierce and robust debate, he would hose the situation down and move the conversation on, with no new or transformative outcomes. Brian knew how to turn the heat down. He just wasn't able to turn it up. Hence, the status quo remained, and the business continued to struggle to change and transform itself. Brian was, in effect, unintentionally enabling the possible future failure of his team, and perhaps his company.

Fortunately, Brian had the courage to address his own personal limitations, and with disciplined and focused effort over time, he learned and developed much more functional responses to conflict and tension, becoming increasingly capable of turning up the heat on others and holding them in it.

Turning up the heat

You can use several techniques to turn up the heat in a productive way. They include:

- **Asking challenging questions:** A well-placed curious question can draw attention to topics and issues that people are avoiding. Such an enquiry is an invitation and a challenge to draw closer to the heart of a problem or examine an underlying issue. Here are some examples:
  - 'What's really going on here?'
  - 'What if that's just a convenient story you're telling yourself?'
  - 'Why are you not talking about *xyz*?'
  - 'What's your role in the mess?'
  - 'What do you think will happen if this continues?'

- **Making provocative observations and interpretations:** Sometimes a question is too indirect. Making an observation of the facts of a situation or making a provocative interpretation of what those facts mean are both effective ways of raising the heat. Examples might include:
  - 'I'm worried that you seem to be avoiding something here. I've noticed that whenever the topic of *xyz* comes up you quickly divert your attention to something else.'

- 'You appear very quick to blame others for these results. I've not heard you acknowledge what part you're playing in the mess.'

- 'You haven't yet acknowledged any accountability you might have for this situation. I'm concerned that it leaves you powerless to change it.'

- 'So far you haven't done anything to change the way you are doing things. So we keep getting the same results. I'm worried that if nothing changes, nothing changes.'

- 'I'm concerned that unless something changes, you'll have to confront some undesirable consequences.'

A key to turning up the heat with provocation is to do it with the right intentions. Being perceived to be agitating or trouble-making purely for your own benefit or amusement can be counterproductive.

- **Showing emotions:** Frustration, annoyance and even anger can be useful for turning up the heat. This is especially true if you're normally calm and emotionally-even and have already tried calmly and rationally dealing with the situation – but, despite this, you are having trouble cutting through a non-responsive and passive dynamic. This might mean you have become predictable, and others now assume you will not dial up your strength. In this situation, an unexpected display of irritation, frustration, annoyance or even anger can get others' attention very quickly and have significant impact.

Importantly, however, your response still needs to remain controlled and proportional to the situation. A story about the former premier of the Soviet Union Nikita Khrushchev illustrates this point. In a messy United Nations debate, he appeared to become so impassioned and angry that he thumped his shoe on the table to get others' attention and make his point. Shortly afterwards, he was seen to leave the chamber wearing both his shoes, even though a solitary shoe remained behind on the table.

- **Plateauing:** Some individuals and certain circumstances require a lot of heat before anything changes. However, you need to keep in mind that applying too much heat too quickly can destroy trust and cause the other person to try to avoid the issue. Similar to paramedics treating a hypothermic patient after a long immersion in freezing water, you need to slowly turn up the heat. Turning up the heat incrementally, with pauses for your observation and reflection, and to allow the other person to psychologically adjust, can be helpful in any situation where you are concerned about the person's ability to tolerate a rapid increase in heat.

Turning the heat down

Being able to control the heat as a leader may also involve needing to turn the heat down. Again, several techniques can be used:

- **Playing the ball not the person:** When emotions run high, arguments often turn personal, with blame and attacks on each other's character destroying trust in the process. In these moments, focusing the discussion on the facts of the issue or problem, rather than the personalities involved, can help reduce the heat to a more productive level.

- **Showing empathy and kindness:** When others become emotional – a sure sign that the heat has turned up in the discussion –the risk increases that they will become less willing or able to stay in the productive zone, and will instead want to escape or avoid the difficult conversation. Showing empathy and kindness can reduce their discomfort to a more manageable level, and allow them to work on solving the issue or problem, rather than being distracted or depleted by their own emotional state.

  The key here, though, is not to fall into the trap of repeatedly rescuing the other person from their discomfort, and thereby letting them off the hook. I have worked with a number of people who use crying as an avoidance technique. In these cases, I acknowledge the emotion and what might be causing it, hand them a tissue and allow a pause, but remain resolute in keeping the person focused on the issue or problem that we are trying to resolve.

- **Meeting Type I needs:** As discussed in chapter 11, we each have deep powerful needs for autonomy, mastery and relatedness. Not meeting them can have adverse effects on a person's energy and commitment to confront difficult issues or make changes in their effort or behaviour.

When the going gets tough, and the disequilibrium is high, redirecting others' attention to how they can continue to exercise autonomy, gain mastery or facilitate their relationships with others can be sufficient to give them the psychological resources to continue to grapple with the issue or problem that you are asking them to address. Examples of how you might redirect attention in this way include:

- 'What options do you have for what you do next to make progress with this?' (Autonomy)
- 'What do you need to learn, or get better at, to be able to get on top of this?' (Mastery)
- 'Who could you lean on for support, guidance or coaching to help you succeed with this?' (Relatedness)

This approach is not so much a means to turn down the heat, but instead a way of making the heat or discomfort more bearable.

Reflection

How do you view conflict – as a natural and essential part of relationships? Or something that you try to avoid because of the discomfort it causes?

Do you generate too much heat and tension, damaging relationships and results along the way? Or are you inclined to avoid turning up the heat enough for anything to really change?

How could you get better at regulating tension, becoming more proficient at turning it up and down according to what is really needed to transform the behaviour, performance and success of others?

Conclusion

Congratulations! You now know what Xtraordinary leadership looks like, where warmth and strength are blended into the Catalyst: Challenge and Empower pattern. You're also well aware why Xtraordinary leadership matters – engaging, influencing and mobilising other people to contribute and commit to the work that really matters. Finally, you understand how the habits of Xtraordinary leaders can help you to release others' energy, maximise contribution and realise their full potential. It's now up to you to put it into practice.

PUTTING XTRAORDINARY LEADERSHIP INTO PRACTICE

Encouragingly, my experience of developing thousands of leaders around the world has taught me that the warm and strong behaviours of the Catalyst leader can be learned and applied, provided you're motivated to do the work and pay disciplined attention.

I've also observed that the greatest progress is made when attention is paid to growing yourself both inside and outside. The inside work involves examining the mindsets, beliefs, mental models and thinking habits you hold that skew you towards or away from either strength or warmth. The outside work involves learning new skills, techniques and behaviours that bring your warm and strong intentions into being more obviously and masterfully.

One thing at a time

Finally, the role of focus, experimentation and persistence can't be overstated. A willingness to try new and different approaches while remaining open to the results of these experiments radically enhances the rate and depth of learning. 'Practice, practice, practice' is a helpful mantra. So too is the advice 'don't try to boil the ocean'.

Do you remember the approach that Andrew Mackenzie from BHP took, which I introduced at the beginning of part 3? Working on making his leadership more remarkable, one habit at a time. You too can make your leadership Xtraordinary – just choose one thing, and get started!

GROWING MORE XTRAORDINARY LEADERS

If you can make progress in growing your own leadership, perhaps together we can make progress cultivating more Xtraordinary leaders. Ralph Nader, the consumer advocate and justice campaigner who successfully took on the might of corporate America in the areas of consumer protection, environmentalism and government reform, noted that the 'primary function of leadership is to create more leaders, not more followers'.

I heard these sentiments echoed recently by a senior officer at the Australian Defence Force Academy, who stated to a group of new leaders that, 'Good leaders influence their teams to achieve an outcome. Great leaders develop other leaders.'

Now, more than ever, we are each called to catalyse, challenge and encourage more Xtraordinary leadership than we have today. We will benefit not only in our own personal practice but also all around us in our teams, organisations and communities as we all gain from more Xtraordinary leadership.

This is where the true potential of Catalyst leadership can be realised. Through its ability to cultivate more empowered, energised and accountable individuals and groups, it effectively produces more leaders. As a result, this way of leading increases the capacity of the group, organisation or community to accelerate its transformation exponentially, and improve the outcomes it experiences.

This is a call to action – we need to move beyond the status quo, beyond the average, beyond the ordinary towards something more remarkable. The time is now to bring warmth and strength together in our leadership and, by doing so, produce something more Xtraordinary in our lives.

Acknowledgements

My heartfelt thanks to …

Tamsin, for being my partner in life, and in the creation of this book.

Lally and Dash, for providing inspiration every day.

Corinne, Suzanne and Lotte, for helping bring this to life.

Anne, Justin, Alby and Simon, for being Xtraordinary.

Michael, Charlotte and Anna, for your publishing expertise.

All of my clients, for making my work meaningful and worthwhile.

Every leader who has taught me something – whether you knew it at the time or not!

Endnotes

Introduction

1 Edmonds, P (2017), 'The fish that mates by direction', *National Geographic*.

2 Schaller, M (2008), 'Evolutionary bases of first impressions', in Ambady, N and Skowronski, J (eds.), *First Impressions*, Guilford Publications.

3 Ambady, N and Skowronski, J (eds.) (2008), *First Impressions*, Guildford Publications.

4 Cuddy, A, Kohut, M & Neffinger, N (2013), 'Connect, then lead', *Harvard Business Review*.

5 Chamorro-Premuzic, T (2019), 'Why do so many incompetent men become leaders? (And how to fix it)' *Harvard Business Review Press*.

6 Including Gentry, W (2010), 'Managerial derailment: What it is and how leaders can avoid it', in Biech, E (ed.), *ASTD Leadership Handbook*, ASTD Press; and Gentry, W & Chappelow, C (2009), 'Managerial derailment: Weaknesses that can be fixed' in Kaiser, RB (ed.), *The Perils of Accentuating the Positives*, Hogan Press.

Chapter 1

1 See, for example: Diehl, M, Owen, S & Youngblade, L (2004), 'Agency and communion attributes in adult's spontaneous self-representations', *International Journal of Behavior Development*, 28; Woike, B (1994), 'The use of differentiation and integration processes: Empirical studies of "separate" and "connected" ways of thinking', *Journal of Personality and Social Psychology*, 67 (1); Woike, B, Gerschkovich, I, Piorkowski, R & Polo, M (1999), 'The role of motives in the content and structure of

autobiographical memory', *Journal of Personality and Social Psychology*, 76 (4); Benninger, A, Cuddy, A and Glick, P (2011), 'The dynamics of warmth and competence judgements, and their outcomes in organisations', *Research in Organisational Behavior*, 31; Diehl, M, Coyle, N & Labouvie-Vief, G (1996), 'Age and sex differences in strategies of coping and defense across the life span', *Psychological Ageing*, 11(1); Guisinger, S & Blatt, S (1994), 'Individuality and relatedness: Evolution of a fundamental dialect', *American Psychologist*, 49(2); Markus, H & Kitayama, S (1991), 'Culture and the self: Implications for cognition, emotion, and motivation', *Psychological Review*, 98(2); Helgeson, V & Fritz, H (1999), 'Unmitigated agency and unmitigated communion: Distinctions from agency and communion', *Journal of Research* in Personality, 33.

2   Wojciszke, B & Abele, A (2008), 'The primacy of communion over agency and its reversals in evaluation', *European Journal of Social Psychology* 38, No.7.

3   Helgeson, V & Fritz, H (1999), op. cit.

4   Smith, G, Kohn, S, Savage-Stevens, S, Finch, J, Ingate, R & Lim, Y (2000), 'The effects of interpersonal and personal agency on perceived control and psychological wellbeing in adulthood', *The Gerontologist*, Vol. 40, No. 4.

5   Helgeson, V & Fritz, H (1999), op. cit.

6   Roohafza, H, Afshar, H, Keshteli, A, Mohammadi, M, Feizi, A, Taslimi, M & Adibi, P (2014), 'What's the role of perceived social support and coping styles in depression and anxiety?', *Journal of Research in Medical Sciences*, 19 (10): 944–949.

7   Kessler, R & McLeod, J (1985), 'Social support and mental health in community samples', in Cohen, S & Syme, S (eds.), *Social Support and Health*, Academic Press

8   Helgeson, V & Fritz, H (1999), op. cit.

9   Sanfey, A & Wout, M (2008), 'Friend or foe: The effect of implicit trustworthiness judgements in social decision-making', *Cognition*, 108 (3) 796–803.

Chapter 2

1   Cuddy, A, Fiske, S & Glick, P (2008), 'Warmth and competence as universal dimensions of social perception: The stereotype content model and the BIAS map', *Advances in Experimental Social Psychology*, Volume 40, 61–149.

2   Batrinos, ML (2012), 'Testosterone and aggressive behaviour in man', *International Journal of Endocrinology Metabolism*, 2012 Summer 10 (3)

3   Frith, C & Frith, U (2006), 'The neural basis of mentalizing', *Neuron*, 50(4), 531–534.

4   Insel, T, Young, L, Witt, D & Crews, D (1993), 'Gonadal steroids have paradoxical effects on brain oxytocin receptors', *Journal of Neuroendocrinology*, 5(6); Arsenijevic, Y & Tribollet, E (1998), 'Region-specific effect of testosterone on oxytocin receptor binding in the brain of the aged rat', *Brain Research*, 785(1).

5   Bos, P, Hofman, D, Hermans, E, Montoya, E, Baron-Cohen, S and van Honk, J (2016), 'Testosterone reduces functional connectivity during the "reading the mind in the eyes" test', *Psychoneuroendocrinology*, 68 (March).

6   Burnham, T (2007), 'High-testosterone men reject low ultimatum game offers', *Proc Biol Sci*, 274 (1623); Zilioli, S, Ponzi, D, Henry, A & Maestripieri, D (2015), 'Testosterone, cortisol and empathy: Evidence for the dual-hormone hypothesis', *Adaptations in Human Behavior and Physiology*, 1(4).

7   Dhakar, M, Stevenson, E & Caldwell, H (2013), 'Oxytocin, vasopressin, and their interplay with gonadal steroids' in Choleris, E, Pfaff, D, Kavaliers, M (eds), *Oxytocin, Vasopressin and Related Peptides in the Regulation of Behavior*, Cambridge University Press.

Chapter 4

1   Kegan, R (1994), *In Over Our Heads*, Harvard University Press; Torbert, W (1987), Managing the Corporate Dream, Dow-Jones.

Chapter 6

1   Willis, J & Todorov, A (2006), 'First impressions: Making up your mind after a 100-Ms exposure to a face', *Psychological Science*, 17, No.7.

2   Cotrell, CA, Neuberg, SL & Li, NP (2007), 'What do people desire in others? A sociofunctional perspective on the importance of different valued characteristics', *Journal of Personality and Social Psychology*, 92.

3   Mark Schaller, M (2008), 'Evolutionary bases of first impressions', in Ambady, N and Skowronski, J (eds.), *First Impressions*, Guilford Publications.

4   Ambady, N, Bernieri, FJ & Richeson, JA (2000), 'Toward a histology of social behaviour: Judgemental accuracy from thin slices of the behavioural stream', *Advances in Experimental Social Psychology*, 32.

5   Nesse, R (2005), 'Natural selection and the regulation of defences: A signal detection analysis of the smoke detector principle', *Evolution and Human Behaviour*, 26.

6   Schupp, HT, Ohman, A, Junghofer, M, Weike, AI, Stockburger, J & Hamm, AO (2004), 'The facilitated processing of threatening faces: An ERP analysis', *Emotion*, 4.

7   Ross, L, Lepper, M & Hubbard, M (1975), 'Perseverance in self-perception and social perception: Biased attributional processes in the debriefing paradigm', *Journal of Personality and Social Psychology*, 32 (5).

8   Haselton, MG & Funder, D (2006), 'The evolution of accuracy and bias in social judgement', in Schaller, M, Simpson, JA & Kenrick, DT (eds), *Evolution and Social Psychology*, Psychology Press.

9   Thomson-Deveaux, A (2015), 'How much can we learn by judging other people from their faces? Psychology: First impressions', *Princeton Alumni Weekly*, July 8.

10 Baumeister, RF, Bratslavsky, E, Finkenhauer, C & Voss, KD (2001), 'Bad is stronger than good', *Review of General Psychology*, 5.

11 Harris, M & Garris, C (2008), 'You never get a second chance to make a first impression: Behavioural consequences of first impressions', in Ambady, N and Skowronski, J (eds.), *First Impressions*, Guilford Publications.

12 Dougherty, T, Turban, D & Callendar, J (1994), 'Confirming first impressions in the employment interview: A field study of interviewer behaviour', *Journal of Applied Psychology*, 79.

13 Ybarra, O & Stephan, WG (1999), 'Attributional orientations and the prediction of behavior: The attribution-prediction bias', *Journal of Personality and Social Psychology*, 76, 718–727.

Chapter 7

1 Gallup (2013), *State of the American Workplace: Employee Engagement Insights for U.S. Business Leaders*, Gallup.

2 Crabtree, S (2013), 'Worldwide, 13% of employees are engaged at work', Gallup, 8 September.

3 Harter, J & Adkins, A (2015), 'What great managers do to engage employees', *Harvard Business Review*, April.

4 Spain, E (2020), 'The US Army's new approach to managing talent', *The Australian*, 5 December.

5 Vance, R (2006), 'Employee engagement and commitment', SHRM Foundation.

6 Gonring, M (2008), 'Customer loyalty and employee engagement: An alignment for value', *Journal of Business Strategy*, Vol 29, No. 4.

Chapter 8

1 Goleman, D, Boyatzis, R & McKee, A (2001), 'Primal leadership: The hidden driver of great performance', *Harvard Business Review*, December.

2 See, for example, Gordon, G & Tomaso, N (1992), 'Predicting corporate performance from organizational culture', *Journal of Management Studies* (29)6; Kotter, J & Husked, J (1992), *Corporate Culture and performance*, Free Press; Ogaard, T, Larsen, S & Marnburg, E (2005), 'Organisational culture and performance: Evidence from the fast food industry', *Food Service*

Technology, (5)1; and Parry, K & Proctor-Thomson, S (2003), 'Leadership, culture and performance: The case of the New Zealand public sector', *Journal of Change Management*, 3(4).

3 Bass, B (1990), 'From transactional to transformational leadership: Learning to share the vision', *Organizational Dynamics*, 18, 19–31.

4 Chemers, M (1997), *An Integrative Theory of Leadership*, Lawrence Erlbaum Associates.

5 Cuddy, A, Glick, P, Beninger, A (2011), 'The dynamics of warmth and competence judgments, and their outcomes in organizations', *Research in Organizational Behavior*, 31, 75.

6 Avolio, B (1999), *Full Leadership Development: Building the Vital Forces in Organizations*, Sage Publications.

7 Dumdum, U, Lowe, K & Avolio, B (2002), 'A meta-analysis of transformational and transactional leadership correlates of effectiveness and satisfaction: and update and extension', in Avolio, B & Yammarino, F (eds.), *Transformational and Charismatic Leadership: The Road Ahead*, Elsevier Science.

8 Deci, E, Connell, J & Ryan, R (1989), 'Self Determination in a work organisation', *Journal of Applied Psychology*, 74(4).

9 Including Baard, PP, Deci, EL, & Ryan, RM (2004), 'The relation of intrinsic need satisfaction to performance and wellbeing in two work settings', *Journal of Applied Social Psychology*, 34, 2045–2068; Deci, EL, Ryan, RM, Gagne, M, Leone, DR, Usunov, J, & Kornazheva, BP, (2001), 'Need satisfaction, motivation, and well-being in the work organizations of a former Eastern Bloc country', *Personality and Social Psychology Bulletin*, 27, 930–942; Gagne, M, Koestner, R, & Zuckerman, M (2000), 'Facilitating the acceptance of organizational change: the importance of self-determination', *Journal of Applied Social Psychology*, 30, 1843–1852; Ilardi, BC, Leone, D, Kasser, T, & Ryan, RM (1993), 'Employee and supervisor ratings of motivation: main effects and discrepancies associated with job satisfaction and adjustment in a factory setting', *Journal of Applied Social Psychology*, 23, 1789–1805; Kasser, T, Davey, J, & Ryan, RM (1992), 'Motivation and employee–supervisor discrepancies in a psychiatric vocational rehabilitation setting', *Rehabilitation Psychology*, 37, 175–187.

Chapter 9

1   Baron-Cohen, S (1994), 'The mindreading system: New directions for research', *Current Psychology of Cognition*, 13.
2   Young, T (2020), 'The last word on leadership', *The Australian*, 25 July.
3   Kegan, R & Lahey, L (2009), *Immunity to Change: How to Overcome It and Unlock the Potential in Yourself and Your Organisation*, Harvard Business Press.
4   Ibid.

Chapter 10

1   Deibert, E, Kraut, M, Kremen, S & Hart, J (1999), 'Neural pathways in tactile object recognition', *Neurology*, 52.
2   Norgren, R, Hajnal, A & Mungarndee, S (2006), 'Gustatory reward and the nucleus acumbens', *Physiology and Behavior*, 89.
3   Sheperd, G (2006), 'Smell images and the flavour system in the human brain', *Nature*, 444.
4   Mehrabian, A & Morton, W (1967), 'Decoding of inconsistent communications', *Journal of Personality and Social Psychology*, 6 (1); Mehrabian, A & Ferris, S (1967), 'Inference of attitudes from non-verbal communication in two channels', *Journal of Consulting Psychology*, 31 (3).
5   Harris, M & Garris, C (2008), 'You never get a second chance to make a first impression: Behavioural consequences of first impressions', in Ambady, N and Skowronski, J (eds.), *First Impressions*, Guilford Publications.
6   Nelson, N (2020), 'All in the mind' podcast, ABC, 20 September.
7   Sutherland, C (2020), 'All in the mind' podcast, ABC, 20 September.
8   Ibid.
9   Ekman, P, Davidson, R & Friesen, W (1990), 'The Duchenne smile: Emotional expressions and brain physiology: II', *Journal of Personality and Social Psychology*, 58 (2).
10 Dimberg, U, Thunberg, M & Elmehed, K (2000), 'Unconscious facial reactions to emotional facial expressions', *Psychological Science*, January.

11 Surakka, V & Hietanen, J (1998), 'Facial and emotional reactions to Duchenne and non-Duchenne smiles', *International Journal of Psychophysiology*, 29(1) June.

12 Strack, F, Martin, L & Stepper, S (1988), 'Inhibiting and facilitating conditions of the human smile: A non-obtrusive test of the facial feedback hypothesis', *Journal of Personality and Social Psychology*, 54(5).

13 Keating, C, Mazur, A & Segall, M (1981), 'A cross-cultural exploration of physiognomic traits of dominance and happiness', *Ethology and Sociobiology*, 2.

14 Carli, L, LaFleur, S & Loeber, C (1995), 'Nonverbal behavior, gender, and influence', *Journal of Personality and Social Psychology*, 68(6).

15 Word, C, Zanna, M & Cooper, J (1974), 'The nonverbal mediation of self-fulfilling prophecies in interracial interaction', *Journal of Experimental Psychology*, 10(2).

16 Nelson, N (2020), op. cit.

17 Neffinger, J & Kohut, M (2010), *Compelling People: The Hidden Qualities That Make Us Influential*, Little Brown Book Group.

18 Carney, D, Hall, J & LeBeau, L (2005), 'Beliefs about the nonverbal expression of social power', *Journal of Nonverbal Behavior*, 29.

19 Ibid.

20 Keane, T, St Lawrence, J & Himadi, W (1983), 'Blacks' perception of assertive behavior: An empirical evaluation', *Behavior Modification*, 7(1).

21 Weisfeld, G & Beresford, J (1982), 'Erectness of posture as an indicator of dominance or success in humans', *Motivation and Emotion*, 6(2).

22 Carney, D, Hall, J & LeBeau, L (2005), op. cit.

23 Huang, L, Galinsky, A & Gruenfeld, D (2010), 'Powerful postures versus powerful roles: Which is the proximate correlate of thought and behavior?' *Psychological Science*, 22(1).

Chapter 11

1   Elliott, T (2020) 'Intensive carers: The health workers behind Australia's COVID-19 success story', *The Age*, June 20.

2   See, for example: Baard, P Deci, E & Ryan, R (2004), 'The relation of intrinsic need satisfaction to performance and wellbeing in two work settings', *Journal of Applied Social Psychology*, 34, 2045–2068; Deci, E, Ryan, R, Gagne, M, Leone, D, Usunov, J & Kornazheva, B (2001), 'Need satisfaction, motivation, and well-being in the work organizations of a former Eastern Bloc country', *Personality and Social Psychology Bulletin*, 27, 930–942; Gagne, M, Koestner, R & Zuckerman, M (2000), 'Facilitating the acceptance of organizational change: the importance of self-determination', *Journal of Applied Social Psychology*, 30, 1843–1852; Ilardi, B, Leone, D, Kasser, T & Ryan, R (1993), 'Employee and supervisor ratings of motivation: Main effects and discrepancies associated with job satisfaction and adjustment in a factory setting', *Journal of Applied Social Psychology*, 23, 1789–1805; Kasser, T, Davey, J & Ryan, R (1992), 'Motivation and employee–supervisor discrepancies in a psychiatric vocational rehabilitation setting', *Rehabilitation Psychology*, 37, 175–187.

3   Slemp, G, Kern, M, Patrick, K & Ryan, R (2018), 'Leader autonomy support in the workplace: A meta-analytic review', *Motivation and Emotion*, 42.

4   Ebrahimi, H (2009), 'Archie Norman: The ex-Asda boss who saves businesses on the shelf', *The Telegraph*, 3 July.

Chapter 12

1   Huang, K, Yeomans, M, Wood Brooks, A, Minson, J, & Gino, F (2017), 'It doesn't hurt to ask: Question-asking increases liking', *Journal of Personality and Social Psychology*, Vol. 113, No. 3, 430–452.

Chapter 13

1   Duhigg, C (2013), 'What Google learned from its quest to build the perfect team', *New York Times*, 28 February.
2   Kakkar, H & Tangirala, S (2018), 'If your employees aren't speaking up, blame company culture', *Harvard Business Review*, Nov 6.
3   Phillips, M (2004), 'Malcom Gladwell on culture, cockpit communication and plane crashes', *The Wall Street Journal*, December 4.
4   Freeland, B (2012), 'When bad communication kills', *Brush Talk*, 6 August.

Chapter 14

1   Gentry, WA, Weber, TJ & Sadri, G (2008), 'Empathy in the workplace: A tool for effective leadership', The Centre for Creative Leadership.
2   Kellett, J, Humphrey, R & Sleeth, R (2016), 'Empathy and the emergence of task and relations leaders', *The Leadership Quarterly*, April.
3   Baron-Cohen, S & Chakrabarti, B (2008), 'The biology of mind reading' in Ambady, N and Skowronski, J (eds.), *First Impressions*, Guilford Publications.
4   Hatfield, E, Cacioppo, J & Rapson, R (1992), 'Primitive emotional contagion', in Clark, M (ed), *Review of Personality and Social Psychology: Emotion and Behavior*, SAGE Publications.
5   Young, T (2020), 'The last word on leadership', *The Australian*, 25 July.
6   Baron-Cohen, S & Chakrabarti, B (2008), op. cit.

Chapter 15

1   Losada, M & Heaphy, E (2004), 'The role of positivity and connectivity in the performance of business teams: a nonlinear dynamics model', *American Behavioural Scientist*, Vol 47, Issue 6.

2   Hasson, U, Ghazanfar, AA, Galantucci, B, Garrod, S, Keysers, C (2012), 'Brain-to-brain coupling: A mechanism for creating and sharing a social world', *Trends in Cognitive Science*, 16(2)

Chapter 16

1   Ullman, H & Wade, J (1996), *Shock and Awe: Achieving Rapid Dominance*, National Defense University.
2   Grashow, A, Heifetz, R & Linsky, M (2009), *The Practice of Adaptive Leadership: Tools and Tactics for Changing Your Organization and the World*, Harvard Business Press.